ISBN: 0-922915-84-9
ISBN: 978-0-922915-84-2

FERAL HOUSE
1240 W. SIMS WAY SUITE 124
PORT TOWNSEND, WA 98368

WWW.FERALHOUSE.COM
INFO@FERALHOUSE.COM

15

THE SATANIC WITCH

ANTON SZANDOR LaVEY

Introduction by Peggy Nadramia

Afterword by Blanche Barton

FIRE
most male core
wide shoulders
long torso
narrow hips
short legs
hard, firm flesh
pioneer
domineering
agressive
impulsive
always onstage
selfish
authoritarian

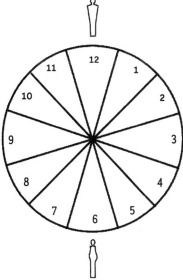

EARTH
emotional
thick sausage built
resilient
rubbery flesh
social
sense of humor
agreeable
concrete
doer, not thinker
practical
ressourceful

AIR
intellectual
narrow, stick build
sinewy
no waist
translucent
social critic
technical
abstract
least social
dour
air splitter
clinical
thinker, not doer

WATER
most feminine core
narrow shoulders
short torso
long legs
wide hips
marshmallow flesh
fluidic movements
carries things out
consistent
dedicated
receptive
dependable
generous
steady

CONTENTS

INTRODUCTION

By Peggy Nadramia
High Priestess, Church of Satan

The book you are now holding was first placed in my hands when I was 17 years old. It had a different format and a different name: *The Compleat Witch, or What to Do When Virtue Fails*. Well, as the careful reader quickly discovers after opening this diabolical tome, virtue is bound to fail, so pull up a seat and open your mind. This is nothing less than hardcore magic; use of its principles and instructions will change reality, but it takes guts.

Throughout my years as an administrator and representative for the Church of Satan, I've had the opportunity to meet and communicate with hundreds if not thousands of Satanists from every walk of life. They've all been inspired by the philosophy put forth in *The Satanic Bible* and were happy to take the label that came with it. Yet I'm often surprised by how many of them let the wisdom of *The Satanic Witch* just slip through their fingers. There are men of the Satanic persuasion who peruse its pages and then shelve it, figuring they'll wait for *The Satanic Warlock* to come along and until then, take their fashion cues from heavy metal videos and vampire comics. Tsk, tsk, gentlemen; the parade is passing you by. Nowhere else will you find such a distillate of LaVey's personal magical principles; with *The Satanic Witch*, you get the real LaVey—more of his wit, irony, observations and quirks than you have in any other of his works (with the possible exception of his music). And then there are those short-sighted ladies who let the point of this potent guidebook fly right over their heads, and actually hint that LaVey might be a misogynist! I've never met anyone who had more respect and admiration for feminine power; as he explains in detail, his advice is directed toward women because they can implement it where men cannot. And to those who like to characterize his tactics as "old-fashioned," I submit that the "Law of the Forbidden" will never go out of style, and women of today are still willing to learn dirty tricks for catching men—hence the new industry that has sprung up around a more recent book called *The Rules*. Thirty years ago, Anton LaVey codified these practices and called them the "Rules of the Chase." And those who put them to use he accurately named "witches."

Legend tells us that the Satanic witch of old received her magic from The Dark Man. While the rest of the world, particularly the men-folk, slept in blissful innocence, she and her sisters would meet Him in secret groves. There He would advise, inveigle and disclose the knowledge that would empower them to work their spells and enchantments. Anton LaVey embodied this tradition during the early days of the Church of Satan when he established Witches' Workshops in his old, black Victorian home in San Francisco. The teachings he imparted in those sessions are distilled in *The Satanic Witch*. Here then are some of those pearls of infernal wisdom and how they empowered me, and how they continue to create ripples in our world today.

> *New standards of non-beauty were formulated by ... ugly women and vagina-less men...* (Page 153.)

The societal androgyny LaVey was fighting against was in full swing when I was a young would-be witch; in fact, things had gone far beyond the chunky heels and pantyhose that had become his *bête noire*. We were walking around in chukka boots and Earth Shoes™; my purse was a burlap bag. Blue jeans were the uniform of the day, unless you felt like getting up early to iron your painter's pants, the ones with the little loop on the side for your hammer. Women who wore red lipstick and nail polish were objects of derision on any day except Halloween; these strong colors offended our quest for the "natural look," unless we were getting ready for a David Bowie concert when blue glitter eye shadow would have been acceptable. Our eyebrows were plucked to a hairline; gobs of black mascara outlined our young, innocent peepers in faces devoid of any color beyond that of our often-troubled teenaged skin. But we didn't just look confused about being girls; we were confused. *Ms.* magazine was saying that if we let a man hold a door open for us, we were accepting a subservient and inferior role. Free to be you and me? But who the Hell was THAT? It was great to have complete freedom over our sexuality, thanks to Planned Parenthood and access to birth control, but we "celebrated" our liberation by covering our curves with the same clothing and shoes guys wore and spit on them when they tried to be chivalrous.

I hung out with a pretty brainy and outré bunch back then; otherwise, it might have taken a few more years for me to get hold of an author like LaVey. I was already exhibiting one of the telltale signs of witchery: I liked being with young men more than young women and got along much better with the opposite sex. As LaVey would say, I succeeded in spite of my choices in couture, and not because of them; blue jeans will still show off a nice derrière, and those slinky Huckapoo blouses were pretty snug. I had already read *The Satanic Bible* and *The Devil's Avenger* and was familiar with LaVey as both a philosopher and a man whose choices and attitudes filled me with hope and excitement. Moved by his concepts, I knew that my future as an independent adult did not have to be a slow descent into the status quo, accepting ever more pre-chewed concepts along with a pre-patterned lifestyle. I saw that I could start having more fun instead of less.

The biggest problem you'll have with this advice is resolving yourself to trying it. (Page 64.)

At any rate, the aforementioned books had only prepared me, because it was *The Satanic Witch* that put the most potent information about magic across the plate. LaVey's system of character analysis, his rules of seduction, his brutally honest means for looking at oneself and working with what you find, instead of against it, all combine to make *The Satanic Witch* one of the most powerful tools a Satanist may wield. This is a book of forbidden knowledge. There are things contained herein that are actually outrageous, and some readers will not have the ego to keep going forward, preferring to toss this volume across the room and write LaVey off as a crank, or as simply promoting his own personal fetishes. At first I know I wanted to. I was smugly confident that my wit and sparkling personality would gain attention from men. But even at such a tender age, the realist in me was unable to deny his persuasive wisdom. LaVey had convinced me to take his techniques out for a test drive.

My Mom couldn't believe I wanted to wear stockings instead of cracking open a L'eggs Egg. "Ugh," she demurred, "we were so happy to get rid of those horrible garters." I remembered LaVey's words about each generation of women sloughing off the burden of their old-fashioned institutions, and just went about my business. LaVey wrote this book in an atmosphere of complete fashion fascism; women were virtually compelled to dress in the style of the day, and that style was decidedly unfeminine. Back then, you wore bellbottoms because that was all the stores sold; you couldn't find wine stem heels for love or money. I had to resort to my Grandma's underwear drawer for a nice cotton garter belt, and to a dusty old Woolworth's for genuine beige nylons. And when I dabbed vanilla extract behind my ears and the man I had in mind moved closer and murmured, "Mmm... you smell like a cookie..." I thanked Anton LaVey. In other words, this stuff worked.

> *The greatest powers you can employ as a witch are
> totally dependent on your own self-realization that in
> being a woman you are different from a man and that
> very difference must be exploited!* (Page 20.)

The world is beginning to find this out. Some newer feminist
writers like Camille Paglia are happy to trumpet the differences between the sexes now that such differences are not
immediately earmarked as "strengths" and "weaknesses."
Science is keeping in step, as neurological studies reveal that
the masculine and feminine brains deal with emotions, ideas
and spatial relationships quite differently. Even educators are
discovering that when girls are taught math in a separate
environment from the boys, they learn it just as quickly and
thoroughly, but differently. Remember the outrage a few years
ago when Talking Barbie ™ said, "Math is hard!"?

> *If you're not ugly enough to make people stare at you,
> then you are able to be an extremely sexy girl.* (Page 5.)

I've watched Satanic Witches slowly open up to the incredible
liberation inherent in this statement. It's only those who have
accepted the media's model of what a "pretty girl" is and reject
the powerful tool their unique femininity has given them who
look down upon those of us who choose to wield it. Any
woman can be sexy, LaVey emphasizes, if she lets herself look
like a woman and works with those traits with which she was
born. She doesn't have to be skinny, or blonde, or large-breast-
ed, or tall, or young, or have perfect teeth. She need only make
her "pact with the Devil," following the tips LaVey is here to
pass on to her.

> *Let me congratulate you. You need starve yourself no
> longer.* (Page 65.)

Since LaVey wrote those words for every marshmallowy, bottom-of-the-clock woman who was going crazy trying to look like Twiggy or Mia Farrow, a whole industry has risen up for those of us who are full-figured and like it that way. Large-size models like Emme host their own television shows. My husband won't let me put my back issues of *Mode* in the recycling bin. A few years ago, I sent Dr. LaVey a copy of a large-size lingerie catalog; he called to say that in his usual pile of mail from those who assumed he'd be interested in more esoteric, occult pursuits, he'd finally got what he wanted: pictures of chubby chicks in their underwear. In any case, he was among the first to say that if you were naturally plump, Nature had made you that way for the men who liked such women, and you should show off your bulges for them. And we haven't looked back.

Through the mannerisms of the nose and its functions, much can be told. (Page 215.)

Anton LaVey hated perfume, but he loved smells. One could rarely get through an evening of conversation without him mentioning a particularly outrageous odor that had wafted through his olfactory organ and what it had evoked in him. His favorite way to describe a place he liked was "stenchy." If aromatherapy had existed at the time he wrote this book, LaVey would have been all for it, but I guarantee you his version would have included less Lavender and more Gunpowder. He advocated the wearing of musk long before it became ubiquitous. More blasphemously, he suggested you allow your own natural scents to play a role in enchantment, and now everyone has heard about the effectiveness of one's own pheromones. Today, any witch can go to her local department store and find a unique line of cologne sprays with names like Gasoline, Grass, Rubber or Chocolate—all scents LaVey points to in his lessons in enchantment. Unfortunately, they haven't yet gotten around to Urine, one of his favorites, but give it time!

> *Respect based on accomplishment can only be given by those who are humble, wise and themselves worthy of respect.* (Page 122.)

How many people have you met who are humble, wise and worthy of respect? I'll wager you didn't use all your digits to count them. In that case, if you want to score points and get ahead in your chosen sphere of influence, you're going to have to use something else besides your intellectual powers to influence the fools who can help you. You can't demand recognition for what's between your ears from those who are not capable of giving it (see above). If you're the typical misanthropic Satanist, you'll have to agree that the majority of people you'll run across in life not only deserve to be manipulated, but are begging for it. They need witches like you!

> *Being realistic is a large part of being a compleat witch.* (Page 180.)

And that's where the true beauty of these principles comes in. LaVey reminds his reader constantly, that while he can tell her how to look or what to say to attract a man according to his position on the personality synthesizer clock, he can't promise that a witch will keep hold of this guy if he really isn't her type—and more importantly, that such a man won't really fulfill her needs, anyway! But in her search for the man who can fully satisfy her, the successful witch may charm plenty of others along the way, adding to her personal potency and getting all the favors and advantages she wishes. Being realistic about yourself also involves being honest about your motivations—drop that "Good Girl Badge" and acknowledge your own selfish desire to live a happy life in the here-and-now, like any other healthy animal.

There is far more magic in witchery than that which takes place during a ceremony. (Page 252.)

The magical secrets the author has to impart are deceptively simple in *The Satanic Witch*; often, they're sandwiched between mundane bits of misdirection. But LaVey drives home the point that the essential ingredient to a successful working is self-consciousness. How then is the witch of today to feel she is among the daring few who walk in the Devil's Fane? Hordes of black-lipsticked goth chicks clad in bondage gear now fancy that they are "initiates of the Dark Side." They think nothing of stabbing mass-produced voodoo dolls, turning crosses upside down, and blaspheming the names of Jesus and Jehovah. They imagine themselves to be so wicked, when they are just another contemporary cliché. The true grimoire is the one you are about to explore; it is utterly heretical in our society to even consider such things as revealing your soiled underwear, gaining some extra weight, or skipping the use of deodorant for a day or two. Here's fair warning: you will be outraged, you will be scandalized, and you may even want to forget the whole thing. But measure the potency of Anton LaVey's tutelage by this reaction, and rejoice. You're about to place your feet on the Left-Hand Path, and this Devil won't steer you wrong.

Prologue

After reading a few pages of this book, many will feel it to be a treatise on man-catching. This is understandable enough as considerable emphasis is placed on the mundane and occult manipulation of men.

But there is a good reason for this. Whether or not a witch needs any man other than the one she has currently chosen is relatively unimportant. What *is* important, however, lies in the fact that if a woman wants anything in life, she can obtain it easier through a man than another woman, despite woman liberationists' bellows to the contrary.

The truly "liberated" female is the compleat witch, who knows both how to use and enjoy men. Any bitter and disgruntled female can rally against men, burning up her creative and manipulative energy in the process. She will find the energies she expends in her quixotic cause would be put to more rewarding use, were she to profit by her womanliness by manipulating the men she holds in contempt, while enjoying the ones she finds stimulating. It's pretty hard to lose, using such tactics.

If she really prides herself on being a woman, she will take full advantage of her station. And the advantages are surely there, if she is bold enough to employ them!

A worthwhile man can be your greatest ally, and even one that is a pompous ass can sometimes be your most productive quarry. Even a man who is virtually devoid of any attributes other than his overt lust for you can be transformed into a bit of witch-power for yourself.

One of my greatest mentors was the late Sir Basil Zaharoff, Chevalier of the Legion of Honor, Knight of the British Empire, procurer of beautiful women, arms merchant, Satanist and the original Daddy Warbucks. Perhaps Sir Basil best understood the formula that I wish to impress upon my witches. Man to man, his advice was brutally simple: "Women are the best allies. They can make a man do what you yourself alone can never convince him is the best policy." For every man there lurks an ideal pattern for a woman. Most men do not even know she is there. She must be served, however, and in order to complete a man's need to fulfill the woman within him, he will see a woman that walks the earth, and not recognizing that woman to be the counterpart of the one within, will be compelled to her. If you know how to imitate the woman a man carries within himself, you may have anything you wish that another human can supply.

THE TEST OF THE THIRTEEN FACTORS

Before reading this book, take this test. It will tell you whether you have the ability to practice the art of witchery. Your present degree of competence towards a career in the practice of the Devil's game can be defined by answering thirteen of the following questions. Only thirteen out of twenty of these questions have any valid significance. The other seven have no bearing on your ability. Choose the questions you will answer carefully, as only thirteen count for possible answers. After you have decided which questions you are going to answer, check "yes" or "no" in the square provided. When you have finished answering the thirteen questions you have chosen, turn to page 266 for the answers, which must be held upside down and read in a mirror.

1. Have others ever referred to you as a witch? ☐
2. Do you have an ancestor or relative who was or is a witch? ☐
3. Are you better off today than you were a year ago? ☐
4. Do you feel you have supernatural forces working against you? ☐

5. Is black your favorite color? ☐
6. Do others seek out your company without your trying? ☐
7. Do you ever have fits of jealousy? ☐
8. Have you experienced what you would consider E.S.P.? ☐
9. Are you strict in your attention to feminine hygiene? ☐
10. Do you find others going along with what you want of them? ☐
11. Were you born under any of these signs: Leo, Scorpio, Pisces? ☐
12. Have you ever been considered "cheap"? ☐
13. Have you experienced anything of a mystical nature while using drugs? ☐
14. Do you have an interest in movies and TV shows with an occult theme? ☐
15. Do you often wear undergarments that are black in color or of a flashy nature? ☐
16. Are you accomplished in commonplace skills? ☐
17. Would you consider yourself to be intellectual? ☐
18. Is there anything you would fear as a consequence of your practice of applied witchery? ☐
19. Do you find that men often make passes at you? ☐
20. Do you wear any kind of amulet or charm that has occult significance? ☐

If you have a score of 7 to 9 correct answers, there is hope for you as a competent witch. If you scored 10 to 12, you are well on your way to sorcery, and if you got all 13 possible answers correct, you are truly gifted.

1. Are You a Witch?

"Be the first on your block to amaze your friends."
Johnson Smith Company Catalogue, 1929

WE ARE LIVING in the only period in history in which it is considered fashionable to be a witch. Given this complete public acceptance, an understandable tendency towards fadism develops. The once-stigmatizing label of "witch" has become a title of positive intrigue and has attained a status never before realized.

But this marks a considerable transition in the image of the witch. The biblical warnings against witches were such that it meant torture and death for anyone accused of the heresy of witchcraft. The Middle Ages was the worst period in history for a person to be accused of sorcery. However, the only similarity to today's witch is the glamorous appearance that some of the condemned women of the witch trials possessed. It is quite obvious from the charges leveled against many innocent girls that their only crime was in being sexually appealing.

Most of the beauties who suffered at the hands of the inquisitors were tormented because they refused to succumb to the right people or were too quick to give in to the wrong ones. Many men who lusted after such women became so guilt-ridden that they would denounce them out of fear that they would fall from grace in the eyes of God. Of course, the most successful witches were usually sleeping with the inquisitors and were never even considered to be witches. Successful as they might be, however, they could never openly take pride in their witcheries, for to do so would mean certain death.

Centuries later, the image of the witch was held exclusively by the old crone, who might not have feared arrest or persecution but certainly wasn't the type to be invited to cocktail parties. Only the ugly, grotesque, solitary and unpleasant carried the name of "witch." This tradition was so strong that to be referred to as a "witch" was an insult only a few short years ago. Now, countless women are coyly boasting about being witches. In fact, one of the reasons I decided to write this book was the prevalence of what sociologist Marcello Truzzi refers to as the "Nouveau Witch." * With so many witches roaming the earth, how can one tell the real ones from the false? It is as if everyone who ever removed a splinter from their finger were to go about proclaiming themselves surgeons! Surely there must be a means of defining and maintaining standards of witchcraft. Granted, there are no universities which are accredited in giving degrees in enchantments. Even if there were such places of learning, which soon there might be, the same problem of proving one's worth would remain as with any liberal arts course. The art student who has graduated from college with honors can usually land a good commercial or teaching position upon leaving school but not necessarily paint any better than an artist who has never come near an art class but still possesses the highest artistic ability.

* Marcello Truzzi, *The Occult Revival as Popular Culture: Some Random Observations on the Old and the Nouveau Witch.*

In any pursuit which deals with talent as an important factor towards success, academic or official licensing is of secondary importance. What is of prime importance is the *result* which is obtained through the use of the medium and how it is received by those to whom it is directed. Pedigrees are of questionable importance when the dog is sleeping while the burglar makes off with the silver. Nor do they help your legal defense when the mailman is bitten. Likewise, it is useless to have a grandmother who read tea leaves and a Scorpio rising in your chart, if you can't land a boyfriend, keep a husband, get a job or avoid pregnancy.

The most common credential used by modern witches is inherited ability, followed closely by "proper" astrological signs. Names and birth numbers of a suitable nature are often employed as testimony to one's ability as a witch, and an exaggerated assumption of E.S.P. powers sustains many a would-be witch's delusions of magical prowess. Other claims to fame include unobtrusive birth marks and blemishes that may be used as evidence of a "witch's mark," unusual conditions at birth, such as the presence of a "veil" and the ever present revelations of older and wiser (and shrewder!) "gifted" readers, whose extremely profitable stock-in-trade is to tell young girls of their latent magical powers.

With all these apparently sound reasons proclaiming one's right to witchcraft, small wonder there are so many witches around nowadays! What, then, *is* the definition of a true witch? I don't see any reason to readily discount the movie and TV image of the witch, because I think whatever popular image is most flattering should be utilized and sustained whenever possible. People will believe what they want to believe, and the current image of a witch is the most intriguing and glamorous that has yet to appear.

Just because every girl who calls herself a witch cannot do the things witches are seen to do on television shows does not mean that she should not take advantage of the public's assumption that she can!

To be sure, there are many who view the witch as a member of an old and pagan religion, more concerned with her beliefs than with her powers. No matter how many words have been written by the spokesmen of the "white witches," however, it is apparent that the public likes their witches to be cast in a fairly standardized image, and this is what it is: (1) The witch is a WOMAN. Men are called warlocks. (2) The witch is usually a wretched looking old crone with warts on her nose or an extremely sexy girl. (3) The witch has made a pact with the Devil and through rituals dedicated to him gains her power. (4) She is often blessed with a family heritage of sorcery in one form or another. (5) She has the power to get what she wants. (6) She has the facility to cloud men's minds and make simpering idiots out of them. (7) She destroys her rivals through the use of curses, thrown without mercy. (8) She has an intuitive capacity which allows her to size up a given person or situation before she proceeds further. (9) She has a familiar in the form of a pet. (10) She knows formulas for various concoctions which she gives to visiting gentlemen. In these qualities will be found a composite picture of the modern witch, whether she be beautiful or ugly.

Now, let us explore each ingredient and see how really accurate this description can be . . . And how you can become a witch in this image . . .

1. *The witch is a woman.* Well, you *are* a woman, so there's no problem here!

2. *The witch is either a wretched old crone with warts on her nose or an extremely sexy girl.* Are you ugly? If so, you qualify. If you're not ugly enough to make people

stare at you, then you are able to be an *extremely* sexy girl. You'll just have to sacrifice some deep-rooted notions and violate a few taboos . . . which brings us to

3. *The witch has made a pact with the Devil and through rituals dedicated to Him gains her power.* In order to be a successful witch, one *does* have to make a pact with the Devil, at least symbolically. She must recognize her very earthly heritage and realize she is working on that level at all times. She must worship the Luciferian element of pride within her, knowing full well that it is her honest ego that impels her to learn the arts of enchantment in the first place. She must also realize that happiness and self-satisfaction in *this* life are the reasons she has become a witch. A strong and non-hypocritical realization of this factor, occasionally pondered, is a potent ritual in its own right.

4. *She is often blessed with a family heritage of sorcery in one form or another.* Everyone inherits something from their forebearers that can be applied as a *useful* legacy. If your parents were good-looking, you may have inherited their looks. If they were ugly, you may have a fearsome appearance (sometimes kindly referred to by friends or relatives as "distinctive").* Someone along the line may have had a particular talent in music or art which you have received. Even if you don't know who your parents were, you still will inherit whatever qualities run concurrent to competent sorcery, but not be bogged down by assuming stereotyped but useless legacies.

5. *She has the power to get what she wants.* Through

---

* Dr. Sandor Feldman (see bibliography) relates the following anecdote: While two men were walking along, one of them called the other's attention to a little boy coming from the opposite direction. The boy had an enormous, distorted head. He was hydrocephalic. The first man said, "Look. Isn't that terrible, the head . . . ?" The other commented, "It is my son." The first, trying to save the situation, hastily added, "It suits him well."

the proper balance, the willingness to temporarily adapt to certain situations (rudely called "prostituting oneself" or "selling out") and a little patience; many are witches without even knowing it!

6. *She has the facility to cloud men's minds and make simpering idiots out of them.* If you have the guts to follow the advice contained herein, this should be the easiest part.

7. *She destroys her rivals through the use of curses, thrown without mercy.* The only way a curse *can* be thrown *is* without mercy, and the power of the curse is most effective. If you are without guilt at having feelings of animosity, there is no reason why you cannot throw a curse and make it work.

8. *She has an intuitive capacity which allows her to size up a given person or situation before she proceeds further.* Those who cannot put their finger on the reasons they feel as they do about certain people or situations, but nevertheless are guided by such feelings, call it "intuition." Alas, in altogether too many cases intuition turns out to be wrong. When we cease depending on half-baked intuition and combine intuitive thinking with certain conscious formulas for recognition, we can literally keep "one jump ahead" of what is about to happen.

9. *She has a familiar in the form of a pet.* An animal, bird, snake, fish or even plant that "tells no tales" is an essential ingredient towards the smooth-running living conditions of the successful witch.

10. *She knows formulas for various concoctions which she gives to visiting gentlemen.* Well, if you haven't guessed already, this means that if you can't cook, you'd better learn (except in the case of the very masculine witch who would specialize in kitchen-oriented males). Commonplace skills are essential.

The Myth of the "White Witch"

Aside from the tricks of the movie or TV witch, usually accomplished with special camera techniques, there is no reason why any girl who puts her mind to it and learns the proper methods cannot become a full-fledged witch in accord with the popular conception. Only those who either do not know the means to success or are too stubborn to use them, once having been told, will persist in defining themselves as witches by using the sanctimonious definitions of so-called "white witches" working for "the benefit of mankind." There will always be those who, furtively desiring personal power but unable to do anything about gaining it, will devise their own definitions of what a witch should be like, seeing to it, of course, that their definition fits themselves.

The "white witch" is the by-product of an emergence in England of an above-ground witchcraft interest at a time when witchcraft was still technically illegal. In order to pursue the "craft" without harassment and prosecution, the spokesmen for witchcraft attempted to legitimize and justify what they were doing by proclaiming the existence of "white" witchcraft.* "White" witchcraft, it was stated, was simply a belief in the religion of the old wise ones, or "wicca." The use of herbs, charms and healing spells was only employed for beneficial purposes.

It was to be believed that the kind of witches that were dangerous to have around were "black" witches. These were supposedly evil in their pursuits and worshipped Satan. The fact that the "good" or "white" witches employed a horned god in their ceremonies was justified because it "doesn't represent the Devil!"

---

* The term "white witchcraft" was first used by William Seabrook in his book, *Witchcraft, its Power in the World Today.*

Of course, no one admitted to *practicing* witchcraft ceremonies of any kind. Anything that was associated with witchcraft was pursued in the name of "study" or "research." This was the climate in England between 1936 and 1951.

With the repeal of English witchcraft laws in 1951, all of the underground witches started creeping to the surface, and as their eyes became accustomed to the light of sudden legality, they ventured forth. Unused to such freedom and heavy with the stigma of illegality, they went about shouting "white witchcraft" even louder than ever, as if expecting at any moment to be snared by a heretic hook.

About this time, interest in the occult was becoming popular in the U.S., so naturally attention was focussed on the Britsh Isles with its rich heritage in all matters ghostly and fanciful. As might have been expected, newly emerged English witches saw the U.S. as a fertile stamping ground for safe recognition of their "witchiness." Concurrent with the first post-war writings out of England came the first diplomats of witchdom, and America was more than curious. Having no other literature but Margaret Murray, Montague Summers and Dennis Wheatley to read, it was assumed the new revelations by Gerald Gardiner and his followers were the straightest stuff available.

"White witch" became a definitive term, and thousands who wouldn't touch the practice of witchcraft with a ten-foot broomstick found a conscience-redeeming opportunity to follow the "art" by using the new rules of the game. Regardless of what these people would like to believe, the image of the witch had been stigmatized for centuries. *All* witches were considered to be agents of the Devil, antagonistic to scriptural teachings, and a direct part of the dark side of nature. As there is always a relative outlook as to what is good and what is evil, once witchcraft emerged from its "all evil" state into neutral territory, a differentiation was bound to occur. The righteous, of course, will always wear the mantle of "good," "white light," "spiritual" and varying shades of holiness.

An analogy might be made concerning "white" and "black" witches. Let us assume that warfare had, for centuries, been called "wholesale murder" and the men who fought called "murderers." One day it was decided that there was something quite noble and dignified about this old activity of wholesale murder. All the murderers, basking in the light of new-found legitimacy, began calling themselves "good murderers." The enemy's troops, of course, were the "bad murderers." The stigma of the word, "murderer," still remained, but at least the good murderers felt a little more at ease. Now, maybe these murderers always had a fairly legitimate reason for going into battle. Maybe they succeeded in saving their homeland from that which threatened it. They might have even had a scholar among them who had traced the origin of the word "murder" to an ancient word which meant "mother." But the fact remained, "murder" was still a negative term in the public's mind. So instead of simply revelling in their subsequent acceptance by the public, their guilts, brought about by long years of stigma, necessitated their placing of the word "good" in front of "murderer" as a sort of self-reassurance that they were doing the right thing!

Whenever a girl becomes a "white witch," you know she is either kidding herself or has much to learn.

The Drug Scene

Another of the most commonly employed self-convincers in the world of witchcraft is the drug scene. After a formidably productive experience under the influence of an hallucigenic drug there is often a profound assumption of mystical or magical power.

The assumption is, of course, confined solely to the user of the drug, but let no one attempt to deter her from her chemically produced reality! If one has sought magical power or mystical wisdom and has experienced an extremely sound enchantment through the use of the drug, chances are, she'll look no further. If she *does* explore new facets of occultism, however, *no* experience will quite come up to that which the drug has supplied, so, therefore, the drug will become the criteria-producing device for her self-assumed prowess.

Let me state categorically at this point that drugs are antithetical to the practice of magic, as they tend to disassociate the user from reality, even though he oftentimes thinks himself closer. It is true that many drugs expand the consciousness, but, in so doing, they make it much more difficult for a person to become selective in thoughts and motivations. In magic, it is imperative that one be able to narrow down his various awarenesses to *one* compelling desire towards which a ritual is performed. When the use of drugs has allowed the mind to run rampant over such "narrow-minded" traits, something very meaningful is lost.

The ideal witch must be able to be singular of purpose, when the need arises, and dogged narrow-mindedness has its just place in the ritual chamber where stubborn emotion must hold forth. Any soma-producing chemical or device negates such an "up-tight" quality. In reality, the more up-tight one is when he enters the ritual chamber, the better. With a lack of hang ups, comes a lack of strong emotional response to the very situations often needed to generate the force necessary to throw your spell. The "free," dreamy-eyed, "beautiful person" type is often the first to call herself a witch but actually is the antithesis of the real thing.

An argument might be given that it is okay to use drugs but not when one is casting spells. This is like commenting on the problem of drunkenness and alcoholism by saying it's all right to drink but not when you're driving. There are many people who are rotten drivers who never touch a drop, and, conversely, many whose lives are ruined by booze who ride buses. *The effects of drugs upon the witch are only definable by the success shown by a witch outside her drug-oriented peer group.*

A common phenomenon nowadays is the prevalence of "witches" involved in the drug scene. The prowess claimed by such would-be sorceresses centers around their in-group activities and not the outside world. One such witch approached me recently, saying she had just performed a great magical working. It seems she had driven her car on the freeway after taking a rather large dose of LSD. Feeling very "magical," she drove across an oncoming six lanes of traffic with sufficient "magical power" to bring each of the speeding cars to a halt! She was totally convinced that her abilities as a witch were responsible for her immunity. When I told her that her safety had been insured by the quick reflexes and sound brakes of the other drivers, it went in one ear and out the other.

Another young "witch" had been at a social gathering where marijuana in conjunction with various drugs was being used. My informant stated emphatically that during the course of the evening's activities she had seen someone who glowed with such a "radiant aura" that she approached him with the "magical" intention of lighting her "joint" from his "radiance." She swore that as she held her marijuana cigarette up to his face, it miraculously glowed alive. Now I have heard all the old gags about one drunk lighting his cigarette from the glow of the other drunk's nose, but never thought I'd hear its contemporary parallel told with a straight face and as a portentously serious account of the powers of witchcraft!

The confusing thing about all this is that we are now living in a climate of occult popularity where such experiences are not relegated to the wards of mental institutions.

For those whose mental imbalance is drug induced and even temporary, a fertile environment for such periodic "miracles" exists. It is but a short step to the employment of such "magical" experiences towards a pedigree for witchery.

Combine the effects of drugs with the search for a religion to supplant one which has never held much meaning, and you will arrive at a *need* to believe, which is strengthened by readily obtainable miracles which can ultimately fulfill that need. Hence, an unswerving faith in magic can be readily manufactured even as it was accomplished by the same means by the shamans of primitive societies but *not* a proficiency in the practice of magic.

If you are to be a successful witch, faith helps, but it takes a good deal more. If, however, you do not plan on practicing witchcraft but only believing in it, use all the drugs you like.

The Married Witch versus the Single Witch

It would be assumed that to be a witch, one would function better in an unmarried capacity. After all, who ever heard of a witch who was married, before a certain television show came into being. Not so, state all the rules of witchery. There is no reason why a successful witch cannot be married—some of the most seductive enchantresses have both husbands and well behaved offspring.

Aside from the security a sound marriage can provide, it is obvious that a married woman exerts a much greater fascination than her single sister. The reason for this is *The Law of the Forbidden,* which will be discussed later and is, after all, the reason you are reading this book.

Unless a witch wishes to appeal through the use of a virginal image, the more "experienced" she appears, the more desirable she becomes. Very few men will be compelled towards virginity in a woman, except as a fillip to the ego. The concept of virginity as a desirable value is viable when one thinks of sacred love and enduring romance. The average male, however, is an animal first and a romanticist second. For this reason, he will always be tempted by the woman whom he considers to be of easy virtue. Whether or not a woman is of easy virtue is unimportant when stating the requirements for the witchhood. What *is* important resides in the hope, the assumption, the promise of sexual availability and experience.

If the woman who is known to be single can be assumed to have indulged in sex, then the married woman surely must know what it's like! It is precisely this "advertising" of one's sexual knowledge that gives the married witch a certain appeal often lacking in the single witch.

Inasmuch as there are very few virgins around nowadays, we can virtually forget the attraction that such a witch could exert. Even the trappings of the virgin that are used in witchery, such as white and pink colors in clothing, must be combined with certain suggestive tricks that will lead to the impression that the wearer is sexually available.

The fertile deities of the Pagans were all transformed, by one name or another, into scarlet woman, witches and she-devils by the good Christians, who wished to make it clear that chastity was a virtue. Therefore, it became the assumption that any woman who exuded sex was of the

Devil. Sex and the Devil must therefore be extended to exemplify the witch, as well.

For centuries, we have associated the single girl with chastity and the married, divorced or widowed woman with carnal knowledge. Such associations will not easily leave the mainstream of the unconscious. All of the traditional wedding pranks are directed toward one common goal, and that is the blatant proclamation that the demure young lady in the lacy white gown will soon be bouncing about in sexual abandon. No wonder the expression, "blushing bride" was once such an apt description! The prurient stares of those who ogled the young woman as she would alight from the dusty Ford coupe with the "Just Married" sign and string of tin cans were bound to produce a crimson face, which, of course, only added even more to the lascivious effect! It was as if the poor girl was carrying a placard reading, "I Have Been Getting Laid!"

Now that our social norms have so radically changed, such phenomena have diminished, but their residue certainly persists. It is for this reason that the married woman, or one who has *been* married, possesses a sensual edge over the unmarried witch.

The *disadvantages* of being married are obvious. A single witch is freer to engage in success-oriented enchantments whereas the married witch must watch her step. The witch with a husband who is either agreeable or out of the running may, of course, use her witchery towards sexual ends. The siren who is content with her husband, sexually speaking, but is career minded has a vast field of opportunity in which to employ her powers. The witch who is, as the last mentioned, sexually content with her spouse but not inclined towards a career for herself can become as the legendary sorceress behind the throne of her husband, the king. In this way, she can enchant those whom her husband could not emotionally reach.

So, you see, marriage is no handicap to witchery. In fact, there are examples that will be shown later in this book of how it actually pays to *say* you are married, even if you are not.

Probably the greatest single disadvantage of the single witch is the often-encountered "desperation vibrations" she throws off. No matter how smug and complacent she may appear to be in her unmarried role, she still carries the underlying stigma of the woman who "hasn't been able to catch a man." The stigma that was once associated with witchcraft has been inverted into an intrigue, but the only sexually positive inversion of the "spinster syndrome" is the recent rationale of being a "swinger." It is wise for the unmarried witch who is well into her twenties to adopt this image, regardless of her personality type, if she has the looks to match it.

Choose an Image

Whether a witch is married or single, she should discover the image that she most naturally and effortlessly represents as a sort of "home base."

Everyone has a stereotyped counterpart that turns up whether in a movie, TV show, novel, comic strip or other form of popular media. You owe it to yourself to ride on the coattails of the established visual image that most resembles you. We see this game played every time a popular female personality is emulated by multitudes of women, who can find similarity in their own appearance, however slight. The knowing witch always capitalizes on the physical typing that has been set up for her or chooses one she feels she can throw herself into. There is an old saying, "If you have the Devil's name, you should play the Devil's game," and if people constantly give you clues to your proper image by telling you who or what you resemble, take it from there.

If you are thin, with raven hair and dark eyes and your face is rather long and angular, you should capitalize on the vampire theme and do all you can to hint at that image. If you find people always wanting to help you and taking a protective attitude towards you, utilize a naive and innocent appearance and bearing to your advantage. If you have a "mean" look and attract meek men, then do all you can to look meaner! Be a veritable whip and leather type. If you're getting on in years and have a nose like a potato with a body to match, don't kid yourself into thinking that a facial vacuum and losing forty pounds will turn you into a seductress. Instead, get yourself a couple of cats, fill your house full of weird bric-a-brac, learn to make cookies, and let it be known you're a witch! Soon you'll have more worthwhile male friends than you ever would have in your personality-less attempt at rejuvenation. If you're truly grotesque, with a face that would stop ten clocks and a voice like a klaxon, turn yourself into a real hag-monster and have fun scaring the Hell out of people!

In many instances stereotypes are based on very real personality traits that are relevant to the appearance presented. Consequently, a witch who chooses an image most conducive to her ready-made appearance is likely to find herself revelling in a very comfortable role. This doesn't mean that a witch must go through life playing only one role simply because she has been stereotyped into it. It all depends on your acting ability, especially when it comes to make-up and facial mannerisms. Any successful witch must be a good actress.

Unfortunately, too many would-be witches who consider

themselves to be good actresses wind up playing all the wrong parts! The role that is the most appealing is often the one that is represented by the "inner" or "hidden" side of one's nature. We see this all the time in the large, dominant looking, glamorous "Amazon" type who tries to act the part of a demure and naive little girl—especially when drunk! We also observe this in the frail looking, helpless appearing, wide-eyed little creature who always seems to be yelling the loudest and stirring up the most trouble. These are both common examples of unsuccessful witches whose lack of opportunity lies in their refusal to "feed back," even temporarily, what their appearance implies. They are living counterparts of the old cliche, "To look at her you'd think she was . . . but just wait 'til she opens her mouth!"

True, there are times when it serves a witch well to disarm her quarry by acting completely different from what is expected of her, but these are specialized cases that will be discussed later in this book.

The general rule is to become a "package deal," thereby allowing the person you are bewitching to think that they have you all figured out. This may seem a bit dismal to you who have assumed that a "witchy" type must always appear enigmatic, but I have observed that the most frustrated, unsuccessful witches are those who work at ambiguity rather than "type-casting" themselves. The only type of witch that can get away with an enigmatic image is the "femme fatale" who has a naturally strange or unusual appearance. Needless to say, the type usually attempting the most mysterious image is the most un-mysterious looking to start with!

Choose an image that goes easiest with your outward appearance and take full advantage of all that has gone before to further establish that image. There is nothing wrong with being type-cast if you can make it work for you!

"Natural" versus "Acquired" Ability

Insofar as "natural" or "inherited" ability is concerned, the only truly built-in advantage a girl can possess is her looks. Looks mean everything, despite delusions to the contrary.

A naturally good-looking girl has the best requirement possible for enchantment. This does *not* mean that an ordinary or even homely girl cannot be a successful witch— it simply implies that if a girl is pretty, she doesn't have to try as hard. This can be many a beautiful girl's downfall, though, as the plain girl has to learn to compensate for her lack of beauty by developing other talents. The most beautiful girls are seldom the stars of any show but are relegated to the chorus. This is simply because the pretty girl sits back, being used to getting by on her looks, and takes advantage of only what comes along, and, as is often the case, winds up more taken advantage *of*! The plainer girl, who depends on her wile, guile, artificial glamor and assertiveness, invariably winds up in the spot-light. Whenever an accurate description has been able to be given of famous and legendary spell-binders through history, these women turn out to be something slightly removed from the stereotyped standards of beauty, and in many cases, they were downright homely.

If you are possessed of the kind of appearance that causes men to stop in their tracks, beware of the tendency to coast along witchcraft-wise on your astrological sign, latest Ouija revelation and neck pendant. You could very likely spend most of your life talking about what a great witch you are, having many bug-eyed male listeners and accomplishing absolutely nothing other than an occasional fling in the sack with some guy who is going to do "great things" for you. You may be sure of being propositioned all over the place—not because you are possessed of magical power but simply because you are a sexy looking girl!

Naturally, an attractive woman will find doors open to her that her more dowdy sisters must pay through the nose to enter. Every pretty girl is used to receiving favors, and if we are to be honest in recognizing the Satanic laws of indulgence, it is understandable that she should receive favors. After all, by her very existence, she is bringing beauty of a visual nature into the life of the beholder—the type of beauty that, if it is accompanied by an undercurrent of sexual excitement, doubly adds to the pleasure reaction. In a sense, she is giving, without even trying. So long as anything pleasant constitutes an indulgence, the viewer of the pretty girl will be indulged. Small wonder, then, that he reacts consciously by having to do something for the girl!

This factor of physical appeal, then, is very important in bewitching. If it is at all possible to indulge whoever looks upon you with a treat that will obviate a reward, you must do so. In practical witchery you must first command attention by your looks. Then, you should be able to create an enticement. If you can't *entice* the viewer into doing what you want, you must *scare* him into doing it. We'll cover that aspect in a later chapter. Right now we'll concentrate on the importance of a pleasing appearance.

Since life is a give-and-take proposition, we must play the game as such; but, as you know, there is often a lot more "take" than there is "give." When a pretty girl "gives" simply by being a pretty girl, she subsequently "takes" when the little favor is bestowed by the nice man. In her often-limited mind she assumes her enchantment to then be complete, not realizing that now it is *her* turn to give for a second time. Completely off guard because of the smugness engendered by her temporary conquest, she then is thrown into a situation where she is unmercifully taken advantage of by the "nice man."

It must be born in mind that the element of sex-appeal is not dependent on perfect face and body, lest many of my readers feel themselves falling short of the mark when it comes to physical perfection. The relative ingredient of what constitutes a pretty girl are seen in many forms. So long as beauty is in the eye of the beholder, we must acertain a little about the beholder and his particular likes.

The universally accepted standards of beauty are those based on certain curves, metric proportions and contours. These are the standards which constitute the "naturally pretty" girl. Through modification, using make-up, clothing, fetishistic devices, etc. a girl who is less than "perfect" can sometimes "out-perfect" the natural beauty.

Oh yes, one last rule before we get into the formulas: NEVER FORGET THAT YOU ARE A WOMAN, AND THE GREATEST POWERS YOU CAN EMPLOY AS A WITCH ARE TOTALLY DEPENDENT UPON YOUR OWN SELF-REALIZATION THAT IN BEING A WOMAN YOU ARE *DIFFERENT* FROM A MAN AND THAT VERY DIFFERENCE MUST BE EXPLOITED! The extent to which you exploit your womanliness must always be in perfect balance with the *lack of womanliness of the man you have chosen to bewitch*! How will you know this balance? The next chapter will show you.

2. Knowing Yourself and Others

The Real You

IN ORDER to properly analyze or size up an individual you plan to bewitch, it is imperative that you understand certain rules. For the purposes of witchcraft, one should conceive of each person having two personalities—the one everyone sees, and the one he carries within him. Actually, these two personalities can be broken down into three layers—the outer layer being the "cover" by which others often "tell the book" and the inner layer, the so-called "true" personality. There is a third layer, however, that is sadly neglected—always there and always apparent. The reason it is not readily noticed is because it is all too visible, much like the old saying about not being able to see the forest for the trees. This third personality represents the inner core, the "reversion to type," and is a direct reflection of the characterization which is seen on the surface, or first layer.

Let us, therefore, consider the first and third layers to be the same, with a big layer of padding between them which makes up the second. This second layer is the "other side" of our nature, the woman within each man, the alter-ego, the "dark side" of our nature, etc. It is also the part of the personality you must learn to recognize in every person you plan to bewitch. Figure 1 shows what it can be likened to, for example, in a short, fat, man.

As you can see from the diagram, layer number two takes the form of a tall, slender, slim-hipped woman. If our short, fat man were to have a best friend, it would be another man who was tall and slender with a personality totally unlike his own. Put a wig and a dress on the tall skinny friend and you'll get a pretty good hint at what the wife or girl friend of the fat man will be like.

Have you ever noticed how a man's best friend will always be his opposite in appearance? The women you have always had as your best friends have been opposites of your own appearance, haven't they? If you are extremely pretty, your best friend was always the one you found yourself trying to convince others of accepting as beautiful even though they couldn't see it. If you are an active type, you will attract quiet people. If you are quiet, you will gravitate towards energetic types. In short, *the reason opposites attract is because we need those opposites to make ourselves whole.*

However badly we might need this opposite of ourselves though, there will always be a two-to-one victory for the outer and inner, the numbers one and three layers of our personality.

This great overbalance, which I shall call the "Majority Self," is the one that will always come through when the chips are down. This is the "reversion to type" and the appearance, personality and general impression we present to others at first glance. To sum this up, WHEN DEAL-

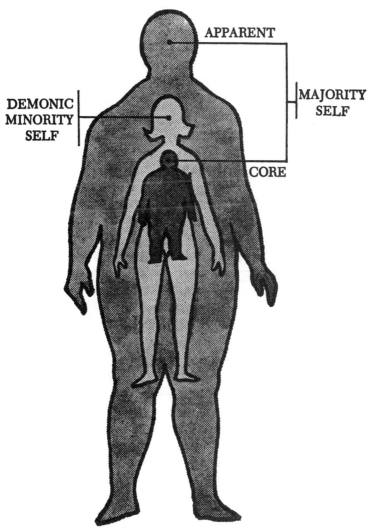

FIG. 1

ING WITH MEN AND WOMEN AS A GENERAL
RULE YOU *CAN* TELL A BOOK BY ITS COVER.

In the practice of witchery, however, you must appeal
to the other's need to express and exercise the *second* layer
of his personality. This is the side of his nature that is seldom fulfilled and, therefore, always hungry. An old phrase,
once popular in underworld circles is, "Treat a slut like a
lady, and a lady like a slut." This is all well and good and
might be considered a profound simplification of what I
have been saying, but it stops only half-way through the
formula, as many destitute gigolos and altruistic reformers
have discovered.

The reason this old vulgarism is only half true is because
in the final analysis, the lady will regain her decorum and
become mawkishly indignant, and the slut will be discovered in one of the upstairs bedrooms away from the rest of
the elegant revelers—her Dior gown up around her hips,
one guest on top, and two more waiting outside the door.

A completed variant of the previous cliche for witches
to remember is, "Treat a bum like a prince, and a prince
like a bum—a little boy like a big man, and a big man like
a little boy—a professor like a prizefighter, and a prizefighter like a professor; *but* don't ever let the bum forget
he's a bum—the prince, a prince—the little boy, still a little
boy, etc. When you begin your enchantment, always approach your quarry with his second, or "Minority Self" in
mind.

This means that you can approach him as an "outsider,"
who will treat him in the manner that his Minority Self
craves, or you can *be* his Minority Self, in a female form!

Returning to our previous formula, instead of treating
the bum like a prince and worrying about holding his ego
down to its proper level for control, leave his Majority Self
as it is and *you* appear as a princess. If your subject is a

captain of industry, a leading financier, a big newspaper publisher—*you* should come on like a domestic, a counter girl, a dancer in the chorus. If he is a Casper Milquetoast who holds a petty clerical job, appear as an efficient business woman and give the impression that everything revolves around you in the office. If your target is a highly intellectual academician, present yourself as a rather brassy, flashy filly with more heart than brains. If he happens to be a real swinger, with Italian silk suits and a fat address book, appear as an intrigued, but naive, small-town librarian. Get the idea? That Minority Self, which you must represent, doesn't stop at personality types but is readily observable in the very physique and movements of your quarry.

To be a successful witch, one must learn how to recognize these things, but first she must know *herself*.

So that you may know yourself, and others as well, we must establish a guide. I have devised a system of character analysis, utilizing the best gleanings from many sources. Researchers such as Sheldon and Kretschmer have helped a great deal by their classifications of body and personality types. Sheldon defined human physique into three basic categories—Ectomorph, or thin, cerebral, and straight up and down; Mesomorph, or wedge-shaped, practical and broad-shouldered; and Endomorph, or roly-poly, social and broad-hipped.

From these basic classifications, Sheldon defined literally hundreds of sub-classifications, all variants of the three basic types. Kretschmer used the same fundamental typing, except he called them "Leptosome," "Athletic" and "Pyknic."

The method I have used for convenience throughout this book I call "The LaVey Personality Synthesizer." By studying the almost limitless areas of human behavior and correspondences, I have arrived at certain capsulizations of human personality. Aside from the previously mentioned researchers, I have observed most of my "subjects" in their natural habitat. My gleanings have been obtained, not as an accredited psychologist or sociologist, but rather as a Devil's advocate, who has spent the better part of his professional life in concert halls, barrooms, police work, carnivals, wild animal training, photography, clinical hypnosis, ghost chasing, burlesque shows, amusement parks, art studios, revival meetings, advancing the cause of Satanism, and just plain *looking!*

I have conducted what sociologists might call an "unfunded research project." Much of what I have synthesized in my sometimes overly-scattered pursuits will to many readers appear utterly mad, ridiculous and outrageous. Much is based on the scientific evaluation of others. Perhaps even more will be condemned as having "no known or accredited scientific basis." Fine. All I know is it works. And if it works, I don't knock it. If some of my "nutty" theories you read in this book work for you, you're ahead of the game. I only present them for what I have found they can do when applied.

The LaVey Personality Synthesizer

Every human type has its corresponding personality traits, and, as you can see, occupies a position on the circle that can approximate the numbers on a clock. In order to simplify things, we will use this clock numbering system when referring to the types we will be discussing throughout this book. (See the endpapers of the book for a diagram of the synthesizer.) Therefore, if mention is made of a "two-clock type," you will know that the person is halfway between a mesomorph and an ectomorph type. I am not adhering to the typing systems of Kretschmer and Sheldon completely, because to do so would eliminate much of the far-reaching opportunities for quick and easy analysis this method will allow.

Before we go farther, the most important rule in using this method of analysis must be stated: the demonic element in everyone is manifested in their choice of a mate. ONCE YOU HAVE FOUND THE PERSON WHOM YOU WISH TO BEWITCH ON THE CHART, YOU MUST DO YOUR UTMOST TO PORTRAY THE PERSON DIRECTLY OPPOSITE YOUR SUBJECT.

You can test the authenticity of the chart by simply observing people you know and their choice of a mate. Wherever you find a difficult relationship between two people —especially of opposite sexes—you will notice they are close together on the chart rather than opposite each other. The classifications that can be defined are limited only by the short-sightedness of the witch. Using this typing system, more can be told about a given person than with any other method ever devised.

Twelve o'clock represents the pure masculine counterpart to the six o'clock feminine. Inasmuch as these types can be likened to Adam and Eve, the satyr and the nymph, etc., very few individuals will find themselves right on those marks. As will be seen, we will not judge so much by three basic classifications, but rather by gradations closer related to four quarters of the circle: twelve, three, six and nine. These four points have personality affinities with the elements of fire, air, water and earth, and their colors: red, blue, green and yellow.*

---

* The clock form has been used effectively in many areas where gradation is required of a continuous nature. Like the color wheel, which we shall employ in conjunction with it, the clock allows for subtle yet readily recognizable gradations.

In employing this synthesis, one will find that the more it is used, the more strictly related elements of personality will be seen running concurrent with each type on the clock.

Predominantly Masculine Types in Female Bodies and Vice-Versa

If you have been born a woman and happen to be in the top extreme of the clock, it indicates you are dominant in your nature and your "Core" takes the form of a male rather than a female person. Here is where we run into a problem if we allow it to exist. The same situation, in reverse, occurs in men who fall into the extreme lower half of the clock. Let us say that the upper half represents the "ideal" masculine Core, while the lower half represents the "ideal" Core in a female. Thus, the three layers of personality in a twelve o'clock woman would look like Figure 2.

To simplify matters, we can say that the twelve o'clock woman will search for (or rather be searched for by) a six o'clock man, and will invariably wind up with one, whether she wants him or not. The fact that she is still carrying about with her a woman's body necessitates an even greater search for a man who is stronger than she, so that she can really "feel like a woman." Naturally, this is a pretty big order to fill, as she is already occupying a twelve o'clock position on the clock.

If a twelve o'clock female, who is used to passive men fawning all over her selects an extremely dominant man—one who is even more dominant than herself—she cannot expect such a man to fall in love with her, despite her temporal needs for such a man, because in order for that very temporal passivity need to be fulfilled, *the dominant man would, by nature, reject her!* Then, the twelve o'clock gal moans and

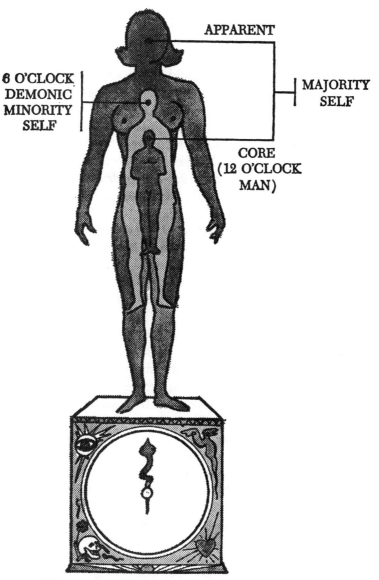

TWELVE O'CLOCK WOMAN   FIG. 2

wails that the *more*-dominant-than-herself man is not returning her raging love! She is often too stupid to realize that his very rejection of her indicates his dominance over her, without which, there could be no attraction towards him in the first place. Thus, she would no longer be dependent upon her stronger man, but in control of the situation —as is her usual standard when dealing with her panting suitors. If, however, she can step aside temporarily from her blind desires and realize her needs to "suffer" run concurrent with the rejection she experiences from her "brutal" and "callous" love object—then, and only then, will she become self-realized.

The parallel to this situation is the six o'clock man (see Figure 3), who secretly desires a woman he can boss around. When he finally finds such a dormouse, *she is so totally like himself in personality and physical typing that he cannot become enthusiastic about her* but continues to long for dominion over a "girl of his dreams," who, as you might suspect, is of a type totally unprepared to see any dominant qualities in such a man! On the contrary, his "dream girl" will always be that most dominant woman who holds him in thrall—not a type who is identical to himself but even more subservient! Then he finds himself tied up in knots and enslaved, as usual, by the kind of woman he bemoans *not* being able to boss about. Little does this unknowing man realize that it is his very pattern to need a dominant woman, and when that woman ceases to dominate him he will automatically drift to a new whipmistress who can!

Here we have discussed two types of human beings, who, being usually unaware of their true nature, go through life complaining about their unrequited love—invariably to none other than those individuals who become the sometimes-disdainful objects of their desires. Unfor-

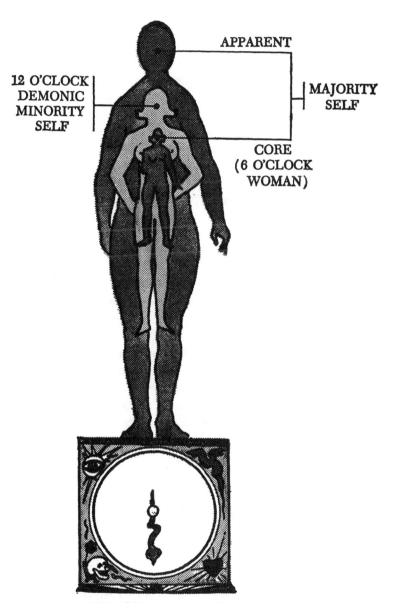

APPARENT

12 O'CLOCK
DEMONIC
MINORITY
SELF

MAJORITY
SELF

CORE
(6 O'CLOCK
WOMAN)

SIX O'CLOCK MAN   FIG. 3

tunately, if their caterwaulings are long and loud enough, and their love objects are nice enough, even though dominant by nature, a very curious phenomenon develops. The dominant love object, in attempting to "keep peace" and divert grave traumas on the part of his or her suitor, becomes literally vampirized by the "weaker" person! Thus, it becomes a situation wherein the master finds himself fast becoming the slave—*but without the benefits of such an arrangement*, as the newly developed "slave" has not based his or her choice of a "master" upon any natural sexual or mental attractions!

Temperament

Going back to the synthesizer clock as we start at one o'clock, we find the person who is dominant by nature, didactic, and with an inquiring mind, becoming even more mental as two o'clock approaches. With two, however, some of the social affabilities diminish, and by the time three is reached, we find an inclination towards haughtiness and cynicism. These people are the least agreeable when it comes to accepting anything at face value and are seldom "joiners." As they are thinkers, rather than doers, there are few absolutes in their lives. Consequently, these three and four o'clock types are the most mystical and abstract in their thoughts. If their Demonic element is allowed to express itself, however, through a non-human vehicle, such as poetry, music, art—great works can be accomplished. Genius dwells within the four o'clock type more often than any other, and the typical "egghead" is a pure four o'clock.

Five o'clock types are less abstract and more practical and have the quality of being able to stick with things providing the going doesn't get too rough. For this reason, they are admirably suited to office roles and clerical work. Steady and dependable, they have the flexibility necessary to keep going day after day. Even more consistent is the six o'clock person. In fact, he is the most consistent on the clock. Devotion to cause and duty is the hallmark of the six o'clock type, and he takes great pride in his promptness. These are the men who stay on a job for so long that everything in the firm depends on their presence. These are the women who stay with husbands that other women on the clock would discard. If a six o'clock man strays from his wife, you may be sure it is another woman's fault—invariably one from the top of the clock.

Seven o'clock persons retain much of the qualities of the six, but with more social inclination, and by the time eight is reached, the emphasis is on doing rather than thinking. The eight and nine o'clock types have little use for hairsplitting debate and will most likely interject a humorous comment whenever the going gets too serious.

The most agreeable and socially likeable eights and nines give up some of these qualities to the ten o'clock type but still have the monopoly. By the time ten is reached, the assertive temperment of the top half of the clock is brought to bear. The need to dominate presents itself, and affability is often sacrificed. The ten o'clock type has no use for "eggheads," but ironically his best buddy is probably a slightly sallow four o'clock, whose introspection is "overlooked" by the ten o'clock. Likewise, his wife is probably a not-too-domestic slender four o'clock girl, who does his thinking for him.

Eleven o'clocks are the stereotyped "he-men" whose authoritarian natures are only excelled by the twelve o'clock, who must be the head man in whatever he does, either constantly or at least periodically. Therefore, authority positions are filled by twelve o'clocks who, because of their needs to be noticed, are always the pioneers in any new undertaking. Whatever they start, it is up to good six o'clock men to keep it running.

Skin and Flesh Tone

Insofar as skin and flesh texture are concerned, the firmest and most dense tone is found between ten and two o'clock. Proceeding towards three, we encounter greater translucency of skin and sinewy muscle development covered by softer flesh. As we move downwards towards five, we find, increasing with six and seven, the extremely soft marshmallow flesh which is characterized in women by small lumps and dimples on the buttocks and thighs even when young. Moving round to eight o'clock we find the flesh more resilient and bouncy. As nine o'clock "Teddy bear" qualities toughen up to ten o'clock, we find ourselves back where we started, observing girls with tawny, firm flesh and oft-times huge bosoms. It is the slim-hipped, big-breasted (and seemingly unattainable yet compelling to great numbers of men) girl of this category that is most often seen in the centerfold of a certain men's magazine not particularly noted for the yielding sexual propensities of its female employees.

General Proportions

Starting at twelve, we find broad shoulders and back, large rib cage, but not necessarily large breasts in women. If the breasts are large, the chest will be also. In a woman who is 5'8" one may find a forty-two inch bust with a "B" cup, whereas the three o'clock girl might have a thirty-five inch bust with a "D" cup. This is because the basic frame of the twelve o'clock woman is wedge shaped, while the three o'clock straightens out. Slim hips will be seen on both men and women of this category, in fact, the slimmest on the clock.

In keeping with the wedge shape, the proportions will be overbalanced on the top half of the body, so that if the person is seated, he will always appear taller than he is. Seen from the waist down, they will always appear shorter. They are often extremely long waisted and short-legged. The reason it is easy to assume them to be athletic types is because (especially in men) they have the facility of always being able to pull their stomachs in and look as though they have been exercising very rigorously! Actually, the majority of real athletes fall into the two to four and eight to ten positions, depending on their choice of sport.

To the right of twelve, we find the chest becomes narrower but just as deep. To the left of twelve, the chest becomes shallower but sometimes wider. If twelve o'clock people gain weight, it will show first in the torso, rather than the legs, the gain manifesting itself in the belly and gluteal region but not readily noticeable except in profile.

As we move towards one o'clock, and the chest narrows, by the time three is reached the torso has shortened proportionately and the legs lengthened. The field of fashion modeling draws from this category, as the women occupying it are almost straight up and down with a slight tendency to be slimmer below than above. Weight is not easily gained, and the nervous temperment burns up calories fast. If any weight should be gained or lost, it will be immediately noticed in the face, with a few scant pounds making the difference between a sunken, drawn look or a puffy appearance.

The four o'clock has virtually no waist and when tall is the traditional beanpole. Short four o'clocks, if inclined at all towards stoutness in later years, resemble little fat tree trunks. Three and four o'clock men who wish to develop their physiques must engage in a strict muscle-building regimen. They will probably never get fat but certainly must work to put on weight and it must be in the form of muscle. If the shoulders are to be broadened, the chest enlarged, the biceps developed, it must be through exercise in those particular areas, for the frame itself is not conducive to such enlargement. Hence, the compensation of the "ninety-seven pound weakling" stigma often results in some very grotesque muscle development resembling balloon-like appendages. The solitary nature of most three and four o'clocks is certainly conducive to the needed hours spent in gymnasiums, on teeter boards, jogging, rowing, cycling, etc.

As we round the bottom of the clock, weight starts to develop without trying, and at five o'clock care must be taken to keep weight *off*! By this point of the clock, the stick-like verticals have bulged at the sides forming an ellipse with the ideal Lunar or Vensuian form at the six o'clock position. Narrow shoulders, wide hips and thighs, long legs and short torso characterize the perfect six o'clock. If mermaids lived, they would all be six o'clocks, for they are as much synonomous with the fluidic quality of the six as the twelve is forged in fire.

Crab-like, the six o'clock is flat and wide, the abdomen and buttocks often disproportionately flat in comparison to the width of the pelvic area. Astrologers would be quick to call this the pure Cancerian type. The first place to gain weight and the last place to lose it are the outer upper thighs. Even with excess weight however, the waist can still be sucked in disproportionately owing to natural tendency towards abdominal flatness, which is a holdover from the beanpole four o'clocks, or if you prefer to come round from the other direction, a loss of stuffing from the sausage eight o'clocks.

As seven o'clock approaches, we see a bit more protruding from the rear end and tummy, and by eight o'clock, the torso has thickened, the waist lengthened, the legs shortened, until we see our "Teddy bear" nine o'clock. His solid body is usually accompanied by a face which is inclined towards rotundity. In fact, eight and nine o'clocks will always enjoy their food and must fight to stay slim. They gain weight in the legs, torso—in fact, just about all over! And the *last* place they will ever lose weight will be in the face. If a jovial, round-eight-thirty type man dropped from 250 to 140 pounds, his face would look little changed, even though he now resembled a lollipop.

The solid, husky fullback is often a nine o'clock, and if he can avoid eating his own food when he opens his restaurant after his retirement from football, he might still look good at fifty. The eight and nine o'clock gals are the type Kretschmer used to glorify as the "real woman" Pyknic types. The most "earthy" farm stock, socially gregarious, PTA going, Kewpie doll, with round hips, round breasts, round bottom—in short, *round all over*—fits this classification. Years ago *Esquire* magazine published an edifying article attesting to the fact that "Pyknics are more fun."

By the time we reach ten o'clock, the hips have slimmed, the shoulders widened, the legs shortened and the *Playboy* princess appears on the horizon with her counterpart, King Kong, holding her in his arms.

Sexual Proclivities

The woman most prone to stereotyped lesbian activities is the twelve o'clock. The man most likely to fit the established image of the homosexual is the six o'clock. *All* types, however, have their respective homosexual counterparts. This simply implies that a twelve woman and a six man are ideally suited for sexual interchange and often are transexuals. When a sex-change operation is performed, it is most complete and successful in these individuals.

Six o'clock professional female impersonators are the rule, whereas the "closet queen" transvestite usually appears in the secret practices of the eleven o'clock truck driver or twelve o'clock movie idol, who couldn't look more ridiculous in his sequined cocktail dress and spike heels!

The most sexually receptive persons fall between five and nine. The most aggressive in their sex drives are between nine and one. These are also the most openly exhibitionistic in a flagrant and contrived manner. Because they are social by nature, they want to be noticed more than the others on the clock.

The least sensual types are between one and five o'clock. The most successful (and frigid) prostitutes are one and two o'clocks. The person most likely to perform sex for spiritual enlightenment, protest, or not at all is the three or four o'clock. Here we find the typical hippie, with clothes carefully chosen to either conceal the figure completely or render it as unappealing as possible to all except others in the same peer group. Old beatnik and older bohemian types have always striven to find the latest style in burlap, war-surplus, Indian blankets, etc. for their apparel. Men of this grouping are the least concerned about sexual attraction by way of clothing; yet understandably, people who fall into this category will be the first to show their "freedom" by taking off all their clothes.

Seventy-five percent of the people you see featured in nudist magazines or girlie pictorials showing indelicately exposed genitalia are in this section of the clock. When the five to nine is exposed it is because he is drunk and doesn't know his pants are unzipped. The woman in the five to nine group always seem to have a way of exposing themselves without really trying and are experts in the art covered by the chapter, "Secrets of Indecent Exposure."

To simplify matters, it all boils down to this: When it comes to sex, nine to ones do it because they want to, one to fives do it for a purpose and five to nines do it because they can't help it!

Here are some additional pointers: The man who is the typical conventioneer and who seeks out play-for-pay gals is the eight or nine o'clock type and is usually the best salesman. Naturally, the gals who will accommodate him will be pro's from the two or three o'clock grouping, unless he should find a "social-minded" streetwalker from the ten o'clock group. Of course, she won't be nearly so appealing as she is closer to his own type. As a last resort, the visiting sales manager might even take a tipsy seven o'clock house-wife, who is out from Madison, Wisconsin visiting her sister. She is staying at the same hotel as he, and, not tired enough to go to sleep, stepped into the cocktail lounge as she walked through the lobby. After downing one drink, she was well on her way to losing her inhibitions. The next day she felt terribly ashamed of herself, and he felt it was okay, but he could have done better!

The fact that the five to nine o'clock girl is the most sub-missive sexually gives the long-legged, fluidic six and seven o'clocks the best swivel-hipped dance movement.

Ballerinas, who are on a more esthetic plane, move closer to five o'clock. The stiff and contorted spasms engaged in by "modern" dancers is exemplified by the three and four o'clocks. Their lack of carnal sexuality is shown in their dance movements, which, in keeping with the "air" influ-ence, are of a flying nature. The body remains relatively motionless, while the arms and legs flail about, sometimes resembling attempts to fly, sometimes to thrust away the "attacker," sometimes appearing as violent protest and always implying a "fleeing to freedom."

Contrast this with the erotic dance forms taken by the other long-legged dancers who occupy the lower half of the clock. If three and four wish to repel sexual advances and fly away, not so with eight and nine. These wiggly earth-worms will be inclined to hold their arms close to the body, limit their leg-thrashings, and rotate their bodies like mad! The arm and hand movements will imply a "pulling in" and "clutching to" and, in keeping with the "earth" influence, the dancer often resembles a groundhog "digging in."

Because the six o'clock is the longest-legged and com-prises a "swimming" compromise between the flying of the four and the digging of the eight, she will often steal the show. The most "perfect" female sexually-interpretive dance forms have been those best performed by six o'clocks through the ages. The Hawaiian hula and the Near Eastern nautch or "belly" dance are prime examples. The most pro-ficient exponents I have ever seen of the grass skirt and finger cymbal school of dance, as well as bump and grind artistry, have been almost "pure" six o'clocks.

When we move up to the top half of the clock, we find the spirit is willing but the flesh is weak, when it comes to dance forms as we know them. Being on the "masculine" half of the circle gives one more of an ability to strut rather than dance. It is for this reason that drum majorettes are usually ten and eleven o'clocks, who do a great job with a baton and "let's give the little lady a big hand." When one of them tires of the grange hall and goes to the city to get a job dancing in a topless club (as these large-chested types often do!), she invariably is much more appreciated for her mammaries than her movements. The twelve o'clock witch would best stay off the dance floor but confine her rhythmic motions to jungle priestess routines where her leopard skins and whip will be appreciated!

The worst natural dancers (who are usually wise enough not to try) are the cerebrally inclined, short-legged anti-social one and two o'clocks.

Incidentally, the higher up on the clock you are, the rougher time you will have coping with your periods. Also, the more you will be unfavorably influenced by the full moon. The lower you are on the clock, the *better* you will function during a full moon!

Sense of Humor

The degrees and type of humor are governed a great deal by the position one holds on our clock. Those with the highest developed sense of humor dwell within the eight to ten o'clock sector. These people can truly enjoy a funny situation without analyzing it. The most dour and humorless types are the two to fours. Whenever we see a comedian who *uses* comedy as a vehicle for bitter social criticism, he falls into this classification. The most responsive audiences are the five to nine types. Nine to ones must be able to identify themselves with the performer before they can appreciate him. And one to fives spend more time analyzing what is before them than experiencing it. Almost all critics are one to five types. Famous comedy teams like Laurel and Hardy, Abbott and Costello, etc. are usually two/eight or three/nine relationships.

Alcohol and Drug Use

Where booze is concerned, eight to tens consume the most and keep the bars in business. Eleven to twelves like it but most can take it or leave it. One and two types are most likely to abstain from alcohol or only drink for professional reasons. However, the majority of alcoholics fall into the eight to one grouping. Threes are prone to drugs, and the biggest percentage of drug abusers are the three and four o'clock types, just as the biggest lushes are the first mentioned eight to tens.

Interestingly enough, if and when a four o'clock drinks it will be cheap wine, because of its "poetic" connotations. If the ten o'clock feels "daring" he'll puff a little marijuana, because, being a basically social type, he will choose a social drug. If bourbon distilleries had to depend on four o'clocks and LSD pushers had to survive on ten o'clocks, they would both go broke overnight.

The folks at the bottom of the clock can take it, but once having taken, find it hard to leave, where alcohol is concerned. In these most easy-going and steady types a few drinks will trigger an oft-times welcome loss of inhibitions more readily than with any other category. These are the normally consistent and dependable types, who have one drink too many and wind up getting in a fight, taking their clothes off, or wetting their pants.

The most important rule to remember, concerning alcohol, is that whatever form it is taken in will have the effect of bringing the qualities of the *Demonic* to the surface. Thus, a normally jolly nine o'clock, when drunk, will become a morose, dour and cynical person. The dry, technical three o'clock will turn into a sort of arrested development life of the party, who might even sing a ribald song he learned in high school. The strong assertive twelve o'clock will become sentimental, nostalgic, maudlin over youthful errors and lost romance and might even cry in his good bonded whiskey. The five o'clock bank clerk will relive the beach at Anzio; and the eight o'clock, who is usually bouncing around like a rubber ball, will be found in a dark-

ened corner, morosely serious over what he feels is his lack
of accomplishment and how people don't know what he's
going through. When that old-time fundamentalist coined
the term, "demon rum," he never knew how right he was!

Professions and Occupations

Persons on the left side of the clock, from six to twelve,
are "social" types. Those on the opposite side are "non-
social" by nature. Therefore, positions in which other people are involved as an essential part of the occupation are
held by six to twelves. Technical, intellectual and clinical
roles are held by twelves to sixes.

Personality-wise, the clock can be divided down the
center, with "heart" people on the left and "head" people
on the right. Of course, the same kind of job *may* be held
by *any* of the different types on the clock. What we are
concerned with, though, is the incidence of certain type
persons for certain occupations, and how a person who is
a failure at his job is often in a profession totally alien to
his typing.

An example of this is the three-thirty salesman who
dreads meeting people and secretly hopes the sale doesn't
go through after subtly criticizing his product to the customer in the first place! His wrinkled suit looks like (and
is) the most unimportant thing in his wardrobe and his dull
brown shoes have never been polished. Here is a man who
should be working in an electronic plant soldering resistors,
so he can go home each night and do some more writing
on his play, which has "a great deal of social comment," or
at least go down to the coffee house and talk about his play.
Of course, the successful extreme of this type *is* likely to
be a successful writer of avant-garde plays.

There can be many sub-categories within the same profession. In medicine, for example, psychiatrists will fall into the two to four group, hospital administrators at five or six, lab technicians at three to five and surgeons one to three (the kind the little eight o'clock meat-balls all want to marry). Nurses that *care* about their patients (sometimes too much!) are six to eights, whereas the tough old birds who brook no nonsense are eleven to ones. The kindly old G.P.'s and most pediatricians are eight to elevens, and gynecologists are usually eights. The twelve o'clock is represented in the graying-at-the-temples, bedside manner physician, who specializes in diseases of the rich.

Defense attorneys are usually nine to elevens, while prosecuting attorneys are ideally two o'clocks. Most attorneys who become judges are eleven to one with the ideal combination of sympathy, analysis and symbolic leadership at high noon.

The lower one is on the circle, the more compatible with his own classification he is, e.g., six o'clocks get along with other six o'clocks. Very seldom, however, will a twelve o'clock be able to tolerate another twelve o'clock for any length of time. This is why a twelve o'clock leader may employ a six o'clock to act as a sounding board for others whom he wishes to influence. This is a common practice in planned political campaigns, where the twelve o'clock candidate employs many six o'clock campaign managers knowing they will be ideally suited to move among the masses of potential constituents. A very important aspect to be considered is the natural acceptance of the six o'clock campaign manager by the potential twelve o'clock constituent, who could easily be alienated from the twelve o'clock candidate should he meet him on a personal level. *In short, the six o'clock will be accepted most universally as he presents no threat to anyone's ego.* Therefore, he is indispensable to any twelve o'clock leader who wishes to reach the most people.

Consequently, the best spokesmen for someone else are always those directly opposite on the clock. The best managers of others are always six and seven o'clocks. "Fans" fall into the five to nine grouping, naturally being the most responsive audiences. The best salespeople are eight to tens, providing there is self-gain involved as well as financial. Most blue-collar workers and laborers are also in the eight to ten category, with professional military men and the best career soldiers falling within the ten to twelve grouping. Policemen and firemen are nine to ones with the majority of policemen ten to twelve. The authoritarian image of the policeman attracts a great many twelve o'clock types, but the majority are closer to ten o'clock.* The military, like the medical profession, has its various in-group classifications. We can observe these variants in any occupation or profession that embraces several different skills within a single field. Music is a striking example of this.

Fads for certain musical instruments will produce players and devotees from all categories on the clock, most of whom exhibit dubious degrees of ability. Usually, however, when they keep laughing long after you sit down at the piano, you give up any career you might have envisioned.

---

* An interesting observation of the author's is that the vast majority of idealistic protestors that engage in campus demonstrations and have a bitter hatred for the authority image of the policemen are four o'clock types, who are diametrically opposite on the clock from the tactical squad officers that clobber them. To the ten o'clocks, the demonstrating fours represent the height of sassy impudence and goading non-conformity; whereas, to the four o'clock demonstrators, the police represent the acme of totalitarian ignorance and brutality. When one recognizes certain factors, however, such actions resemble more of a sado-masochistic encounter exercise. As one self-aware eleven o'clock police officer, who had participated in such actions, told the author: "They're spitting at us and calling us names and acting like masochists, and we're just the sadists than can take care of them."

Assuming that not everyone can be a Paderewski, Segovia, Menuhin or Casals, we must consider the driving emotional force that produces great musicians. It has been said that a great musician must make love to his instrument, woo it like a mate, and bring out the best it has to offer. This is the secret of any great concert artist. The musical instrument is a substitute for the lust object. The Demonic element of any musician will be exercised in his musical instrument. Small wonder professional musicians exert a strong appeal over women. They (the musicians) are already "in love" and present an attractive challenge.

Here are the instruments which correspond to the numbers on our clock: 1. french horn; 2. saxophone; 3. clarinet; 4. harp, guitar; 5. flute, dulcimer; 6. violin, viola, cello; 7. oboe; 8. piano; 9. tympani; 10. snare drum, tom tom, etc.; 11. trumpet; 12. organ, trombone, tuba. As you can see, the instruments are listed with the most assertive near the top and the most passive, fluidic and pastoral near the bottom. Now, the choice of a musical instrument is much like the choice of a pet. When one has no other love, he will employ a representation of his Demonic layer in the form of the musical instrument he will "make love to." This will always take the form of the instrument *opposite* his position on the clock. If, however, he has his Demonic element properly exercised in another manner, he will choose, as a sort of "familiar," the instrument *closest* to himself on the clock. In this way, he is getting to the very Core of his personality.

An illustration of this entire concept is thus: There are two excellent professional violinists. Violinist "A" is a bachelor, twelve o'clock, slim-hipped, broad-shouldered, suave—in other words, a typical Hollywood stereotype of a gypsy, who has a job serenading diners at the Bit of Transylvania, a restaurant with atmosphere. As Laszlo (for that is his name) lovingly caresses his fiddle's "erogenous zones," the women present gaze longingly, their once-hot stroganoff mouldering cold on its plate. "For heaven's sakes," complains hubby, "eat your dinner!" The words die unheard, though, as all female eyes are on Laszlo making love to his violin. Little does Laszlo need any of those women right now, as his heart is taken.

Violinist "B" is George, an unassuming, rather short six o'clock, with a friendly smile and diligent approach to his art. George is happily married to a rather tweedy twelve o'clock, who sees to it he is well taken care of. He has a couple of young sons, who are his great pride, and holds a respectable position as concert master in a large symphony orchestra. He has his Demonic element indulged, so his violin is his "familiar," the real Core of his personality.

Occupationally speaking, the most retiring individuals are the academic researchers, critics, technicians, civil service clerks, ivory tower professors and collectors of welfare checks, who all fall in the three to five position. Most craftsmen who deal in delicate or intricate operations fall into the one to three grouping; however, we occasionally see the same phenomenon as pertains to the musician who is in love with his instrument. Typical of this is the round little eight o'clock inventor who is "married" to his laboratory. In painting and sculpture, we see this Apparent Demonic dichotomy quite frequently. In these cases the situation is easy to spot, because there is visual evidence of it in the product of the artist.

An interesting case which comes to mind is that of a nine o'clock man who was in the antithetical profession of electronics engineering—one usually occupied by three o'clocks. It turned out that electronics work was the manifestation of his Demonic self and despite the compulsion he felt towards this field, he half-heartedly undertook many sidelines: real estate sales, boat leasing, vending machines, etc., in addition to his cherished technical profession. His side-activities were clearly more natural adjuncts of his basic type, but still he courted electronics, excelling brilliantly. After many years of pouring himself into his Demonic pursuits, he started dating girls—and what was the means he used to meet his female companions? An electronically computerized dating service! In this way he could maintain his electronic "mistress," yet consort with "other women" with her approval, as she was instrumental in supplying him with his lovers! Needless to say, all the girls with whom the computers supplied him were three o'-clocks.

A good test for personality typing, if the individual who is your subject has any drawing ability, is this: Ask your subject to draw a picture of a woman, assuming your subject is a man. The result you see will be the Demonic layer of his personality, from which you may take your cue, should you wish to bewitch him. Artists and sculptors of all types show their Demonic side most readily. If some of you recall the pictures of girls you used to draw when you were in your teens, you will remember how the girl on whom you drew your favorite hair style or eye make-up always looked as you would have liked to look—which is always like a girl opposite you on the clock!

Sports, Athletics, Aches and Pains

Sports involving teamwork are played by those on the left side of the clock, except for boxers, who are usually around eleven. Wrestlers, on the other hand, can be twelve o'clocks, as due to the nature of most present-day wrestling, both performers "win," and a twelve o'clock cannot stand to lose! For this reason, the twelve o'clock, whom Kret-

schmer misleadingly called the "athletic" type, is the one
least likely to engage in any sort of competitive sport. However, if the twelve o'clock can be the sole or stellar performer, he excels.

Just as there are more twelve o'clock orchestra conduc-
tors than any other type, so you will find similarities in the
sports and athletic world. All of the famous weight lifters
(not the earlier mentioned three and four o'clock body-
builders) were twelves.° The Achilles heel in the case of
the twelve o'clock is the lower spine. All those famous
strong-men had to wear stomachers under their leopard
skin tunics to keep their sacroilliacs from acting up. The
reason for this and the reason most men in the ten to two
group have back problems is because they were never
meant to walk on two legs as well as the others! Their long
torsos and short legs are not equipped for such trained animal shenanigans.

The long-legged people at the bottom of the clock never
have such problems, as their bodies are relatively small for
the big legs that carry them. Their weak spot is usually the
feet and ankles—especially in the five to sevens. Being like
mermaids, dolphins or others unaccustomed to walking on
their tail flippers, these people are great when it comes to
wiggling but keep the podiatrists in business.

Six o'clocks are the most comfortable in water and therefore often expert swimmers. Mountain climbers would be
thought to be twelve o'clocks, but usually are intellectual
twos and threes with a desire to leave the lower world behind and get into the rarified air. The pioneering twelve
o'clock must have an audience, and mountain climbing is
usually too solitary for his ego needs. Explorations are also

---

° One-of-a-kind circus performers, like featured jugglers, whip-crack-
ers, human cannon balls, finger balancers, wild animal trainers, trapeze
artists (usually "catchers") are notoriously twelve o'clock types.

more for twos and threes, who often limit their human companionship anyway.

In sports, the ideal referee or coach is the six o'clock who, like the twelve o'clock judge, has the emotional/analytical balance needed but must give the actual show to others. The audience will watch the orchestra conductor, but seldom do sports spectators get worked up over the referee. Most referees and coaches manifest their Demonic layer in the participants of the sport.

Baseball players are usually nine to elevens, who can keep their weight down. Football players range all the way from eight to eleven, depending on the position they play. Always remember, the further down on the clock, the better the runner, as the legs are longer. In soccer, the same grouping as with football holds true. From one to three, we find tennis and handball players, and pole vaulters, (flying) broad jumpers, trampoline, track runners, and surprisingly enough, basketball players * are threes and fours.

Auto racers fall into different groups. Sports car racers are usually two o'clocks, while stock car, rod and street racers are ten and elevens. The big Indianapolis jobs are usually driven by elevens and, naturally, where nobody else is in the race (like a salt flat trial of a specially built car), as you might expect, it'll probably be driven by a twelve.

Horse race jockeys are usually scaled-down one o'clocks, and a wondrous example of the horse being their "famil-

* Basketball is a strangely paradoxical situation, as in order to find the most ideally physically suited individuals (tall, fairly limber, long legs for running, quick and violent arm movements), four o'clocks are custom-made. Fours, however, are not the least bit competitive and are solitary by nature. Hence, many basketball players are "pushed" into the sport by parents or friends (or themselves), who feel *every* boy must have a sport of some kind. Could this be why basketball referees have to do more goading, running around and shouting than the often-morose, non-social players themselves?

iar," rather than their Demonic element. Usually, jockeys' Demonic elements come out in the choice of a rather large, overweight blonde, seven o'clock floozy.

We will leave fad sports like: miniature golf (now full-sized), water skiing, go-carting, and hula-hooping, with the advice that, like musical instruments, in these fads only those who excell can give us an accurate personality typing.

Are You Passive or Dominant by Nature?

By now you probably have a pretty good idea of your position on "The LaVey Personality Synthesizer." Now, let's consider your relative position as a sorceress.

When assuming the role of witch, it is important to re-member that you are acting in an ultimately dominant capacity, even though you are passive by nature. Every woman is essentially passive, but only insofar as her bio-logical functions are concerned. Many women, and espe-cially those who are inclined to be predators, are decidedly masculine in their drives. The biggest threat to any man is that which attacks his ego in a feminine form. The most aggressive male will be a willing "slave," so long as his ulti-mate male ego is allowed to remain intact. Once a man has been charmed by a witch, he should be unable to resist whatever her wishes might be.

The more sexually secure a man is, the less sexually ag-gressive he is likely to be. This is a rule all witches must learn well. One of the first signs of a need to be dominated by a woman shows up in the overly-aggressive male, sex-ually speaking. We can liken this to the mistaken recog-nition of the sadist and the masochist. It would be assumed that the sadist would be the man who goes about insulting and baiting others, while the masochist quietly sits back without offending anyone. Actually, the person who torments others at the drop of a hat is the masochist, because he secretly wishes to be beaten for his rude and offensive behavior and does what he can to engender such retribution. Such is the overly-aggressive male, who paws every woman he comes near and could vulgarly be described as an "ass-grabber."

This type of man seldom gets his come-uppance at the hands of a real witch, because women instinctively think of him as a dominant and aggressive type, when actually, he is crying out to be mastered. *His aggressive behavior is more a challenge to fight than to make love,* and we see his type chewed up the most in the animal kingdom where the shots are called with more accuracy! If you want a man you can master easily, this is an ideal type to stalk, as he will fall right into your hands, without your even trying. All that needs to be done is to act as brash and insulting as possible and he will fall helplessly in love with you. If, however, you succumb to his first advances and do not symbolically slap his face (which is what he wants), he will have had the unrewarding satisfaction of defiling another "stupid broad," thus sustaining his disappointment in women and frustrating his search for a woman he can "respect." What he really means when he refers to a woman he can "respect" is a woman who's tougher than he is!

If you are an outwardly dominant type of woman, you are probably used to being approached by this type and wonder why that, just when you think you have found a real dominant male who can make you feel like a helpless creature, he turns out to be another little boy, who clutches at you like his nursemaid. The submissive type of woman is never too disappointed by this type, because she usually gives in to him before he has a chance to show his true colors. Neither will she ever reap any rewards from him, though, as he can feel no "respect" for his submissive partner. For those of you who are passive type witches, it is important that you hold off a bit just to see how really dominant he is. If he shows interest in you and tries to put the make on you and you refuse, if he is truly dominant by nature and sure of himself, he will move on to someone else whom he feels is mutually interested and thereby indulge himself in a most selfish manner. This is the man worth setting your spell for, as he is truly independent and will complement your passive nature. Then, it is your turn to act as the aggressor and, as if an afterthought, agree to accept his advances. You have made the important submissive move that gratifies his dominant nature, yet genuinely not allowed him to think you are a pushover. If, however, the man you have thought to be dominant becomes *more* frantic after you have rejected his advances, forget it! You will wind up with a wailing suitor who will stifle your chances to find the man you really need.

The sexually over-aggressive man can be collected easily by the naturally dominant woman, who can accumulate an entire slave camp simply by allowing herself to appear on the scene wearing the accoutrements of the "push-over" as bait. Many successful career witches have acquired their male adjutants in this very manner. This is why many of the best positions in sales and executive managership are held by such "ass-grabbers," whose sexual combativeness is sublimated in the business world.

The Power of Certain Names

It has long been considered *de rigeur* that witches have "magical" names. The reasons for this are varied. Obviously, many witches do not want their true identities known, so a secret name used only in the company of other witches often insures anonymity, lest one of the less-discreet witches in the coven spill the beans.

We are not concerned in this book with the names of witches listed in Margaret Murray's *Witch Cult in Western Europe*, as these names (Margaret, Bridgit, Janet, Isabel, Katherine, Ann, etc.) tell us nothing insofar as the influence of certain names is concerned. What testimony they present lies in the fact that *any* and *all* girl's names are found on the rosters of the inquisitors. During the days of witch trials, it mattered not what your name was. *Any* name could be used as evidence of witchery, just as any freckle or blemish could be considered a witch's mark.

Latter-day witches, however, seem to favor names with an exotic sound or demonic connotation, and you are more likely to encounter witches named: Lilith, Hecate, Astarte, Devilla, etc., than Nancys or Lindas. My experience has shown me that the Nancys and Lindas are often the most competent witches, though, and for a very good reason.

As I have previously stated, the most important thing to any man is his ego. In dealing with a man in the top half of our clock, a witch must realize that she should do nothing to threaten this ego. In charming a man on the lower half of the clock, however, the witch must *supply* and literally *be* his ego; so here a "strong" name can be employed. Dominant men will seldom respond sexually to a strong female name, whereas passive males will excitedly tremble at the sound of one. Therefore, don't blame anyone but yourself if your name is Frankie, or Rita or Casey or Hilda and all you attract are fawning men! You can't place the blame on your parents' shoulders, because even if they named you an ill-fitting name, there is nothing stopping you from either modifying or changing it. In order to present a consistent image, you must use a name which corresponds to the role you are playing. If, temporarily, you step out of your image, remember to modify your name accordingly.

There are many stupid misconceptions under which inexperienced witches labor. For example, if your name is Roxanne and you are a ten o'clock witch, your name is fine, so long as you confine your bewitchments to men lower on the clock than yourself. Suppose you should want to enchant a one o'clock man. It won't be easy in the first place, and you will have to do all you can to present yourself in the image of a seven o'clock woman. This means you must modify your appearance slightly, your voice, and your name. Yes, you heard right, your *name*.

But being a ten o'clock, your ego won't allow you to extract a simple old "Anne" from your existing name, thereby allowing the one o'clock man to feel "on stage," instead of yourself. No—you start thinking about names that are "soft," less dominant, less ego-threatening, because someone has told you about this book. The next time you see your quarry you decide to use your new-found formula and spring this sort of thing on him: "You know, my name is Roxanne, but people that know me real well call me 'Kitten.'" Talk about out of the frying pan into the fire! You would have thought "Kitten" would be just the thing with its soft fur and purr but still the hint at claws; but you missed the point completely! YOU *HAD* TO THINK OF SOMETHING "DIFFERENT"! And by choosing something different, you're back with your big whip threatening his ego! Instead, you should have hit him with something like this: "You know, my name is really Joanne, but it sounded so ordinary, I changed it. But sometimes I really wonder if I did the right thing."

There have been few studies on the power of certain given names over their owners, but the few researchers in the subject have turned up some startling, but easily-understood findings. What is equally as important as the commonness or unusualness of a name, in witchery, is its "hardness" or "softness" and unconscious semantic connotations. A name like "Roxanne" is a "hard" name because of the "x" sound and its semantic connotation to the word "rocks." Therefore, it is an excellent name for a twelve o'clock witch but totally antithetical for a six. Consonants that constitute "soft" sounds, where names are concerned, are those that either project the tongue against the back of the teeth or pucker up the lips. "Hard" consonants are those that do not require that the mouth be closed or the tip of the tongue employed, but rather where the glottis does most of the work, as in "k" and hard "g" sounds.

A "dominant" name need not be one with a hard sound, but can be anything of an exotic nature—in other words, anything that will "steal the show." Witches who are playing the roles of four to eight types would do well to avoid such names but confine their originality to changes from usual spellings rather than in the sound of the name, e.g., Jane = Jayne, Tammy = Tami, etc. Here are some examples of ideal names for ten to two o'clock witches:

Abra	Amina	Clorinda
Acacia	Anatola	Cosma
Acantha	Arabella	Crescent
Adelpha	Ardath	Crystal
Adora	Argenta	Dagmar
Agave	Arachne	Dale
Aida	Atlanta	Derelys
Alanna	Ava	Desiree
Allyn	Azuri	Devilla
Alexandra	Bathsheba	Dextra
Alexis	Brunhilda	Dorcas
Alison	Calista	Eartha
Allegra	Calypso	Elektra
Alpha	Carmen	Eleanor
Alura	Cassandra	Elysia
Alzena	Celeste	Erika
Amber	Chandra	Fabia

Fanchon	Lilith	Sibyl
Faustina	Lucretia	Sydney
Fleta	Ludmilla	Sonya
Fortuna	Lunetta	Sorcha
Freya	Lysandra	Terry
Gail	Mab	Thalia
Galatea	Majesta	Theda
Gemma	Marvella	Tiberia
Gillian	Mercedes	Titania
Hecate	Morgana	Tracy
Hera	Nadja	Ultima
Hypatia	Nike	Ulrika
Ilka	Nyx	Urania
Ilona	Oona	Valda
Imperia	Omphale	Valerie
Isis	Ozora	Valkyrie
Isolde	Palmyra	Vampyra
Jinx	Pandora	Vanessa
Jocasta	Perfidia	Velvet
Kama	Pyrena	Veronica
Karla	Quilla	Vicki
Kali	Regina	Volante
Kelly	Rexana	Wallis
Kevin	Rita	Winifred
Kim	Rowena	Wynne
Kimberly	Roxanne	Xylona
Kirstin	Sabrina	Yolanda
Karma	Samantha	Zandra
Leonore	Satania	Zara
Leona	Scarlett	Zeena
Leslie	Selena	Zora
Lexine	Shelly	Zyklonia
Libby	Sherry	

Naturally, if you want to really get obvious, an out-and-out man's name can be used, thinly disguised, such as Georgie, Frankie, Tommie, Bobby, Freddie, Billy, etc. It has long been a predilection of young girls to nickname their best friends with male variants of existing names, e.g., Winifred = Freddy rather than the more feminine "Winnie." In such cases where the root name was a man's, the nickname will be a reversion to the original male name as in many of those previously mentioned. This is nothing more than an unconscious manifestation of the Demonic element.

Ideal names for witches who are either within or playing the role of the three to nine grouping are many. Here is a sample list with the "borderline" names (marked with an asterisk) that can be safely employed by women in any position on the clock:

Adelle*	Dixie*	Lois
Alice	Donna	Loralee
Alicia	Doris	Louise
Angela	Dorothy*	Lynn
Anita	Earline	Margie
Anne	Eileen	Marilyn
Annette	Elaine*	Marla
Arlene	Erin*	Marlene
Babette	Eve*	Marsha
Barbara*	Evelyn	Marylou
Beth	Frances	Melanie
Beverly	Georgina*	Melissa
Blanche*	Gerry*	Maureen*
Betty	Gwen	Nancy
Bridget	Helen*	Pamela
Candy	Irene*	Pat
Carol	Iris*	Peggy
Cathy	Jackie*	Phyllis*
Charlene	Jane*	Roberta*
Charlotte*	Jean*	Sandi*
Cheryl	Jill	Sheena
Christine*	Joan*	Sheila*
Cindy	Joanne	Shirley
Claire*	Joyce*	Susan
Clarice	Judy	Tammy
Claudia	Julie	Vera*
Cleo	June	Verna
Connie*	Karen*	Vickie*
Corinne	Lana*	Virginia
Cynthia	Lani	Vivian*
Darlene	Lorna	Wanda*
Debbie	Linda	Wendy
Denise	Liz	Yvonne
Diane	Lisa	

These names have been carefully chosen, all nuances of sound taken into consideration. Where a nickname variant

of another name is shown, it is because the variant is more
effective for our present purposes than the original name.
In some instances slight changes in a name, which will
make it more conducive to another image, should be obvious, e.g., Marge or Margie can admirably be "strengthened" by a change to Margaret or Margo. Softening or
hardening of the "g" makes a vast difference. Marge ends
on a soft "g." Margie has a soft "g" followed by the diminu-
tive in the "ee" sound, which adds a further note of "helplessness" to the already obvious unpretentiousness of the
name. Such a name can never present an ego-threat to a
top-of-the-clock male. Margaret, however, has the hard "g"
coming right down like a mallet in the center, followed up
with a hard-to-form "ret."

His Name

A lot can be told about a man by his name. It is amazing
how few persons realize the impact a name can have on
success or failure. Names are very much like looks. You can
either have what W. C. Fields referred to as a "euphonious
appelation" or an extremely ugly-sounding name and make
it work for you. If a name is nondescript, it has its advantages, but they lie principally in their element of camouflage or protective coloration.

A man with a name like Gregory Belmont will often see
the advantages in such a pleasant sounding label, whereas
a fellow named Phil Peckerdick might have a rough time
of it *if* he allows himself to! The man who really must try
harder to get ahead is the "Bill Johnson," and those who
do succeed are often the same man but "D. William Johnson" or "Will Desmond Johnson" or "W. Desmond Johnson." Such a man would be likely to succeed, simply because he could remain aloof to occasional comments like:

(60)

"What's he trying to give it with that 'W. Desmond Johnson' crap"! For a witch bent on enchanting such a man, it would prove disastrous to come on with a name like "Zorita." When dealing with a man with an unpretentious name, however, it is usually safe to have a more exotic name than his. Despite the connotations of certain surnames and their influence in a person's life, we will deal here primarily with first names and the diverse forms they take.

In America it is the rule to employ first names as an assumption of familiarity, so the form these names take gives much indication of the personality of their owners. Testimony to the importance of the first name in contemporary American culture can be illustrated by the anecdote about the man who went before the judge, petitioning that his name be changed. "What is your present name," the judge asked. "Joe Schitz, your honor," replied the applicant. "Well," commented the judge, "I can readily understand your desire to take another name. What is the new name you would like to assume?" The man answered, "Vincent Schitz, your Honor." Astonished, the judge asked him why he wished to change his name in this manner. "Well, your honor," the man answered, "Every time I see anybody I know they yell at me, 'Hello Joe, whatta ya know'!"

To say that a man's name is an extension of his ego is true, and many men will employ a fancy name as a cover-up for lack of ability or achievement. Again, this is very much like good looks in a girl. If you have the knowledge of applied witchery, such beauty can be invaluable, but if you are laboring under misinformation, self-deceit and exploitation, good looks can be a curse. There is nothing more ludicrous than the familiar, self-deluded, talentless, puffed-up twelve o'clock type man with a fancy name, presiding from his regular bar stool at the corner saloon.

Equally as common in our society is the plodding five o'clock office clerk with a face no one would notice and a name to match, whose importance is such that the firm would practically collapse, should he ever leave.

A good test of a man's nature is whether he uses a nickname, and if so, the enforcing of such a nickname over another possible variant of the same root name. Examples of this are the diversities of personality types bearing a name such as "Charles," relative to whatever nickname, e.g., "Charlie," "Charley," "Chuck," "Chick," "Chazz,"—or a foreign variant that has been bestowed by parents, e.g., "Karl," "Carl," "Carlos," "Carlo," "Karel," etc. There are certain personality connotations in such nicknames and foreign variants that readily present themselves to the aware observer. "Charlie's" are usually easy-going, "Chuck's" more assertive, "Chick's" inclined towards cockiness, and "Charles's" reserved and sophisticated. "Will's" always have more depth than "Bill's," and "Willie's" retain a boyishness, while "Billy's" often go looking for trouble. "Carl's" are usually serious, and "Carlos's" are inclined to chase after anything in a skirt. "Richard's" are bookworms, whereas "Rich's" are usually a trifle conceited. "Ricky's" are womanchasers and "Rick's" are often swaggering toughs. "Dick's" still predominate, however, and can be found hanging around, no matter what type you are dealing with. "Tom's" are usually quite stable, but "Tommy's" are cut-ups. "Bob's" are easily bewitched, but "Robbie's" fancy themselves as romantic leads, as do "Steve's," "Gary's," "Lance's," "Kirk's," and other assorted sex tags. "Mike" is an allaround guy, whereas "Michael" is serious and romantic.

Foreigners who maintain their original names upon coming to America are much more headstrong and harder to bewitch than those who leap right into an Americanized variant of their original name. They are magically very sound in retaining their foreign names, as the element of intrigue is always present. The meaning of the word, "exotic," we mustn't forget, is simply "foreign." Any witch who is an exotic type to start with can do well with a foreign variant of her name. A dashing-looking Frenchman named Laurent Gautier would have to be crazy to start calling himself "Larry Walters," the Anglicized version of his name. Likewise, a sexy witch from Ireland named Sheena would have rocks in her head if she took up its popular American variant, "Jane."

The Law of the Attraction of Opposites

It should be apparent by now that if you wish to enchant or charm a man, you must portray an image diametrically opposite on the clock from him. The only exceptions to The Law of the Attraction of Opposites are in cases where either one or both of the individuals involved has not yet matured sexually, even though they are fully equipped for sex, physically. The natural process of selection arranges things so two persons of the identical physical types will not mate and wind up in a few generations with the same problem as over-pedigreed dogs. History, however, shows us many examples of improper breeding, due to imposed standards of decorum or fashion. It's not that I'm against such things; genetic control is not only a necessity, but an eventual certainty. But it won't come in the form of breeding twelve o'clocks with other twelve o'clocks or six o'clocks with six o'clocks. So if you're hung up on a cute two o'clock boy and you happen to be two o'clock yourself, you want a big brother, not a lover, and you're probably very young. Wait a couple of years and your tastes will change!

As obvious as it may seem, most people are still unaware of the attraction of opposites. In order to appear the opposite of your quarry, you must resort to many techniques. If you are naturally attracted to him, chances are good that your physical choice is close enough, already. If you are bewitching for ulterior purposes, though, you will sometimes have to start modifying your appearance at bedrock —your physique.

First, though, let's go back to the witch who is naturally attracted to a certain man. If she is a ten o'clock, being basically a woman, she will secretly want a man who is more dominant than herself, which only leaves eleven and twelve o'clock men. She will gravitate towards and therefore compel men to her who are lower down on the clock than herself, as they represent the Demonic element within her. You see, she must fully bring out the Demonic, before she can recognize the Core, so here is what happens: She constantly attracts four and five o'clock men with whom she toys, sometimes basking in the welcome attention and ego-gratification they give, other times disdainfully avoiding them as pests. It is quite obvious that this type of woman has her share of her Demonic counterparts in ready abundance. She then sees a man, one who is "different" from the others and who doesn't seem to be the least bit interested in her. Naturally, this strength of independence brings out the little girl in her and places her in a role other than her usual one of control. What is she to do to get this man?

First, she must give up any notion she may have of "mastering" him as she has been able to do with all the rest. The minute she masters him, she will lose interest in him and be right back where she started, searching for a man who can serve as a counterpart to the missing third ingredient of her personality—the strong man that lurks beneath both her female Apparent layer and her four o'clock male Demonic layer. Having realized that she has found a temporary "master" (and it can never be other than temporary), she must get every bit of mileage she can from such a relationship. The next thing she must do is look in the mirror—that old tool of the Devil—and see what must be done to bring her physically closer to that place on the clock where his "ideal" mate would be—about five or six o'clock.

As she stands, her legs are fairly slim, her hips trim, a long waist and well developed breasts. She's never had any trouble attracting men, but they never seem to be the ones she really wants. First of all, she'll have to fatten up in her hips and thighs, do something to make her posterior appear bigger and her breasts appear smaller. *Heresy!* Who in the world ever heard of purposely putting on weight in the butt? Well, I have! And I've seen the positive results that ensue. You say you can't gain weight in the legs, it all goes into your breasts first? Well, then, there are tricks that will make you look bigger below and smaller above, which are familiar to most women. The biggest problem you'll have with this advice is resolving yourself to trying it.

Women (especially in America) have been brainwashed for so long into thinking "thin" that it is unfathomable to them that there could be any sane men with other standards. Most women can gain weight in the legs, hips and thighs without too much trouble but fight against such apparent lunacy. What is even worse is that witches of the very type that nature intended to be a little on the chubby side fight constantly against their own success by adhering to this sort of foolishness. Thus, many seven and eight o'clock girls will diet themselves sick, wear figure-concealing clothes and have convinced themselves that they really look best that way.

When one wants to believe something, it takes little encouragement, and what these girls don't realize is that the only men that are going to be giving them the most encouragement in their new slim roles are the men who are closest to their own type on the clock!

At least half the women who read this book will occupy positions on the clock which are conducive to weight gain. If you happen to be one of them, let me congratulate you. You need starve yourself no longer. Unless you have a specific enchantment to perform that necessitates being a slim type, take full advantage of the bulges you have been so long in hating. The only men you'll attract are the ones you yourself would be interested in, and what's wrong with that? Don't ever forget that compulsion is but a short step from attraction, and whosoever you can attract you can compel!

Whatever physical type you naturally happen to be, represents the Demonic in some man, and if you adhere to your basic type and allow yourself to exploit all of its attributes and eccentricities, you will evolve into a compleat witch!

By His Automobile Ye Shall Know Him

Several years ago, Marshall McLuhan scratched the surface on a blatant facet of American culture—the automobile. The book was *The Mechanical Bride,* and the victim of his attack was a then-popular large automobile replete with obvious sexual symbols in the form of portholes and chrome phalli. Several years later, Vance Packard blew the lid off the entire subject with *The Hidden Persuaders* followed by John Keats' *The Insolent Chariots.* While these two writers have given us superb commentary on the sexual symbolism of the automobile, there is still much to reveal concerning personality analysis based on the car one drives.

American men *are* motivated into buying certain cars

because of the need to extend their personalities into whatever meaningful accouterments they acquire. Just how meaningful *any* accouterment is has much to do with a witch's *modus operandi.*

To the man who is on the top half of our clock, the automobile is most meaningful as a personality assertion—or so it would appear. This is often true, but we will see many apparent contradictions to such a generalization—and for good reason. The automobile is much like the example of the musical instrument mentioned earlier. It has been said to be either a wife or a mistress, but the old analysis predicated upon wife/sedan, mistress/convertible stopped far too short of our present mark.

Let us consider the automobile to be a manifestation of either the Demonic or the Core. This base of operation will be necessary in order that you may define much about your quarry and what your chances will be of landing him. If a man's car is also his lust object, or Demonic, he will either be easy to woo away from his lacquer mistress or stick by her like fiberglass, depending upon his position on the clock. If a man's Demonic is catered to in another form, leaving him with a car like himself, he may not need you at all, but at least you know you won't be competing with an automobile!

Let's get started on the formula. The type of cars listed are those representative of the various numbers on our clock. Certain factors must be taken into consideration when observing an individual's car, such as: Is it his own or loaned? Is it his choice or his wife's? Is it used for a specific purpose other than personal transportation (camper, carryall, pickup, good humor truck, road grader, etc.)? Is it a holdover from a previous marriage or romance that is being kept for reasons of a convenience or financial nature? These are all questions that must be kept in mind. Then, the typing can begin:

One o'clock: showy or extravagant cars of an expensive nature, often of foreign make. The *type* of car is more important than *newness* of car.

Two o'clock: quality sports cars of foreign make, but not ostentatious.

Three o'clock: imported economy cars, "strictly transportation" older low-priced American cars.

Four o'clock: imported economy cars, often beat-up, older model low-priced American cars.

Five o'clock: low priced newer American cars, foreign economy cars, American compacts.

Six o'clock: American compacts and later model low priced American cars.

Seven o'clock: more elaborate American compacts, low to middle priced American cars.

Eight o'clock: newer American medium-priced cars or "top-line" compact.

Nine o'clock: upper-medium priced American cars, usually newer models.

Ten o'clock: larger American cars, large American sports cars, special or "hot" American compacts, all generally newer models.

Eleven o'clock: large American cars, often older luxury models, older large luxury sports cars.

Twelve o'clock: cars guaranteed to stand out, whether through size, luxury, etc., so long as there is a look of importance.

Ten o'clocks wash and polish their cars the most; fours the least. Eleven o'clocks trade their cars in most often, fives keep them 'til they fall apart. Whenever you see a man driving a car that is antithetical to his type, you know the car represents his Demonic side, his secret yearning.

Examples of this are unkempt four o'clock hippies who own (for protest, they think) a gleaming Rolls Royce; the rotund six o'clock office manager who drives an Eldorado (while chewing on a big cigar), etc. Most important, though, seldom will you encounter this Demonic transference going from top to bottom on the clock. Invariably, it will take its form in cases where the automobile-Demonic element is *above* the individual's position on the clock.

The person occupying the higher position on the clock would not allow himself to be viewed by others while exercising his Demonic, should the Demonic lower him in the eyes of others. The person on the lower half of the clock has nothing to lose by roaring around town in a fancy car.

In addition to the choice of car, there is much revealed by the driving habits of motorists. If the car is used as a Demonic exercise, the driver can often become a demon on the highway, quite literally. When the car is used as an extension of the self in a Demonic form, the driver can easily disregard all others on the road, as he is too busy carrying on his affair to be bothered with such trifles as speed limits. Everyone has seen the sallow-faced youth screeching down the freeway, weaving in and out of traffic, his right arm resting on the back of his seat while he steers with his left, huddled tightly against the corner where the back of the driver's seat meets the door. I have heard highway patrolmen who spot such types refer to them derisively (but accurately) as "humping the steering wheel."

Whatever you do, *don't* attempt to bewitch a man who is in love with his car. I have read advice in certain magazines and newspaper columns, telling concerned young girls that they should "learn about his car and talk about it with him and let him know you take an interest in it," and everything will be all right. Well, let's explode that kind of advice once and for all, for any readers who have ever employed such tactics know well the folly of them! At best, you will be allowed to hang around as an extra accessory rather than as a *new* interest and wind up the best dressed mag wheel on the block.

Sleep Patterns . . . and Other Bedroom Activities

Here is a test you can run using your friends as guinea pigs. You can always tell the mate who is most dominant by the side of the bed on which he or she sleeps. When two people are sleeping together, the dominant personality will always be on the right side of the bed, assuming both parties are lying on their backs. Thus, if the man is sleeping to the right of his mate, he will be the most dominant. If the woman is to the right of the man, she rules the roost.

Often such patterns start when couples are first married and never change, even though the personalities of the individuals have. At least you'll know what the situation was when the initial attraction occurred. Males who sleep on the left side of the bed are more interested in oral sexual activity than men who sleep to the right of their partners. Likewise witches who like oral sex will find their best partners sleeping to their left. Exceptions to these rules are cases necessitating one or the other person's convenience, such as nursing mothers, telephones, illnesses, etc.

If you can find a man's fetish, you can spellbind him. Everyone has some sort of sexual fetish, even if it is not even known to the person himself. Unfortunately, too many people assume that a fetish must be an overtly sexual accouterment. This is hardly the case, as the most compulsive fetishes are often those devices or situations that the average person would never consider to be in any way connected with sexual activity.

We are all too familiar these days with the usual types of

fetishes, such as long hair, high heels, garters, bondage, whipping, spanking, corsets, etc. A competent witch should not even consider such devices and acts as fetishes, however, as these represent the skeletons in far too many mental closests to be considered "abnormal." The Shadow used to claim he knew "what evil lurks in the hearts of men," and you too must be aware of his knowledge if you are to become a witch.

Some so-called fetishes are so universal, it seems unfair to consider them anything other than human manifestations of behavior that has its parallels in all areas of the animal kingdom. Outside of the most common attraction factor of all—dominance to a passive person and receptivity to a dominant person—the surest yardstick for fetishistic success is his reaction to certain phases idly dropped in conversation.

If you are around a man long enough to get into conversation, key phrases may be injected that will make his eyes light up and invariably ask to hear more about it or hem and haw for awhile bringing the topic back later in the conversation. Key phrases stating the obvious are unnecessary, as in the case of comments about an article of clothing you are wearing at the time that could be construed as fetishistic. Certain so-called fetishes should be employed *all* the time a witch is on the job, or she cannot claim to be a witch in the truest sense. These obvious fetishes will be discussed in later chapters.

Here is a list of fetish-finders from which you may take your cues. Remember, ONCE YOU HAVE ASCERTAINED HIS FETISH, DRIVE IT HOME BY SUBTLE REFERENCES AND IDLE COMMENT. If you are clever, an opening in conversation can always be created to inject these fetish-finders, phrased in your own manner. Reference to:

How you won't take any guff from a man (boss, husband, other suitor).

How you told someone off.

Shame at being chastised by boss.

Being spanked as a child.

Deserving a good spanking (either you or him).

Hair-pulling match with another woman.

A nasty dog you know who is free with his snout.

How some stupid people think you're a lesbian.

Your feet being all hot and sweaty.

Not being able to bathe in several days.

How some poor man you know is all excited over you.

How it must be fun to be a man.

How he'd make a very pretty girl.

How shocked and embarrassed you were to see a man exposing himself.

Accidently exposing yourself.

Accidentally wetting your pants.

Cutting your hair if it's long, letting it grow or getting a fall if it's short.

At least *one* of these topics is guaranteed to elicit an obvious response when subtly injected into the conversation. The ones that are meaningless to your quarry will be glossed over—in one ear and out the other or rejected with a shrug or idle comment. It is when you see (and the eyes tell) him pick up the cue and feed it back with grim or nervously-wrought interest that you know you've hit the mark.

Once you know you have accurately reached that mark you have a magical weapon at your disposal that will serve you if all else fails. You might even wind up having to actualize such fetishes if bewitching your quarry is important enough to you. It's the old question: Just how meaningful is it to gain what you want? You might be all wrong in every physical attribute for his taste, but if he is turned on by a girl who will dress as a nursemaid and will paddle his bottom while he is dressed as a little girl and *you* act as though you love doing just that, you will walk away from any competition from other gals who only have their looks and proper position as his Demonic counterpart to present.

If you're too embarrassed to employ the aforementioned fetish-finders in relationship to yourself, you can always inject them into conversation by way of a third person. The way the eyes light up when you tell him about what happened to your girl friend or another woman at the office, will let you know you're on the right track. There is only one thing wrong with using a third person account when fetish-finding, and I have seen this problem occur many times over. You must remember that you're dealing with *compulsions,* when you are exploring fetishes, the fetish being just what the name implies—a device or situation that completely overwhelms any other more selective sexual stimuli. If you tell your quarry that your best friend is such a pretty girl, but when she removes her shoes while she's typing at the office, you have to open a window, he's liable to get so horny that all he can think about is meeting your friend with the smelly feet!

I have found that women who seemingly have "nothing to offer," yet "bewitch" a man away from a perplexed wife, who can't possibly understand what kind of power the "other woman" has over her husband, are very often utilizing fetishistic compulsion. A wise witch should know that if the fetish she is catering to is one that the man would not readily disclose to others, she has little fear of competition from others. Professional prostitutes are very careful about divulging good customers' "special requests" to other girls if the financial rewards for such services are substantial.

And substantial they usually are, for fetishistic activity commands (and gets) the highest fees in the profession. EVERY MAN IS A FETISHIST. YOU SIMPLY HAVE TO *DISCOVER* HIS FETISH.

3. E. S. P.: Extra Sensual Projection

IN RECENT YEARS there has been a growing inclination to interpret any human awarenesses that cannot be readily explained as E.S.P. or Extra Sensory Perception. Of course, it is admitted in even the most polite circles that animals have this faculty. Rather than admit that animals have full use of one or more of the so-called five senses, they are credited with a sixth sense, which we call E.S.P. But I believe that the majority of things that are attributed to E.S.P., or a sixth sense, are nothing more than unconscious manifestations of our existing five senses: sight, hearing, smell, taste and touch. The reason the techniques of utilizing these five senses to the degree that would explain away much of the sixth sense nonsense are not learned is because to do so would mean admitting that animals had something we don't have and they might be able to teach us a few things.

Man can't quite bring himself to learn from the animals, though, because he has been brainwashed into thinking he is something special, a higher type of being. He can't beat his chest and play god, because that's reserved for the guy upstairs, and he can't learn from the animal kingdom, because he is supposedly emancipated from it. If something comes along he can't explain, he asks somebody else, and, if there are still no satisfactory explanations, he looks to his gods for one. If faith in his old gods wanes, because of doubts in his mind as to the validity of his religion, he can no longer call strange happenings "miracles." But his ego won't allow him to lose what little self-respect he has acquired, by regressing to animalism in any way, shape or form—even if it means he might learn something. So he thinks of a new "scientific" term which will break away from the religious terminology of "miracles" that has lately left him so disenchanted. He still knows little more than he ever did, but he feels better because he thinks he is on the right track—not dependent on his old god and not trafficking with the Devil, who represents the "lower" elements of man.

In this section we will consider these "lower" aspects of our development—the animal awarenesses that have been so badly neglected that we mistakenly call them "E.S.P.," or "sixth sense," or "sympathetic vibrations." I am not attempting to say that telepathic communication does not exist. It certainly does. It's just that the average person who throws the term E.S.P. around so readily is often confusing it with what one might better call "H.S.P." or Heightened Sensory Perception, which simply means that we receive impressions through our existing five senses that we do not recognize as coming through these agencies.

We can't just say we don't like someone because he smells bad if we don't pick up a strong enough odor to consciously recognize it. Nevertheless, we will react to our H.S.P. If we meet somebody who has a slight, almost imperceptible sneer on his lips and a look of hostility in his eyes, we might not even consciously recognize it, but our animal nature, or H.S.P., relays the message to our brain that this man is no good, basing our judgment on many more factors than we could ever imagine have influenced us.

The tone of one's voice as he talks may be in direct contradiction to the emotional acceptance of the person spoken to or a sound in a room might be of a frequency that will cause anxiety to all present.

In this volume we are concerned with bewitchments and that means acceptance or rejection of certain things by another that will allow the witch to attain her goals. The entire mechanism of acceptance or rejection can be controlled if one learns the proper use of H.S.P. The most effective way to get someone to do what you want, is to let him think it is of his own doing. You cannot command people to do what you wish of them at all times, but you *can* set up and arrange sensory cues so that they will automatically do your bidding. The following chapters will deal with the FIVE senses and how the witch can employ them to her advantage.

The Pupils of His Eyes as a Measurement for Success

Another of the old tricks of carnival fortune tellers, card sharps and con men, is the ability to read a person's emotional response through his eyes. We all have this ability to a greater or lesser degree, but few recognize it, and even fewer consciously employ it.

Dr. Eckhard Hess of the University of Chicago formulated the science of pupillometrics, as a result of his researches into this subject in 1960. Basically, the principle is this: When a person is confronted with something or someone that meets with his approval, the pupils of the eyes will become larger. When disapproval is registered, the pupils will get smaller. Subtle as the movements are, they can still be ascertained, and it is likely we base much of our approval or disapproval of others upon their eye response to us. When introduced to another person whose pupils suddenly get bigger, it is an unconscious reaction on our part to accept him. If the pupils close up tightly upon encountering the same person, we will perceive that something is not quite right with him and be on guard or downright hostile.

There used to be a number of cliches like: "a real eye-opener," "give him the eye," "a real eyeful," etc. and the lore of the evil eye has persisted to this day. The eye as an extension of the brain is verified by the changes in the size of the pupil that occur when other of the senses are stimulated. The old idea of love at first sight is based on the components covered in this book, not the least of which is the response triggered by the appearance of the eyes. If the proverbial "green light" is given with the eyes, it is a sure sign that the pupils will be noticeably larger than they would normally be.

Two people sitting in the darkness of an intimate restaurant, looking across the table at each other, with only a candle for illumination is a romantic stereotype. Both persons' eyes are reacting to the dim setting, so the pupils expand. Combine this with the romantically ideal light of the flickering candle, and both persons will be thrown into an artificial acceptance of each other especially if a bottle of wine is added. Fireside sessions at ski lodges also might be mentioned here. Guillaume de Salluste, a French poet, referred to the eyes as the "windows of the soul."

It doesn't take a great deal of eye movement for even the most unaware person to know something is wrong with another, when the eyes narrow down, a shifting occurs or gaze becomes erratic. There are actual tests which can be devised that will give you a good idea of where you stand witch-wise with the subject you have chosen for you enchantment. First, if you notice his pupils have enlarged, you know you're on the right track.

A good test of what he likes to see in a woman can be conducted employing a magazine (a scrap book is actually best) with a different girl pictured on each page. It takes a little sneaky doing for a girl to just happen to have an album of other girls' pictures around without casting doubts as to your sexual intentions, but such a scrapbook can be made up of clippings from magazines ostensibly for the purpose of a homework project for a make-up or hair-styling class once attended, etc.

Have such a portfolio lying where it is sure to be reached for, and where you can observe his reactions from a close vantage point. While he casually thumbs through the book, watch for a change in his pupils, also noticing if more time is spent on one picture and remember the one that got the green light. The girl reacted to most will give you some indication of what appeals to him.

At least twenty different types should be represented, all wearing clothes. If you use pictures of nudes or scantily clad girls, his reaction is likely to be based upon something you will be unable to readily change—or if he is very pure, his pupils will be the size of silver dollars with every page he turns. Equally useless will be an array of clothed girls with one or two garbed in outlandishly grotesque (pupils contract) or extremely suggestive (pupils enlarge) outfits.

Aleister Crowley, the English occultist and poet, wrote, in his "Hymn to Pan," "Give me the sign of the open eye, the token erect of thorny thigh." This "sign of the open eye" served as a mating signal long before man's scholarly

concern with such matters, so you might as well utilize it
to its fullest.

Another trick a witch should know is how to actually
make her pupils appear larger, therefore motivating your
victim into succumbing to your spell. Near-sighted girls
are more successful than others at charming with their
eyes, because the strain exerted in trying to see without
their glasses, (which are usually left off when they are trying to make their sexiest impression) automatically dialates
the pupils and gives the appearance of the high-sign. Also,
because of the difficulty in seeing, these girls must fix their
gaze more intently on their subject, adding to the effect of
letting the man think she is inviting his attention.

If you are not near-sighted but want to enlarge your
pupils with a certain degree of control while looking at
your victim, here is how: Look directly towards him, as if
you were gazing right into his eyes, but instead of focusing
your eyes on his, pick a tiny area like the corner of his eye,
an eyelash, a pore—and try your hardest to study it intently.
This exercise will enlarge your pupils the little extra bit
needed to do the trick.

On the other hand, if you wish to appear as a dominant,
ruthless witch, and you can see that your quarry will respond to a whip-mistress, you must learn to develop a hard,
impassionate look that will leave him trembling with fearsome anticipation. Instead of focusing on a small area, look
directly at him just as though you were gazing directly into
his eyes but don't even look at his eyes or his face either.
Pretend he isn't even there (this should be easy) and allow
your eyes to pick up all the light and reflections of the
entire area in which you stand, utilizing your peripheral
vision (the things you barely pick up at the outer-most
limits of your vision on either side of your head). The more
area you can perceive, the more light attacks the eyes,

causing the pupils to contract. This will give the effect of looking right through the person, which, in a way, you are. Don't be misled by the old notion that a "piercing" stare is the kind that indicates mastery. The only kind of look that denotes such power over others is the one that seems to say, "I don't need you nearly as much as you need me," and that is the cold, see-through look just described.

The "come-hither" look of the witch that seems to imply lusty treats must not be confused with a "masterful" look. When the pupil is open full, it conveys the promise of sexual abandon in a woman to the man who is the recipient. It also implies the eager lust of a man towards the woman he looks upon in this manner. When you confront a man who does not look you in the eye, it usually means he is preoccupied with other things and isn't interested in you—not that he is too "weak" to confront your gaze. If you can hold the other person's gaze, even after you have averted your own, you have him spellbound.

Successful witches will choose the most likely candidates in a room and then individually give them the sign of the open eye long enough to whet their respective appetites for the pleasure she seems to promise. When one man is "fixed" by her gaze, she moves to another. She knows when she has transfixed her victim by the way he keeps looking at her after she has contracted her pupils and subsequently looked away. The mere action of closing down the size of her pupils is like pulling the bait in after the fish has bitten. She gives each man the idea that she wants him, simply by the use of her eyes, then reels him in by saying with her eyes, "I don't need you unless you have something special to offer." If he has nothing else, he has *himself,* and will spend the rest of the evening giving himself away!

The face and head look more seductive when turned and tilted in the proper way. A lot in how you position your head depends on the type of man you are bewitching. Bearing in mind the rules you have just learned concerning the size of your pupils, we shall proceed. If you are a dominant type who is bewitching a passive male, the most seductive look must be bold, as well. This is best accomplished by placing the front of your face in a direct line with him, so that both sides of your face are equally visible when he looks at you. Your head should be tilted slightly up, so you appear to be ever-so-slightly looking *down* on him. Don't try to look like Theda Bara and lower your head so you scowl out from under your brows. This just looks *weird,* not dominant.

The only witches who should resort to the vampire look are those that look like vampires and that means more bizarre than pretty. The vampire look is achieved by slightly slouching the neck and head forward, with the head tilted well downwards and the gaze coming darkly out from the scowling eyebrows.

If you wish to maintain your dominant look and you feel you must lower your head, be sure your neck and head are held well back on your shoulders. Then, keeping your neck back, tilt your head downwards, taking care that your neck does not slouch forward. You will find that your head is not really lowered so you are looking out from under your brows but that it is actually almost level. It just seems like it is tilted more than it is because of the neck being held well back on the shoulders.

If you are a passive type, or playing a passive role, you must use your pupillary action in the same manner previously described, but position your head in a different manner. Remember, you're supposed to be the girl that can't help it, non-aggressive, shy, a bit furtive, yet decidedly naughty. Unlike the other witch who *commands* her man to her, you must let him think he is taking advantage of you and there's nothing much you can do about it. Little does he know!

Just as the bold girl will look directly at her quarry, so must you, but your head and face must be aimed in a slightly different direction. Rather than facing him head-on, you must turn your head a bit to one side, slightly tilting it downwards, and then look at him. One side of your face should predominate in a three-quarter view. Your eyes should show plenty of white on one side. This has a connotation of wide-eyed innocence, but the angle of the head adds a saucy quality.

If you use any of the old standbys like fluttering your eyelids, batting your lashes or other melodramatic poses, make damn sure there are no inconsistencies in your basic appearance. There is nothing more ludicrous than a big, buxom, eleven o'clock witch flapping her eyelashes, whereas a very small girl can sometimes get away with such antics.

When confronting your quarry, *don't* make the mistake of wearing sunglasses, thinking you will appear more intriguing. The reason poker sharks often wear dark glasses or eye shades is usually so other players won't pick up any betraying change in the eyes if an exceptionally good hand should be held. A poker player can often bluff his way through a bum hand by raising his bet, but chances are good such a player's pupils will be constricted, whereas if the hand was really a good one, the best "poker-face" in the world wouldn't help much if the pupils were dialated from the excitement. In witchery, your eyes are a powerful weapon, so don't muzzle them with sunglasses. Wear sunglasses all you want in the sun or in cases where you don't want your eyes to betray your true feelings, but take them off when you swing into action.

Incidentally, let's not forget that there are men who are

turned on by girls wearing glasses, and despite the old say-ing, they *do* make passes. The stereotype of the bespectacled intellectual has been criticized many times over by op-tical firms and optometrists whose business it is to sell glasses. However, some witches can capitalize on an intellectual image and be thankful for their glasses. The typical nine and ten o'clock male will automatically be attracted to a cerebral type woman of three or four o'clock. This type of man usually needs a thinker, even as a best buddy, so the pair of glasses you might be wearing could well be a fetishistic asset.

One last word about eyes: the fact that the eye is the most flagrant transmitters of sexually motivating situations to the brain can be attested to by the religious and super-stitious taboos involving it. No other organ has been so closely linked with the genitals as the eye. If you can read a person's eyes, they are more naked before you than if you were to remove their clothes.

Sound

A witches voice must be consistent with her appearance. Inconsistency of voice is one of the most common causes of failure in would-be witches. It is one thing to be incon-sistent in ideals, topics of conversation, attitudes, etc. These are the kind of inconsistencies which are often helpful in intriguing your quarry. We must remember, though, that these are the inconsistencies that simply say you are "dif-ferent" from everyone else, not the sort that will be picked up automatically by the other person as the wrong cues to your basic personality type.

It is not simply *what* you say, but *how* you say it, that counts in witchery. Have you ever noticed how the girls with the largest bodies often have the tiniest voices, and conversely, the smallest women usually have the loudest. Of course, this phenomenon is most noticeable in extremes, but then, it is the extreme nature of such cases that makes them noticeable in the first place. Loudness of voice relative to the size of the individual is secondary, as loudness is usually controlled by emotion. *Pitch* is the important factor to consider when establishing your proper image as a compleat witch.

One of the essential elements of comedy is inconsistency. If a man sits down to play the tuba and the sound of a piccolo emerges, it is ludicrous. Likewise, the little man with the big foghorn voice seems ill-suited. Yet we see short plump little women coming forth with husky, pseudo-sophisticated, femme fatale voices; thin, aesthetic types with whining, nasal voices; big Amazons with little squeaky voices; petite Dresden dolls with hoarse bellows—misfits all!

If you are tall, aggressive, with red hair and prominent bone structure, you must cultivate a big, outgoing voice. If you are short, blonde and well-rounded, then your voice should be softer and pitched higher. Don't overdo it, though, as it only requires a slight raising or lowering of your normal pitch to make all the difference in the world. Assertive and dominant women can get away with using regional and foreign accents much easier than witches on the lower half of our synthesizer clock. The higher one is towards the top of the clock, the more suited they are for dialects, accents, strange or unusual speech characteristics, etc. The lower down on the clock one is, the more readily will plebian, slangy, folksy, child-like talk pay off.

As for what you say, eleven to ones can say just about anything, and the more of it, the better. Two to fours better make sense when they talk and can be as cool and cynical as possible. Five to sevens should speak little and agree plenty, and eight to tens must be moderate in the quantity of words used and have a sense of humor. Let me give you a couple of examples of witches I have known, and how one simple change in their speech patterns made them compleat witches.

Witch A is an unpretentious, round-faced girl in her early twenties, with brown hair and rather pretty features —about eight-thirty on our clock. Wishing to be a real witch and viewing all the late-shows on TV as a guide, she acquired a sultry, husky voice. Her conversation was steeped in ambiguities and esoteric intrigue, and she fancied herself a rather plump enigma. Everything started going from bad to worse as she got witchier and witchier and if failure was any criterion, she had made it. When she consulted me for guidance and training, my secretary thought Katherine Hepburn was on the phone. Her case was easy. All she had to do was learn to laugh, raise the pitch of her voice a half-tone, make an occasional funny comment (or at least try), get rid of the slinky black dresses and learn to "say what you mean and mean what you say." After about two weeks of practice, things started looking up, and she went on to some real witchery.

Witch B is a big-busted sex-bomb, in her thirties, with red hair. She is 5'8" with slender legs and hips and the kind of chest expansion that elicits comment and whistles wherever she goes. She has an extremely sensual face to go with it. She is a perfect eleven o'clock type—a lot of woman, with an ebullent outgoing personality and is happily married to a respectel naval officer. When she came to me for coaching in the black arts, she had a tiny child-like voice with all the inflections of Shirley Temple, Jane Withers, Wee Bonnie Baker and Betty Boop all rolled into one. Actually, an intelligent girl, she sounded as though she didn't have a brain in her head and could be accepted only on her looks.

Delving into her past, it turned out that when she was a little girl in New York, child stars were the rage, vaudeville was still around, the movies were in their heyday and Hollywood was at the end of the rainbow. Our witch's mamma was sure her little dollink was going to give all those other kids a run for their money and wind up with her name in lights. After a lengthy succession of try-outs, agents, amateur shows, kiddie reviews, bowing, curtsying, tap-dancing, baton-twirling, eye rolling—not to mention sitting on the lap of every producer on Broadway, our witch had developed the voice that was to issue from her vocal chords for many years to come. She, unlike witch A, had the humor, charm and bountiful looks to keep her happy until she decided that there was something missing—something perhaps easily learned, which would enable her to excell in applied witchery, as she had long been fascinated with sorcery and magic.

After talking with her, it became apparent that she could talk in other voices and *intelligently*! All she needed, with her childhood dramatic training backing her up, was a little encouragement and the proper part to play. She had spent enough time in England to imitate every kind of regional speech pattern from Manchester to Brighton. We decided that the most important thing she needed was a new voice; so slowly at first, so slight as to be almost imperceptible, she started lapsing into her best Hampstead dialect. Within two months her voice was a full tone lower, her accent was established, and she was calling the shots in a way that surprised herself more than anyone. Now her role was established in perfect harmony with her true type—worthy of inclusion in any Ian Fleming novel.

The question I hear now is "How can I possibly get away

with changing my voice when everyone knows me as I am." There are several methods you can employ. The easiest, of course, is to simply change your pitch slightly and no one will notice, but you'll have the fun of seeing their change in response to you. If you are the type that would benefit by an accent, but you can't effectively carry it off, don't even attempt it, as it could make matters worse. If you *can* carry a dialect well, don't worry about what your friends will think. Start it out as a joke, then lay it on so often that it becomes part of you. *Anything that cannot or will not gain acceptance if presented seriously will ALWAYS be accepted if properly presented as a joke!*

Those with a sense of humor will respond with laughter. Those devoid of humor will only appear as grouches. Those who really like you and don't resent your success or happiness will understand if your technique is explained to them. If things aren't going the way you'd like and you change your speech pattern and your few so-called "friends" say they "liked you better the way you were," you may assume that means they liked to see you held down and getting nowhere fast! This applies to all changes this book might bring about in your appearance and personality that will gain you new powers of enchantment.

The *real* results of your new voice will be most apparent around people who don't know you. Oddly enough, a voice change is the most difficult modification of your image to bring about, because it takes the most guts. It can well be the very change you need to perfect your image. Insofar as vocabulary is concerned, the worst thing you can do is to affect a sophisticated manner of speaking and use atrocious grammer and bad pronunciation. This is as ludicrous as the aforementioned inconsistencies in pitch, relative to size. Countless comedy routines have utilized the character of the woman who is trying to be cultured and puts her foot

in her mouth every time she opens it. The difference between using comedy as a magical weapon or being ridi-
culed by others is all in the self-awareness of the individual.
In one case they think they are laughing with you, but the
joke is on *them*—as per my advice concerning accents. In
the second case, they are laughing *at* you, you *know* they
are laughing at you, but your ulterior motives will give you
the last and loudest laugh! In the third case they are laughing *at* you, *and you don't even know it*! This last case is
obviously the one that must be guarded against.

The predominance of many hippie "witches" who don't
know the first thing about the manipulation of others, let
alone the forces around them, has given rise to the assumption on the part of many of these would-be witches that a
few choice astrological terms plus a ten-word vocabulary
is the official speech pattern for magic and mysticism.
These poor things who are often convinced they have the
"formula," stop their mantras only long enough to utter
such profundities as: "groovy," "wow," "oh wow," "heavy,"
"yeah," "right on," "far out," plus a few once-choice ob-
scenities that have long-since lost any impact. Don't get
me wrong, slang has always been and always will be the
language of the people, but sad indeed is he whose vocabulary is reduced to the use of *only* slang expressions, and a
pitiful few at that!

There will always be those who, in their collective search
for identity, employ only the most hackneyed of popular
expressions. We had flappers whose speech was limited to
"Oh you kid," "twenty-three skidoo," "the cat's pajamas,"
etc., but they claimed no magical power—only the hip flask,
the fast joy, the devil-may-care attitude so dear to the heart
of F. Scott Fitzgerald. Nor did the hep cats with the zoot
suits and the drape shapes and the reet pleats profess any
magical awareness while *they* were "in the groove."

If you want your witcheries to work, avoid overuse of such expressions like the plague, as they throw a wrench in the gears of *any* basic personality image and type you are in a truly prejudicial manner. Of course, if your witchery is centered within such a group as the aforementioned, then you must employ such expressions as a means of gaining acceptance. If a witch comes up to me some day, enlarges her pupils, and says: "With a hey nonnie nonnie and a hotcha cha," she'll be sure to get *my* attention!

Music is one of the surest means of enchanting someone, and there is no doubt that music is the universal language. A smart witch can enchant a man she cannot even talk to, if she can play (even badly) or sing music that is analogous to his country. Through the proper choice of music, one can transcend all language, cultural, economic or ethnic barriers which might otherwise be limiting factors.

Unfortunately, most people think this means "You will love me if I play you some of *my* kind of music, and I will appreciate you for yours." Get such stupid ideas out of your head. This assumption is like expecting everyone to think *your* baby is as pretty as you do every time you bring out a snapshot of your child. Very few babies are ugly, and very few types of music you could play would appeal to no one. But one of the biggest and most common mistakes a witch can make is to assume the music she likes best will be equally appreciated by the man she wishes to enchant.

The fact that one's taste in music resides in the Core of his personality gives credence to the statement that the soul of a nation resides in its music. Therefore, if you want to bewitch someone, play him *his* kind of music, *not yours*! If you play him your kind of music, you are playing what represents your true personality, but not his. If he *does* exercise his Demonic element in its corresponding musical form, rather than in a woman, you are in the same position as the woman in the restaurant listening to the violinist mentioned in a previous chapter. You will simply be another instrument added to the ensemble on the record—a fellow "fan" who adds to the enjoyment of his *real* love—the type of music that is only a substitute for *you*! Therefore, *you* must take the place of your musical counterpart. The only way to do this is to musically distract him with the *opposite* type of music from that which you represent while you move in for the kill. This is simply like getting his old girl friend out of the house so you'll have room to operate.

What is far *more* important to consider than the sort of music to which a person will respond, is the *type* of response itself, relative to personality types. With regards to musical response, I have quartered our synthesizer clock into these basic characteristics: Eleven to one—motivational; two to four—intellectual; five to seven—participating; eight to ten—social.

If you want to please a person, it helps to stress the kind of music that would be closest to his position on the clock. Strong melody and rhythm are necessary to charm those on the left, with the beat taking precedence over the melody at nine o'clock. Rhythm to these social types is more important than melody if one or the other must be sacrificed. The music is companionship; the incessant beat, like chatter. This runs concurrent with the element of earth that we find at nine o'clock. Being the most social, music represents companionship more to these people than any others, hence eight to ten o'clock types are most likely to have their car radios going at all times. By the same token, these people, like the three o'clock opposite, are *least distracted* by music. The nine o'clocks need music for companionship but are more likely to pursue other activities while listening. Even while making love these types will have a radio going with no distraction whatsoever.

Two to four o'clocks sometimes listen to music while they pursue other activities, but not for companionship, as do the eight to tens. Two to fours appreciate and study music rather than respond to it. The mental aspect of the right side of the clock sees to that. This is why they like music of a mathematical bent, such as Bach and Brubeck, whereas the fluidic influence starts about four o'clock, with an emphasis on ballads and folk songs by the time five is reached. Being of an esoteric nature, as a result of the air element, most adherants to experimental music and avant garde forms will be found at three and four o'clock. Music critics fall into the two to four category as would be expected.

The eleven to ones and five to sevens are compelled to listen to music and are directly influenced by it the most. These are the types that are unable to listen to music without responding and seldom will be able to pursue any other activities while music is being played without giving attention to the music. The big difference in these two opposite types is this: The five to seven is enveloped in the music and becomes a medium and reactor to it, whereas the eleven to ones are also swept up in the music but become *moved to action by it*! Don't expect to sexually inflame these types through music, as it will distract them from anything you have in mind.

Quality, rather than quantity, is more important to the six o'clock, whereas the reverse is true of the twelve. A good example of this would be a Sousa march, which could be enjoyed and reacted to equally by eleven to ones or five to sevens. The twelve o'clock would rather hear the march played with the emphasis on loudness and therefore could appreciate hearing it slightly out of tune on a broken-down merry-go-round band organ so long as it was loud. The march would then be used as a triggering-off mechanism to get the show (the twelve o'clock) on the road rather than as a *whole* experience as in the case of the six o'clock. This is the reason that when hearing music, the six o'clock will dance to it and the twelve o'clock will go out and do something as a result of it! The nine o'clock will *need* it, and the three o'clock will *analyze* it.

The dance used to be one of the most practical uses of music in witchcraft. Now that physical contact while dancing has become a thing of the past, we have reverted to an older form, in which each person dances individually—either for their own expression or for the entertainment of someone else. The social elements of dancing are stressed by the number of people who are dancing in an area or room instead of by physical contact between dancers. This should present no problem to the witch, though, as most men are voyeuristic and will be much more stimulated by watching a woman moving about suggestively than by dancing with her. The exceptions to this rule are dances which are designed to place emphasis on contact with erogenous zones, and one can only trust that the day will soon come when dancing between couples will return. Before such a pastime ensues, however, a new and epicurian set of sexual repressions must be developed. Until then, dancing will serve as an art, entertainment or means of rhythmic expression but not the overt form of social sexual enchantment it once was. Don't forget, though, the music that motivates people to dance contains the same rhythms that motivate the muscles and tendons of the body to fornicate. Horizontal dancing will always be popular and the intervals of sound that humans call music have helped to maintain that popularity. As an old-time clergyman once said, "The Devil has always had the best tunes."

When we think of music we seldom think in terms of the normal speaking voice, as such. Nevertheless, everyone's basic personality has its own rhythm, and that rhythm is exemplified by the normal cadence and tempo of the voice. If someone is in high gear all the time, you probably notice how it shows in his way of speaking. One of the greatest tricks of human manipulation is to be able to adjust the speed of your voice (and the relative pitch and inflection) to match that of the person to whom you are talking. You should be able to learn the art of mimicry well enough so that you can lapse into a subtle, almost imperceptible echo of the other person's voice.

To do this, you begin your conversation with the other person, in your normal voice, which should, of course, be consistent with your basic type, as we have discussed previously. That much, then, has been established and your image, as you would have your quarry define it, is exactly what his Demonic element calls for. Within the first few minutes of your conversation, you allow your voice, tempo and inflection to merge slightly with his. He won't even notice this if you are gradual enough. Accompany your conversation with very slight nods of your head, indicating you are in agreement with him. If he is a sour-puss and displays certain mannerisms that brand him as a pessimist, don't nod your head when you talk. This type wants someone with whom he can commiserate and usually shakes his head from side to side even when telling of something wonderful that happened! If you run into this type, shake your head from side to side, too, as you talk, letting him think he has met a fellow loser.

Within five minutes of conversation, you should have thoroughly established yourself on the same speech frequency. You have then performed a very potent magical maneuver. There are no longer two people talking, but only one. Your quarry is now speaking as a whole person, using both his Apparent and his Demonic self. You have given him his Demonic voice by appearing in the guise of yourself but speaking as him. He will be disinclined to contradict whatever you suggest to him, as now *he* is the only one doing the talking and his ego—the crystallization of his true self, his Core personality, the Devil who sent out the Demon you represent and the thing that must inevitably be served—will not allow him to speak out against himself! He cannot disagree with what you say, because to do so at this time would mean to disagree with himself. He will find himself saying things you want him to say and thinking they are his own ideas. Don't neglect to nod your head ever-so-slightly at regular intervals except when with a pessimist. Don't forget that the most effective suggestion can come in the guise of a question accompanied by a nod of the head.

If you're dealing with one of the aforementioned grumps, keep your voice dropping at the end of each phrase and keep shaking that head. Let him feel that you are the only person on earth who understands how crummy everything is. Remember, if he didn't see in you the traits opposite from those you are now projecting when he first confronted you, he wouldn't be charmed by you now. After you have kept up your mutual bellyaching and head-shaking and you've arrived at the point in your conversation where you think it wise to interject whatever it is you want from this man, your next step is to raise the pitch of your voice very slightly as you force your card on him. As you speak, this time, you *nod* your head instead of shaking it. Drive your point home in two or three sentences, all the while nodding almost indiscernibly and speaking with brightness in your voice. *Then*—drop right back into the role you *were* playing, your voice dropping, your head shaking, your shoulder ready and everything but the crying towels.

You have your suggestion shoved into his brain in such a

way that he can never get it out. If he doesn't follow your suggestion right away, it will haunt him until he does. You got him when his defenses were down, and the door to his unconscious was wide open when you tossed in your desire, all neatly packaged. The sooner he does your bidding, the better, because that's the only way he will ever get it out of his head.

Use your voice. It is one of your best magical weapons. If you do, you will quickly discover that not all ventriloquists keep their mouths closed while talking.

On the Importance of Odors

"O, Nose, how you have deceived me!"

Iwan Bloch, *Odoratus Sexualis*

I realize that this is a somewhat delicate topic, but it is one sense in particular that women have most neglected to use, hence more powerful for the witch who uses it.

Of the five senses, the sense of smell is the most neglected. An odor will evoke an entire state of consciousness more thoroughly than any other form of communication. No other form of sensory cue has been so shrouded in guilt, misinformation and self-contradictory definition as have the things we smell. The paradox of perfumery stands as the most fragrant example of the olfactory deceptions wrought in the name of finery and good taste.

As a witch, you should learn some basic principles of enchantment through odors. First of all, DON'T SCRUB AWAY YOUR NATURAL ODORS OF SEDUCTION. It doesn't matter how much brainwashing has been done to make certain bodily odors undesirable. Millions of years have seen to it that such scents will never be reacted to in a negative way. The most successful witches are those who smell like women. This doesn't mean that you shouldn't bathe or wash your underwear, but one can overdo a fear of "offending" to a point that negates any opportunity for success. This obsession to scrub away dirt (and with it sin) is a by-product of the kind of puritanism and Calvinism that defies all the laws of nature. The Huguenots even had a hymn equating bodily odors with sin, called: "Everybody Stinks but Jesus." There is no doubt that to many women, a bar of soap has replaced the confessional.

Women who are accomplished and pay strict attention to personal hygiene are successful *in spite* of their habits, not because of them. Usually such cases revolve around established groups—business, social, professional—where acceptance has already been gained. Then, out of protocol and decorum, stringent hygiene is maintained in order to perpetuate one's status. In the animal kingdom this phenomenon would be illustrated by the smelliest animals achieving status, then once having attained favored positions, sniffing each other critically to see who smelled the worst!

We are no different. When we meet a person to whom we respond favorably, invariably he smells good to us, even though we may not consciously recognize any odor. If there is such an attractive odor present, it is usually one that would be considered disgusting, disgraceful or repellent if its origin were known. If the odor that attracts us in the form of a perfume or cologne, it is usually made from the sexual odors and mating scents given off by beavers (castoreum), cats (civit), whales (ambergris), muskrats (Musc Zibata), deers and goats (musk) and numerous plants and flowers whose odors, we mustn't forget, are intended by nature to attract for the purpose of survival and pollination.

It is inconceivable to think that human beings could be the only creatures without appealing sexual odors, yet odors that originate in the sexual parts are considered anathema by a large majority of them. Millions of dollars are spent each year on substances that will remove any trace of "offensive" human odor, and more millions are spent on purchasing the bottled sex-smells of animals, to replace the scrubbed-off and astringently removed perfume that is the most bewitching of all!

Women also find male odors tremendously appealing. Some women for example get turned on by sweaty men. In fact many folk dances contain a gesture in which a scarf held under the armpit during the dance is waved about the man's partner.

I find it ironic that the science of perfumery was developed in days when such extracts were applied *in addition* to the natural odors of the body. Many perfumes were employed because of the lack of sanitation and hygiene, which necessitated the strong odors being covered up by stronger ones. As clothing became more cumbersome and elaborate, people perspired more, and the accumulated secretions that lack of bathing left to ferment made perfumes highly desirable in polite circles.

If everyone went around with an overabundance of clothing and six months between baths, it would get pretty uncomfortable in a crowded room. The main reason for the discomfort, however, would not be because of the odor of the individuals in the room to whom you would be sexually attracted. It would be all those others present who were *not your type*, that would make such a gathering a highly unrewarding experience.

Who or what would constitute those who wouldn't be your type? Generally, assuming you are heterosexually inclined, members of your own sex. This is the reason virtually *all* heterosexual women are concerned about personal hygiene. You don't get excited, only repelled, when you smell the female odors of another woman—and damned if you want to smell that way too! Men and lesbians *love* that aroma, however. But other heterosexual women and homosexually inclined men find it repugnant.

If you could portray the Demonic element within you, you would favorably respond to your own odor as a man would. Your built-in perfume should be a perfect blend of acid and alkaline substances generated by the secretions of the Bartholin glands, perspiration, and urine. Nature has constructed you in a manner that leaves folds of flesh in the proper places so that a blending of the three just-mentioned substances is assured. If you doubt what I say, heed the fact that the most common article of female clothing that is employed as a fetishistic substitute are panties, and the ritual accompanying the acquisition of same invariably consists of the sniffing of the crotch, performed in an epicurian fashion. Don't be misled into thinking it is the heady scent of the perfumed soap or sachet in your bureau drawer that makes your undies appealing. They are appealing *in spite* of the spice and lavender, not because of it. Perfumes should be used *over* existing odors, not in place of them; and the perfume you choose should *bring out* your own odor, not neglect it.

Some of you may have noticed that men seem to swarm around you most when you have your period. Undoubtedly, such a situation has proved disturbing to many of you, as you feel it an inopportune time to really get involved, especially where sex might be concerned. Here again, we must rely on the animal kingdom for our knowledge. The female of the species is always most appealing to the male when she is in heat, which corresponds in some ways to the monthly menstrual cycle in a woman. The changes which take place in your system at this time are such that the normal sexual odor is highly intensified and, because of this, carries further. This is why such a big fuss had been made about offending at this time of the month —*but* are you *really* offending?

It is true, some women have an odor that can cause very decided rejection during their menstrual cycle, but this is because: (a) it is mingled with other odors that are incompatible (certain foods, tobacco, etc.); (b) little or no hygienic measures have been taken, insofar as regular changing of tampons or pads; (c) a naturally excessive menstrual odor. (It has long been part of folk wisdom that burnettes have a stronger natural odor than blondes.) The last two reasons relate to the *intensity* of the odor rather than the odor itself; and I cannot stress enough that *any* odor, if strong enough, becomes unpleasant.

The most pleasing scents, when intensified enough, become noxious; and conversely, many of the most alluring scents are reductions of otherwise objectionable odors. The basic menstrual odor is *not* offensive. It is only its *over-intensity* which makes it so! The actual scent given off at this time is the most potent aphrodisiac a woman can employ *if* properly used.

Many old witches' charms call for the use of menstrual blood invariably along with other ingredients thought to be necessary. Magical potions, salves and even charms usually contain only one or two ingredients that really count but several others that are thrown in because: (a) the more complicated something is, the fewer people will try to make it even if the instructions are available; (b) the unnecessary ingredients serve to misdirect the uninitiated or unenlightened from the truly effective ingredients; (c) the more difficult it is to make, the more dependency rests on the powers of the witch; (d) the credibility of the substance will be greater—nobody believes in things that are too simple to understand; (e) a higher fee or price can be charged by the witch; (f) the originators of the potion didn't even know themselves that out of their complicated mess only one or two ingredients were doing the trick.

Unless the human animal is to be considered the only exception in nature, you are theoretically appealing, rather than offending, during your period. The only offending you need worry about is where your scent becomes *overbearing* or in having to refuse an ardent male with whom you would like to go to bed. A fine trick, utilizing your menstrual cycle, requires taking a tip from the makers of perfume. All the substances mentioned earlier in this chapter are the bases of oils and waters which are considered pleasant-smelling. In every instance, the original substance from which the perfume is made is over-powering in its odor. Only when scaled-down will such a strong odor be accepted as pleasant.

If your period produces an extra-strong scent, which potentially has tremendous drawing power perfume-wise but at a time when you can't gracefully do anything about it, put some of that aroma in a doggie-bag and save it! If you can think of a more romantic name for a magical pouch containing some of your menstrual blood, go right ahead. The method my witches have found most practical is to retain a sanitary napkin or tampon which has been well saturated and cut it down to a size small enough to be unobtrusive. Cover it with a very light material with an open weave so the odor will not be stifled yet the contents will be unrecognizable if it should be discovered. The finished product should be in the form of a tiny pouch or amulet about two inches square and sewn together at the top.

When you go forth to confront your quarry, tuck your sachet inside your blouse or sweater where the cleavage between your breasts will hide it and also supply enough heat to activate the scent. Don't worry about the smell being too strong, as it will be cut down considerably from the intensity produced during your period but still retain its effectiveness. Don't expect to like what you smell if the odor wafts up to your nostrils. When the rest of your body is not experiencing such exhalations, you will not be attuned to the odor as you would be during your period. Also the close proximity of your breast area to your nasal equipage will make it seem stronger smelling than it is. If it really bothers you, place a small dab of Vicks in each nostril and you won't smell a thing, and the slight trace of camphor sometimes even adds to the effectiveness. If anyone should ask you what it is, should it be seen, tell them it is an old witchcraft charm bag containing powerful herbs and powders. Sometimes a leather thong, a string or thin chain attached that will allow the pouch to be worn around the neck is a good idea providing your clothing will cover it.

Here are some other helpful hints in smell-binding: Gauge your use of bodily scents by the occasion and environment within which you will be operating. If you're going to be around nothing but other women, and it is among them that you must pass inspection, keep yourself pure and (ugh) fresh. If you're going to be in the company of men, however, let the effective perfume that nature gave you work its wonders. I am appalled at the way a woman will reek of various odors such as strong foods, cigarettes, liquors, etc. yet maintain a fanatical concern for her personal hygiene insofar as sexual odors are concerned. Of course, the literature of sexual pathology contains much reference to men who revel in all manner of strong, overwrought and abnormal odors.

Aside from the natural fragrance of your genitals, certain other odors can be employed to subliminally turn on a man. One of the most effective of such essences is gasoline. When used in combination with other odors, it will surprise you with its results. Gasoline is best employed where its odor can be subtly wafted into the room in which you are throwing your spell. He shouldn't be able to detect it strongly but almost imperceptibly. Dried grass and weeds, balsam, eucalyptus, pine, rubber are also very stimulating to many men. Urine is another odor which has only been erotically by-passed by the human animal, and there are more men who are stimulated by the smell of urine than will ever admit to it. The odor of chocolate is sure to win children over to you if you are teaching or working around them. To a child, no one can smell as nice as the person who smells like candy.

You are probably wondering why I haven't mentioned specific scents that are well known as perfumes when you like many of the oils and fragrances of an exotic and elegant nature. After all, you have been using perfumes all your life and most certainly have your favorites. There is the answer to your question. We are not concerned here with *your* favorites, but what will bewitch the other person. We have made our full circle from where we started at the beginning of this chapter, and this rule stands sure: THE SCENTS THAT YOU LIKE BEST ON YOURSELF ARE INCONSEQUENTIAL. THE ODORS YOU LIKE LEAST ARE THE ODORS THE MAN WHO REPRESENTS YOUR DEMONIC WILL LIKE BEST.

Those wonderful exotic fragrances: Bergamot, Jasmine, Jonquil, Tuberose, Heliotrope, Frangipani, Ylang ylang, Sandalwood, Saffron, Lilac and all the exquisite creations of the world's finest perfumers are largely manifestations of the wearers' *own vanity* rather than tools of the witch's trade. The same perfume you select as your favorite smells good to *you*, and if a man selected it for you, it is because it smelled good to *him*. Has a man ever presented you with an expensive bottle of perfume? Can you honestly say that the perfume he gave you was the kind you would have chosen yourself? Or was the stuff used once and then put in the drawer? Maybe he knew what you liked, because you told him, and bought it for you, but did he really prefer it to others or buy it simply because he knew *you* would like it? Who was charming whom with the perfume? Think about these questions and you will see that perfume is like candy—enjoyed the most by the consumer.

It was once fashionable for all gentlemen of consequence to wear perfume. There is no reason why men should not wear the same perfumes as women if they like the scent. Unlike differences in men's and women's clothing, perfume has been employed by men as well as women throughout history, and it was not until late in the eighteenth century that its use among men declined. Now a revival of male use of perfume seems apparent which is good. Women are more influenced by perfume than are men anyway. Perhaps if men wear more, women will wear less, as they will be able to smell their favorites on their lovers and husbands, thereby putting their own scent glands to work instead of some beaver's.

Taste

When a child smells something he likes, his natural impulse is to taste it. This also applies to human adults, repressions notwithstanding. It is simply repression of one kind or another that keeps an adult from following up his desire to taste an object which smells pleasant. Most repressions are those which are taught, some wisely, others out of ignorance.

We refrain from taking poisonous substances, because someone has told us of the consequences. The old witch who lulled her victim to helplessness through a potion or elixer was very much like the classical poisoner, who made sure that the substance to be drunk was, indeed, pleasant to the taste. When the same witch was called upon to perform some miraculous service, she knew the opposite would be needed and made sure the drink she gave her client was noxious and bitter. If something wasn't difficult to take, her customer would assume its effect to be worthless. This chapter shall deal with your quarry rather than your customer. Therefore, whatever you employ for your bewitchment must be easily ingested.

The first requisite for any four to nine o'clock witch is that she learn to cook. Witches who are in the ten to three o'clock category on our synthesizer clock need not know how unless they are playing the role of another type. Their talents should lie in potions, and it is more important for a dominant type of witch to be able to make a good drink than to cook.

In dealing with food, a witch should realize that a great deal can be told about a man by his eating habits. Once his tastes are known, his food preferences can be catered to. Though it is true that a man's heart is reached through his stomach, it is more important that he be fed the *right* foods, relative to his personality, than those you find the most appetizing. Like perfumery, foods that *you* like best are not necessarily those that *he* will like best. Many a poor witch has slaved over a hot cauldron, preparing what she considers to be the most delectable meal in the world, only to have it unappreciated. What is even worse, though, is to spend a lot of time on a meal, watch him eat it with apparent enthusiasm and then notice a decided coolness the next time you see him. What this often means is that he said he liked the meal to be polite. Chances are good there are more reasons why he took a powder than your cooking alone, but the wrong choice of food could have been just the nudge he needed to stay away. Had you served the perfect meal, you might have had another chance, and the next time his mood could have been conducive to your success.

The only time you will find a man with a taste in food identical to your own will be when you have found a man who likes exactly the opposite type of girl from what you are! I have seen many aspiring witches fix a meal that is exactly to their guest's taste using their own taste as a yardstick. These witches are terribly pleased when their gentlemen friends gobble up every crumb then ask when the next dinner will be. Mistakenly, the witch thinks she has found a man who really appreciates good food, in accordance with what she thinks good food should be. Little does she realize how well she has succeeded as a chef, but failed as a witch, until she awakens to the brutal fact that he is around only for the food, not for her, and is not the least bit interested in anything but what she can supply him in the way of non-romantic indulgences. These chow-hounds can't possibly get interested romantically, because so long as you have chosen the menu from your personal taste, and they like what you have selected, you have the wrong man! These are cases where the witch's ego can really get in the way, and the gals that do the most boasting about their special way of preparing a certain dish can often be spotted as the ones who fail witchery-wise. Until you are able to learn what *he* likes, don't goof up by throwing him what *you* like!

I have devised a pleasant test by which one can tell whether a person is dominant or passive by nature. I call it "The LaVey Salad Dressing Test." No matter what kind of meal is served, the salad course can allow for personal choice if a basic type of salad is served and various kinds of dressings are offered. Or if you are dining out, there are

only a few fundamental dressings available in most restau-
ants, and from these (French, Russian, Thousand Island,
Roquefort, bleu cheese, oil and vinegar) you may well discover more about a person's character than you would ever
think possible.

Men who are dominant and masculine archetypes prefer
sweet dressings, such as French, Russian, Thousand Island,
as do women who are dominant *or* latent or practicing
lesbians. Women who are passive, submissive, and feminine
archetypes prefer Roquefort, bleu cheese, and oil and vinegar, as do males who are passive *or* latent or active homosexuals. Salads are seldom liked by small children unless a
sweet dressing is applied.

The taste of sweet dressing, with its minty, tomato, spicy
taste (plus the fact that it is most often used when seafood
is incorporated in the salad) resembles the odor of a
woman's sexual parts and is therefore agreeable to the
archetypical male. Conversely, the aroma and taste of the
strong, cheesey Roqueforts, blue cheese, oil and vinegar,
etc. is similar to the male scrotal odor and reminiscent of a
locker full of well-worn jock straps. This is naturally subliminally appealing to predominantly heterosexual females,
passive males and males with homophile tendencies. If a
chef in a restaurant has a specialty dressing, it will not only
tell much about his sexual pedilections but often serves to
classify the management of the restaurant. Of course, there
are many people who like *all* types of dressing, but there
is usually a slight preference in one direction.

A lot can be discerned from the kind of candy or cake a
man likes. Dominant, self-indulgent, greedy types like
candy, cake and cookies with smooth texture—no nuts!
They might love nuts, but by themselves, not blended with
smooth textured foods. These self-indulgent types don't
want to have to work while they eat and obstructions in

their food distract them from their pleasure. They will gladly attack a steak with enthusiasm but rebel when something like nuts come along to break up the tranquility of an ice cream cone. These types have the least problems in life, as they will not readily allow them to develop.

Submissive males, who are often used to sexual abstinence, like food with rough texture and prefer cookies, candy and cake with nuts, health foods, food that is either very bland or extremely hot, strong or sour. In other words, these types must either get no definite pleasure and taste from food (abstinence) or become submissive to its strength. This is your cue that they want to be dominated by *you!*

A dominant male will order his steak rare. One who is prepared to cater to your every need will order his medium or well done. The truly dominant man will eat the frosting and throw away the cake even though it doesn't seem the "he-man" thing to do. The man most likely to give you your own way will eat the cake after he has scraped off the frosting.

In the old days, witches used to place great confidence in an edible effigy of the person they wished to charm. Even such festive confections as hot cross buns had a sexual meaning that isn't talked about at Sunday school. Hence was born the gingerbread man. Ginger has always been considered an important ingredient of love potions, and a love potion should rightfully be called a "lust" potion. Whether ginger works as an aphrodisiac or not, when a gingerbread man was baked a great deal of ceremony went into the preparation of the toothsome morsel.

First of all, it was assumed to be the proposed lover of the witch who prepared it or of the witch's client. Most of these cookie men were made for the use of lovelorn girls, by an older, experienced witch, who was wise in the ways of the world. The general procedure was to have the girl disrobe and lie on a long wooden bench as would likely be found in a kitchen. With her client flat on her back, the witch would procure a board about a foot square and place it over the girl's genitals. Then, she placed a small iron stove, similar to a Japanese hibachi, on the board and stoked it up. Forming the little figure from the dough, and placing it over the glowing coals, she covered it and began to chant.

As she talked, she spoke of the lusts that would fill the man who was represented, the things he would like to do, the exaggerated state of his member and the consuming desire of the girl on the bench. Telling the young woman that the heat from her loins and groin must merge with the glowing coals, she goaded the girl with erotic suggestion until a climax was obtained. Sometimes the orgasm was assisted by the witch, who was often a lesbian who found that caressing her customer's breasts was nice work; or occasionally a "demon" assistant would appear to help, in the guise of a local dirty old man.* Knowing the time needed to bake the cookie, and gauging it accordingly, the witch removed the brazier and board from the now-spent woman and produced the finished product.

Wrapping it carefully with a few more incantations, the witch got her customer dressed and sent her on her way. The young woman was to present the cake to her young man as soon as possible, while it was still fresh, then sit back and wait for the results. It got so whenever a guy got a gingerbread man, he knew what was up, and more often

* In those days if a girl had been properly schooled in theological topics, she would have learned all about various demons, including the dreaded incubi. Such things as orgasms were automatically defined as demonic possession, so a witch could always produce a "real" demon or so under such circumstances. If an orgasm occurred under sacred circumstances, it was an ecstasy.

than not took full advantage of the opportunity! Chances are good he believed in witchcraft in the first place and the knowledge that a spell had been wrought on him could not be glossed over. Combine this with the confidence of the witch when she proffered her spicy cookie, and you can easily see why such enchantments seldom failed.

The tradition of bride's biscuits is directly linked with the use of a cake for purposes of instilling sexual desire in a new husband; and any girl who bakes goodies for a man she likes is keeping an old witch-custom alive.

The term "cookie-lady" is synonymous with "witch." The association of edibles with sexual desire will always make the ingestion of a certain food or drink the most desirable short-cut to romance in the popular mind. When the story got around about the Garden of Eden, it only helped propagate beliefs which had been around for thousands of years. Consequently, love potions are supposedly the stock in trade of the sorceress.

As previously stated, the function of a so-called love potion is only that of an aphrodisiac. Each day I receive several letters from persons who think that a good love potion will solve all of their romantic problems. At best, all a love potion can accomplish is sexual stimulation. Any lasting love which develops will not be induced by the potion but by the person. Many of the old recipes for these drinks were nothing more than instructions in the preparation of liqueurs similar to many that are now available on the open market. Commercially available "love potions" are:

Advokaat—an egg and brandy liqueur.

Chartreuse—a French liqueur supposedly containing 130 different herbs and spices in its secret formula.

Creme de Noyaux—almond-tasting liqueur made from

crushed seeds of apricots, cherries, peaches, and plums, with an orange peel flavoring and a brandy base.

Drambuie—a liqueur with a Scotch malt whiskey base, flavored with spices and honey.

Goldwasser—a spice liqueur containing actual flecks of gold leaf, long considered both virility producing and curative.

Kümmel—a German liqueur made from caraway and other seeds.

May Wine—Sweet white wine flavored with woodruff.

Metaxa—a dark, sweet resinous Greek liqueur with a brandy base.

Mezcal—a Mexican liqueur, stronger than tequila, but also distilled from the fermented juice of the maguey cactus. The traditional variety made in Oaxaca has an actual worm from the cactus floating in each bottle, attesting to its authenticity.

Parfait Amour—a violet flavored liqueur often actually sold as a love potion.

Sloe gin—a liqueur made from the sloe berry (blackthorn), an old ingredient commonly employed for love potions.

Vermouth—a wine containing most of the herbs and barks of ancient love potions and well known to all. The name originated from wormwood, one of its original ingredients, called "Wermut" in German, meaning "essence of man."

If you want to save a lot of time, just go out and buy one of the aforementioned liqueurs. Each contains ingredients that have long been considered essential to love potions, and some are identical to preparations once dispensed as such. For those of you who want to make your own, here are some well-tested recipes:

Syrup of Priapus: One-half ounce of flowers of stoechas;

twenty-five myrtle berries; two-thirds of an ounce anise; two-thirds of an ounce of wild carrots; one-half ounce of saffron flowers; fifty dried dates; four egg yolks; and one pint of pure spring water.

Warm in an earthen vessel well sealed for twenty-five minutes.

Take off the fire, filter through a napkin and when tepid, add: two ounces of pure honey.

Let macerate twenty-four hours, shaking vessel three or four times, pass through a sieve.

Serve him one to two teaspoons in the evening.

Pousse-l'Amour (Liqueur of Love):

Prepare in a wine glass: a quarter glass of Maraschino; add the yellow of an egg; a quarter glass of Madeira and of Creme de Cacao; a quarter wine glass of brandy. Serve without mixing, taking care to leave the egg yolk whole.

Gentian Wine:

Grate one ounce of gentian roots and let macerate for twenty-four hours in three and one-half pints of brandy; add a little red table wine, seal vessel, leave it in the sun for eight days, filter well.

Wine de l'Amour:

Take a fifth of white table wine and incorporate the following substances: two vanilla beans, one ounce cinnamon bark, one ounce ginseng, and one ounce rhubarb. Let macerate for two weeks, stirring daily, then filter and serve.

Hypocras Aphrodisiaque:

One ounce crushed cinnamon bark, one ounce of ginger, one-third ounce of clove, two and one-quarter pounds of granulated white sugar, and one and three-quarters pints of red table wine.

Let these ingredients macerate for five days, strain the whole through a cloth and pour wine through a funnel.

To consume, pour one ounce of the mixture into the wine habitually drunk.

Abyssinian Liqueur of Love:

Prepare in a glass: two lumps of sugar, four drops of Curacao, one wine glass of red Port wine.

Fill the glass with water and let warm almost to a boil.

Serve with a slice of lemon pierced with four cloves and a little grated nutmeg.

Eliser Satanique:

Take one fifth of vodka, pour into a jug, and incorporate the following: one two-ounce jar of instant coffee, prepared with one quart of water that has been brought to a boil, one vanilla bean, one-half ounce Mandrake root, one small tin of sesame seeds, and one pound of granulated sugar.

Let these ingredients macerate for one month, stirring daily, but otherwise kept stoppered. Strain and serve.

If you are having a party and want an easy-to-make punch that will be consumed copiously by those who don't even drink and has a decidedly sneaky effect, I have used this to great advantage for many years:

Goblin Juice:

Mix together one fifth of rum, one fifth of vodka, one large can of pineapple-grapefruit drink (prepared under many brand names), one small can of concentrated frozen orange juice, diluted as per instructions on container; and four ounces of grenadine.

You will produce a drink every bit as potent as the most exotic Polynesian concoction. Serve with ice and lots of salted goodies.

Whatever you do, don't make the mistake of thinking that a love potion will work when everything else has failed. If you expect to find a magical elixir that will enable you to have whoever you want without lifting your little finger to help, forget it! There *are* hormonal extracts that can work wonders, but they require considerably more knowledge for their use than meets the eye.

When employing any type of aphrodisiac, many factors must be considered, chiefly side-effects and personality variants. Knowing all about love potions but nothing about *people* can lead to a situation very similar to the classic anecdote about the man who was never successful with the ladies, who one day accidentally strolled down a narrow street in an old section of town—an area he had no knowledge even existed. Noticing a small shop, its windows so dusty and dirty it was almost impossible to see beyond them, he stopped to peer inside. What he saw intrigued him—all sorts of glass vials, stoppered jars, stuffed birds, battered clocks, etc. Trying the door, he found it opened quite easily, and upon entering, was greeted by the stereotyped little old man with gray hair standing behind the counter, almost as though he was expecting him.

Getting down to business, the wizard (for that was his profession) told the man he had just the thing he needed, to which the man replied that what he needed was a good love potion, and he doubted that he would find it there or anywhere else. The wizard then informed the man that he did, indeed, have a love potion and a good one. Asking the price of such a rare commodity, the man was informed that it was only a dollar and forty-nine cents. Saying he would take one, he waited while the wizard went out back to get it.

That following evening the man had an opportunity to try his elixir. Much to his surprise, it worked, and the girl he was with fairly raped him on the spot. Well, what do you think the man did? You're right! He went right down to the old wizard's the very next morning and it was so early the store wasn't even open. A small pencilled sign on the door informed him that if no one was at the store, to ring the upstairs bell as that was where the proprietor lived. Doing so, he was admitted cordially by the old man and then saw a sight that took his mind off his new-gotten fulfillment. The old man lived in splendour! Everywhere his gaze fell, the man saw incredibly valuable and beautiful furnishings and *objets d'art,* and the decor of the place was in the most extravagant but elegant taste imaginable.

Commenting on what a nice place he had, the man regained his composure and announced that he had stopped by to pick up a few more of those love potions. Agreeable to the sale, the two adjourned to the shop, where the wizard produced six more doses.

A month passed, and the man again appeared at the wizard's shop. This time he was worn, haggard, sallow and bent. His eyes were bloodshot and strained. The wizard had been expecting him. The man had become involved with many women—seven to be exact. All provided by the wizard's love potion. Now he could not get rid of them! They had complicated his life beyond belief! He even feared for his safety. The wizard knew what the man had in mind. He was very wise. He told the man he had a potion that would make those girls forget he even existed. He assumed the man wished seven doses and was correct.

Wondering if he would have enough money to cover the purchase, the much-relieved man asked what the cost would amount to. The wizard mentally added the price up, as it required no great accounting. Seven doses, at five thousand dollars per dose, came to thirty-five thousand dollars. Shaken, the man said he thought it was awfully steep and allowed as how he would have to sell his house to raise that kind of money. He then asked the wizard why his love potions were so cheap, but the antidote so expensive, to which the wizard only commented, "How do you think I get all that nice stuff upstairs!"

Touch

> "And her hands are bands for binding; for when they place their hands on a creature to bewitch it, then with the help of the Devil they perform their design."
> —*Malleus Maleficarum*

Skin softness, like the proper perfume and perfunctory hygiene, is an almost exclusively feminine preoccupation. Men, the animals that they are, are seldom really concerned too much about whether a girl's skin is baby-soft or not. Unless a man is fetishistically attracted to smooth skin, he will always give preference to a woman who represents his Demonic element, even if her skin is less than perfect. Certainly, very few men like coarse, rough skin on a woman, but the average gal has much more to look after, as far as her witch-power is concerned, than her skin. The obsession for soft skin is a throwback to the days when women who were respected were those who never used their hands, and soft skin was a mark of gentility.

Don't get me wrong, I think it's a decided advantage for a witch to have reasonably smooth skin. I simply find it magically unsound to pay homage to your femininity by way of your skin and completely forfeit it in other more important ways. A woman will use gallons of lotion each year to soften her hands, face, arms and legs, while keeping her weight down to a skeletal figure that will practically leave punctures and bruises on a man making love to her.

Regardless of what the ads tell you, not all men like creamy skin on a gal. The men you'll find up around twelve o'clock on the synthesizer usually have a predilection for soft skin, soft flesh, and yes, even flabbiness. Six o'clock men, however, like their women muscular, firm and sometimes like shoe-leather!

Take a tip from these extreme types. If a man likes extra-soft, translucent skin, chances are good he won't like you skinny, whereas if he goes for girls with a boyish figure, he'll not mind if your skin is a trifle weather-beaten. The *consistency* of your flesh is far more important than the delicacy of your skin. What makes the skin men love to touch is the flesh that lies beneath.

There are four basic types of flesh, and each type corresponds to a position on the synthesizer clock. These basic types are: three o'clock—sinewy; six o'clock—flabby; nine o'clock—rubbery; and twelve o'clock—hard. The older a man gets, the more he likes extremes of his Demonic type. He starts out as a boy, liking the kind of girls that are almost female duplicates of his Apparent self. Then suddenly, he will find himself falling for a girl that is exactly the opposite of every one he has ever liked. It is at this time that he has reached true sexual maturity. He no longer is attracted to girls who are "sisters," but to those types he could never hope to find in his immediate family.

The same selective sexual maturity can be seen in girls, when a succession of childhood sweethearts of the type analagous to the girl is followed by the one great love that is represented by a totally different type—the Demonic. We often see cases where a girl has married her high school sweetheart and several years later the marriage falls apart when the woman meets a man who is completely the opposite of her husband. The reason for this kind of occurrence and also the common failure of childhood romances that later develop into bad marriages should be obvious. In instances such as these, a decided difference in the flesh tone will be noticed between the wife and the other woman.

The first manifestations of an Apparent/Demonic change-over are seen in the hair and complexion. The boy who has always liked girls who were fair and blonde will settle down with one who is a brunette with olive skin. The girl who has only dated boys with dark hair and eyes will suddenly get serious about one with fair skin and sandy hair.

Just as these flesh and complexion variants are observable in a white environment, so will they be readily discernible in an oriental culture or within the black community. All of the rules of personality analysis in this book apply to black people as well as white. The same subtle differences exist in all races. One only has to open his eyes to observe them. The old cliche that "all _____ (fill in the blank with whatever race or nationality will be appropriate to the conversation) look alike to me" can only be applied when one is prejudicial in the truest meaning of the word. Where one doesn't *want* to see the difference in types within a given ethnic group, the people comprising that group would, indeed, "all look alike." An insect, asked by another insect, to describe what it was that almost squashed them might reply that it was a person. Asked to elaborate, he would probably drop the subject with, "How should I know? All humans look alike to me!"

If a man likes a firm, boyish figure when he is twenty-five, by the time he is forty he won't mind a few muscles and tendons that show—in fact, he'll secretly like them. If, in his younger years of adulthood, he goes for a baby doll type, by the time he is twenty years older, he will revel in your dimpled thighs and little rolls of fat. If he won't admit these things to you, it's only because he's afraid you'll think him "odd."

Nothing can unconsciously turn a man off more than a musculature and flesh tone that is antithetical to his Demonic type. This is why clothing is such a blessing, as it allows you to camouflage a great deal of your actual appearance. How much or little of your flesh should be displayed, and under what conditions, will be explained later in the book. If a man likes his women tawny and firm, nothing will repel him more than a cute, chubby body with milky skin. He will think of it only as "sickenly flabby." Conversely, the man who prefers his woman to be made of marshmallows and jelly will find little stimulation in a gal who "feels like a guy."

Of course, there are happy mediums, you are thinking. Yes, there *are* compromises between extremes, but don't try too hard to be "perfect" by spending all your time toning up your flesh and skin. The so-called perfect girls are the ones that scare men off because they are neither fish nor fowl. The old saying really applies that advises, "If you try to please everybody, you often wind up pleasing nobody."

The importance of tactile communication is more important to women than to men. A man's sexual and romantic interest is generated principally through the sense of sight, followed by smell and hearing, with touch and taste last. It is interesting to note that women place far less emphasis on male appearance; his odor, voice and touch are sometimes even more important than how he appears. Witches should accordingly not make the mistake of thinking that massaging a man will turn him on, unless it is actual manipulation of the sex organ. Most women respond strongly to massage, so therefore think a man will. The men that respond sexually to a body massage are those whose Core is that of a woman. Heterosexual men who like bodily massage invariably are stimulated by thoughts of lesbian activity between women and find lesbians very appealing. Homosexual men are almost all stimulated by body massage as are virtually all women.

Rather than concentrate on actually caressing a man to charm him, allow him to think he is getting away with something. Arrange it so that your body will touch his in a manner that can appear as by accident, or if you feel bold, use the old trick of touching feet or legs under the table. This type of action, corny as it may seem, is infinitely more stimulating to a man than hand caressing. It is partially because of the intimacy of having contact between parts of the body that would normally only touch during sexual activity. Even while dancing the legs and feet seldom touch. Social contact with the hands between persons of the same or opposite sexes occurs regularly in everyday life, so the hand loses a great deal of its potential as a magical weapon.

To a woman, the emphasis is on the pleasure she *receives* through the tactile maneuvers of others. To a man, the erotic emphasis is on the stimulation gained from *feeling*. Women like to be felt. Men like to feel. Don't reverse the procedure, unless you use your feet or legs for contact.

There are always those masochists who love a gal who will take a firm hand with them. These are often the types I mentioned earlier that act the most sexually aggressive but really are pleading for a slap in the face or a bust in the mouth. Wrestling matches are their thing, and the witch must use plenty of physical contact with them and treat them like the combination of demanding mother and nurse they crave. Because these type men are often the most stable in the world of business and finance, they are frequently good catches for the witch who is handy with her mitts and aggressive enough to use them. Lady judo and karate experts are always tremendously appealing to these men, and masseuses likewise find themselves catering to such types.

Wherever you find classes in touching and feeling, which seem to be popular now under a variety of esoteric names, you will find them populated with people who are only one step removed from the topless bars and Playboy Clubs they deride as being "look-but-don't-touch." In the case of these feely-academies, the standard of conduct is "feel-but-don't-do." Because intellectual or pseudo-intellectual males would be attracted to caressing and pinching on a scholarly basis, don't expect to see much other than two to five o'clock types, both male and female, attacking their inhibitions at your local Center for Tactile Enlightenment. The person running the show, however, will often be a socially gregarious bisexual eight to ten o'clock, who likes to watch ten to twos feel each other up. Men in the eight to ten o'clock bracket will respond to a clinical approach to sex, as their Demonic counterparts are on the intellectual side of the clock.

The one final tactile trick of the witch who is brazen has always been to reach down and touch a man's penis, even if he is clothed. Such a tactic requires a great deal of nerve, but is so blatantly outrageous that it will be guaranteed to get results. Don't grab or grasp, but subtly place your hand on it. If you are lady-like (yes, that's what makes the difference!) he can't become offended, only flattered, spellbound or tremendously stimulated. Men are *not* subtle creatures by any means as the most successful witches know.

4. Looks Mean Everything

You Don't Have to Be Ugly

> "She goes forth from her hut, clad in a coarse
> garment, bare of foot, hair unbound and flowing
> on to her shoulders."
>
> —*Ovid*

THE QUOTATION you have just read might be referred to as
the "Curse of Ovid." It is an affliction common to witches
who feel they must adhere to the description of the Roman
satirist, whose tongue-in-cheek description has been accepted as *de rigeur*.

If you have good looks and you want to be a witch, then
you must exploit your beauty at every opportunity. Very
few women actually realize just how much emphasis a man
places on appearance. You don't have to be flashy to get
visual attention either. Despite the sound of your voice,
your scent or the texture of your skin, your appearance
must command attention. If you are really ugly, you must
capitalize on your grotesqueness.

The truly ugly girl has others at a disadvantage, because
rather than hurt her feelings, they will do things for her
out of guilt. If you are homely and light-hearted and call
others' attention to it, they will think you are a swell sport,
talk about what a shame it is behind your back and try to
avoid appearing patronizing in your presence by not doing

anything special for you. If you are strange looking and act like you don't really think so, trying to look as much like the others as possible, they will still talk behind your back, but a little more cruelly. When you are in their presence their guilt at having done so, combined with the fear of weakening your apparent self-confidence, will cause them to be extremely patronizing. Neither of these patterns really gains you respect but only sympathy.

Respect based on accomplishment can only be given by those who are humble, wise, and themselves worthy of respect. From those who have achieved little or nothing and are ego-starved and insecure, respect can only be gained through fear. If you are genuinely grotesque in appearance, the two ingredients you must possess in order to gain respect are accomplishment and awesomeness. Through accomplishment, you will gain respect from those who are just. With your awesomeness, you will gain respect from those who are small-minded.

For centuries deformed and homely people were considered spawn of the Devil. I learned the present day formula while working in carnivals, where I grew to know and love the people of the side show—the "human oddities" or "strange people," as they are called. The passing of the side show has left a void that psychologists could well study. It seems that public sentiment and guilt at exhibiting deformed people caused the demise of this institution.*

No one ever consulted the performers themselves, however, as to their feelings on the matter. "They should not be exploited." It was "cruel," it was said, "in bad taste," "sadistic." So the side shows folded and the freaks became "unfortunate people who had a right to live just like anybody

* Interestingly enough, almost all side show performers who were able acquired a skill or utilized a talent in conjunction with the obvious drawing-power of their appearance, thus combining accomplishment with awesomeness.

else"; so instead of getting paid while people stared, they got to go into supermarkets with their normal niece, just like anybody else, and people nudged each other, and did double-takes, and ran down the aisle to get their friend, and did exactly the same thing that twenty years earlier they would have paid to do and done openly—not surreptitiously.

I say that if you are in any way beyond the help of glamorizing techniques, take the Devil's name and play the Devil's game and let people know it, for you are the witch that Ovid cast for the world to see. Learn a skill. Paint, play, sculpt, write, draw, read—so that those who matter will respect you because you are strange, wise and capable. Let your status as a witch be known, not sanctimoniously, as a "good" witch or a "white" witch, but as a *stereotyped* witch, who has taken her lessons straight from the Devil himself!

Wear the colors that would be consistent with your type on the synthesizer. Do everything else in accord with your type. You will then be perfect, but strange looking, and that will confound others. You will be outrageous, because everything about you will fit, despite your homeliness; and with your hint of secret powers, the small-minded will fear you, and well they should, for should you follow this advice, you will have those powers.

If you're pretty enough to attract men at all, you'll be able to take advantage of the formulas contained in these chapters on glamour. One of the most commonly asked questions by students of witchery, upon learning some of the tricks which follow, is "Why do I have to do that? I get enough attention as it is!" My answer to that is: A witch can *never* get too much attention, and if you have a surplus, you not only have more victims from which to choose, but an abundance of potent lust-power being poured into you. I will discuss the meaning of "lust-power" later on.

Another frequently asked question is "If I do all these outrageous things you say, what kind of men am I going to attract?" The answer to this is, *all kinds!* If your objections to utilizing some of the methods I tell you are founded on your fear that the only kind of men who will respond to you are the worst kind, get that thought out of your head. A pretty girl will be propositioned wherever she goes, and the best or worst in men, depending upon your definition, will be influenced by the environment in which you operate.

If you are a sexy witch, employing all of the accoutrements of outrageousness, and you go into a bar in the worst part of town, all of the drifters, hustlers and winos will be goggle-eyed over you, and you will think, "That Anton LaVey is nuts! Look at the kind of characters I attract when I come on like this!" Just try going to a fashionable cocktail party the same way, though, and you'll have all the women glaring at you and all the men swarming around you. Attend a business convention and have businessmen clustering about; and present yourself at the Fourth of July planning committee dinner and find yourself the darling of every Elk, Moose, Odd Fellow, Legionaire, and Veteran of Foreign Wars.

What I'm trying to say is that you will steal the show, and the kind of men you attract will depend upon the type of theatre you're working! Don't forget that sex appeal is a universal appeal and is not limited to certain economic or cultural levels. If movie goddesses worried about only appealing to finer and more exclusive males, they would never get anyplace. This doesn't mean they have to got to bed with every guy that ogles them on the screen, much less even ever speak to them. It's just that if you utilize certain tricks that will create compulsion in enough people, you'll soon be able to see the right face in the crowd, and the old adage, "Them that has, gets," will take on new meaning.

A most devastating stigma that can confront any witch is the fear of being "phoney." If you're afraid of being considered phoney, you will surely fail. No matter *what* you do to appear otherwise, if you succeed in anything, there will always be the charge of phoneyness leveled against you by those who either can't stand your success, don't have the guts to do what you're doing or wish they'd thought of it first! If you remain within the bounds of public propriety (and most outrageous tactics are!), perform your tasks or responsibilities in an efficient manner and are civil and courteous, you'd be surprised at the things you can get away with in your appearance.

The witch has always been a rebel, but not in a way that she can be stereotyped. Her actions and appearance are far more non-conforming than the wildest hair, grimiest clothes, mismatching attire and body-art of the most far out stereotyped hippie. Yet with her subtle violations of taboos, the witch, in all her non-conformity, cannot be labeled a non-conformist!

This very paradox is one of the reasons for her power. She is, but she isn't! She is a complete woman, a perfect capsulization of her synthesizer type, yet she defies sacred cows the other women kneel before. Let's see how she does it.

Make-up: Projective Coloration

How often we encounter the man who has a fit when his wife uses glamorous make-up or revealing clothing yet will get all excited when he sees another woman doing the same thing! This is not an isolated phenomenon and is especially prevalent in men who have been raised in an ethnic group that still places great value on a wife as a mother, cook, housekeeper, nurse and piece of property—but not as a woman! All you gals who advocate a "natural look" and disavow make-up are playing right into the hands of these fellows, and if you're "lucky" might wind up with one—and also wind up a personality-less drudge.

You may be sure of appearing as good, safe, stay-at-home wife material, and he will have the utmost respect for you, as he would for a faithful cook, but he'll not respect you for the one most important asset every woman who has the wherewithal to employ it—your looks! Vanity not only keeps a woman young, but also gives her something to live for, and if you get saddled to a man who stifles this basic female urge, yet ogles its effects in other women, he could well be knocking years off your life.

This doesn't mean you should keep up with every new style in an attempt to keep a youthful appearance. It simply means you should appear in a manner that you can identify with sexiness at some time in your life, for that is what really counts.

The woman in her sixties, with her funny hat with the cherries on it, her rouged cheeks, battleship corset and whitely powdered nose is to be admired, for she is sustaining herself by way of what she considers to be an expression of glamour, analogous to the most sensually-appealing period in her life. Her vitality is continuing because of what let's call "Erotic Crystallization Inertia" or ECI.

Just about everyone displays some form of ECI in their appearance except for those who seek to escape it through their adoption of every new style in clothing, make-up and hair that comes along, and I have found *these* to be the most insecure and truly unhappy of all people. Women who affect total appearance changes on a frequent basis are looked upon by others as being "vital," but alas, their vitality stops at their appearance, actions and speech. Underneath their stylish facade they are groping, grasping, searching, yearning, tragically unhappy creatures.

The first place to start and least expensive is with your make-up insofar as bringing out the witch in you. If you want to look like you have just died, go easy on the make-up, because vitality is associated with color. That's why they overdo the make-up so often in preparing the body for a funeral—to make it look alive! *Of course* the body looks like "it's just sleeping," rather than dead—it undoubtedly has more color in the face than it did when alive! The resulting "life" in the skin color often imparts an appearance of actual breathing.

If you are a vampire type, you should learn a few things about vampires. The vampire is pale and wraithlike, with sunken dark eyes, while it is unable to get some nice juicy person to suck on. A successful vampire (and that is the kind you want to be!) always has a feast waiting. Remember, in all types of witchery, them that has, *gets!* This even applies to vampires. So don't *look* like an unsuccessful vampire, and you won't be one. This means you've got to accentuate your mouth, as that is the only orifice of your body into which large things (food) can be inserted that is visible in polite society. Call attention to your mouth, but not through the overuse of your vocal chords, because then everything is going out and nothing is hinted at entering. Wear *red* lipstick. Not pale red but bright enough and dark enough to be of decided contrast to your skin. Even if you're not a vampire type, remember that witches and vampires have long been identified as one and the same, and many languages have only one word for the two terms. Your mouth is one of the most erotically stimulating parts of your body, so don't neglect it by making it look like it's something that's just there because you can't help it. Wear the brightest, reddest lipstick you can find.

The protests to what I'm saying will be at least one of these: (a) It looks "cheap"; (b) It doesn't look "natural"; * (c) It detracts from the eyes; (d) It makes you look older; (e) It's out of style. My answer to (a) is, "cheap" is just a synonym for "available" and every witch who is good-looking should look available. That doesn't mean you have to *be* available! Anything that will make you *look* available, without your actually coming out and stating you are, is fine. You must make every man that sees you think he would like to go to bed with you, and the only way you can do that is to give him sneaky cues that will lead him to think he can.

My answer to (b) is that a man doesn't care one hoot if you look "natural," so long as you look sexy. I have proven many times over that the "painted hussy" will steal the show from the more "tasteful" girls. Many years ago, I had my witches wearing false eyelashes with heavy eye make-up,** and though they were always criticized by other women as looking "artificial," they got all the attention from the men. When a man sees a make-up job that is

---

* Aside from the vampire look, another indisputable reason for wearing red lipstick is that it conforms to the classical image of true beauty. Through the ages certain things have been perennially considered marks of a *naturally* beautiful woman, such as soft, rounded curves; delicate hands, shining hair, small feet and . . . *ruby* lips!

** The reason I'm not instructing you in how to apply eye make-up is because this area needs no exploration, as the current style is to wear any type of eye make-up one chooses and as much as she likes without being considered a floozy. As far as the eyes are concerned, the only area that has been neglected somewhat in the past few years are the eyebrows. This is one of the most expressive features on your face, so don't pass up a chance to utilize this very useful feature, by glossing over it out of preference for what you consider to be more important, the eyes themselves. Make your brows as well defined as possible. If you are a blonde, use dark brown or black eyebrow pencil and don't fear looking "unnatural."

blatantly and obviously make-up, he is automatically flattered, because he knows that the woman is *trying* to look sexy. Men like to see a sexy-looking woman and it pleases a man to think that a woman is knocking herself out trying to please him. (If you are attempting to enchant purely for your own physical or romantic self-indulgence, don't turn the guy off by being fearful that your make-up will get smudged during the course of your love-making. First impressions *are* lasting, so once the emotional crystallization has taken place, be glad that all your projective coloration has done the trick. Contrary to what you might think, a man won't be disillusioned by seeing you without your make-up.)

Red lipstick signals the fact that you're trying to please. Whatever turns a person on is "natural," and we had better get rid of that hackneyed term. You should only consider what is socially acceptable and what is not socially acceptable! Then, from the socially un-acceptable things, decide what is harmful and what is harmless. To most people, the term, "natural," means "naked." So if you really want to be "natural," walk around with all your clothes off, but be sure if you're wearing make-up it looks natural!

If you think dark red lipstick will detract from your eyes (c), you're crazy! What's wrong with displaying one of the most erogenous spots on your body, if you can get away with it; for that is what your mouth represents. You surely don't worry about your mini skirt detracting from your eyes, nor your forty-two-inch bust, do you? Those things are a Hell of a lot bigger distractions than a crimson mouth. If you wear enough eye make-up, you'll have a double threat going for you, as the gazer will be tempted to both your eyes *and* your mouth. An expressive pair of lips with an occasionally provocative exposure of the tongue can drive a man wild, and between such an eye/mouth barrage, he can be reduced to putty.

The mouth can often be a worthwhile detraction from the nose. If you have a nose that you consider imperfect, the best thing you can do is hide it in between a tempting scarlet mouth and a pair of inviting eyes.

Insofar as bright red lipstick making you look older (d), if you ever put on your mother's lipstick when you were six years old, you knew then that it made you look older. The very budding of sensuality that prompted that act was enough to create a lasting impression, which was retained to this day. Little children invariably choose the color red first and the redder the better. When you wanted to put on your mother's lipstick, you certainly chose the brightest color she had, as it would serve better as overcompensation for your youthful years—it would make you look that much older. Therefore, you now equate lipstick with a strong contrast to your skin with an artificial aging process.

Combine this with the element of "availability" and "tawdryness" that bright red lipstick connotes. A woman who is "available" is usually one who is "experienced" and here again we can easily equate "experience" with "age." Don't worry on that score, because unless a man put on his mother's lipstick when *he* was six years old, in an attempt to look older, he won't have the same association as you do.

Concerning being "out of style," the only time a witch will ever be completely "in style" is when there exist enough influential women who apply the principles of dress and make-up set forth in this book. The "painted woman" has been the sex symbol throughout history, so don't be afraid to use that warpaint. The *real* witch has always been a "scarlet woman," despite the popular image of the old hag. Whatever you do concerning make-up, avoid grotesqueness unless you are downright homely to start with. Make-up should be employed to exaggerate your existing charms—not to camouflage them!

Your Fur

Your hair color and style must be consistent with your image. Dominant men generally respond to long hair, passive men to short hair. If you have long hair, putting it up will make you appear more dominant. If you have short hair, buy a fall when you wish to bewitch a dominant man. Dark haired witches are more appealing to passive males than blondes, who are always considered to be softer. Many of the most famous sex symbols have been blonde twelve o'clocks (The late Jayne Mansfield was a perfect example.), whose vast appeal lay in a deceptively blonde-haired baby face such as one would expect to see on a six o'clock, resting on a slim-hipped, long-waisted, big-busted twelve o'clock body.

In typing people, one cannot go by the face, only the physique. The shape of the face, however, should have much to do with the hair style and color one chooses. Hair style more than anything else but clothing is the most effective means for a witch to safely modify her basic or Apparent type. There are certain stereotypes with which every competent witch should familiarize herself. These will serve as a basis upon which to choose the proper hair style for the specific bewitchment she has in mind.

The nature of a blonde is detected largely by the way the hair is worn, so don't think just becoming a blonde will do the trick. It all depends on *what kind* of blonde image you present. If your features are soft, and your hair is flaxen, you will convey a virginal and innocent appearance —especially if your skin has a pinkish tint. If you are large, your flesh tone firm, with a well-defined bone structure, and you have the same flaxen hair as the last girl, you can make like Brunhilde. If your hair is too coarse for the Valkyrie image, you'll be best in exotic roles like a jungle goddess. If your face is just ordinary, with pleasant, regular features, an all-out platinum shoulder-length wig with lots of contrasting make-up will turn you into a real blonde bombshell. All it takes in most cases is guts! A rather tousled dishwater blonde job, possibly frosted, with a roundish face and the properly witchy eyes and mouth will be just the thing to pose as a bored housewife looking for excitement even if you're not married.

Remember, if you can't present the image you want with your own hair, wigs are the thing to employ. First impressions are lasting ones, and your appearance is the biggest part of any first impression you will make. I want to stress that your image as a witch must be synonymous with enchantment, seduction and fascination which all adds up to glamour. You don't have to even consider going to bed with anyone you enchant. You are simply a purveyor of fantasy —fantasy in the mind of the person you bewitch, and if you can give a man a good fantasy, you will have succeeded in throwing your spell.

One of the main complaints about wearing a wig is that you have to be careful that it doesn't get displaced when you are in the sack. I assume that most of the women who read this book want to bewitch. I'm not going to tell you how to make love or even advocate promiscuity, because any gal can become popular if she sleeps with every guy that finds her appealing. A fool and his money are soon popular, and a girl who feels she must go all the way to be accepted falls into the same category.

Have sex with whomever you like and as often as you wish, but don't feel that you have to use sex indiscriminately to be a compleat witch. Some of the most competent witches I know have one man and are perfectly satisfied with him, but *use* the folly of other men who can't accept the fact that such a relationship is possible.

Getting back to your crowning glory, the average American girl has long been stereotyped as having brown hair and a name like Betty or Sue. The traditional girl-next-door has a tremendous appeal, and always will, so don't sell brown hair short. Brown has the advantage of being a good base from which to start. Styled in a soft manner, it will always give a feeling of assurance that some of the best men need from a woman. Piled high, brown hair will give you the most efficient look. Because this is the color of human values, you will fit into social activities with the least trouble and attract the person who might be more anti-social around a blonde or redhead. There *are* some men who can't stand blondes, and many who like redheads even less.

Many men consider girls with black hair too exotic or tire of it easily. A little jet-black hair goes a long way if a man looks at it as a novelty, and there are many cultures where there just isn't much else from which to choose. There are so many different shades of brown, ranging from molasses or maple to deep mahogany, that an infinite color variety is available to the brownette with various rinses and tints.

The witch with black hair is the most frequent stereotype, and if you actually plan on advertising your craft, black hair is best. No matter what will be done to dispel the old depictions of witches there are thousands of years of pre-paid publicity for the raven-haired witch. Ask any child to describe a witch and, TV shows notwithstanding, you most likely will be told that she has black hair. The semantic and religious angles are well established, so if you have black tresses and want to bewitch, bear this in mind. Did you ever see a good fairy in a story book that didn't have blonde hair? Or a saint? Or a heroine? Not many, I'll wager, yet invariably the wicked woman, witch, femme fatale, vampire, head matron, dean of girls or female spy has black hair! Of course, there is always Snow White. If your face is sweet and innocent, with pale, translucent skin and you have soft doe-eyes (they *can't* be the least bit wicked!), then see what you can do with such an image. But keep in mind that Snow White kept company with some very strange men.

Black-haired gals have an overwhelming appeal for masochistic males, exceeded only by redheads. Red-haired women are the *enfants terrible* of the witchhood. If a girl has auburn hair she can pass as a brunette, but still call herself a redhead if the situation warrants it. Likewise, a strawberry blonde can take credit for red hair if it will be to her advantage. But the witch with flaming red hair had better be something special, or her fiery looks will stand in her way. It is not easy to maintain the image that is required of the redhead. Consequently, many girls who are not natural redheads can't stick with it for any length of time once they have dyed their hair red. This is probably the only hair color that one must either be born into or be an excellent full-time actress to carry off. Because redheads are all supposed to be hot tempered, this self-fulfilling prophecy sees to it that they are.

A redhead's image is cut out for her, so there is no other role she can play. Redheads are natural witches, because they have literally been forced into a totally consistent type. Usually the shy retiring redhead has been a freckle-faced carrot-top since birth. These gals occasionally can't live up to the fiery redhead image and sometimes will tint their hair to tone down the red. On the other hand, I have seen instances where introverted girls got just the spunkiness they were lacking by dying their hair red.

The main disadvantage of red hair is the fact that most men either love it or hate it—nothing in between. The chance that you'll turn off the right man is more of a hazard than with other colors. But fetishistically, red hair is high on the compulsion list, and he who goes for it will be your slave. Masochists adore redheads especially if you are up around the top of the synthesizer clock. Many men believe that redheads are more highly sexed and passionate than other women. This assumption has proven detracting from the real qualities of many a redhead, whose suitor becomes disgruntled when he finds she is not some kind of sex-maddened, lust-ridden, motel acrobat but only a passionate, responsive woman. Appearance wise, redheads cause more conjecture than any other, and a cute seven o'clock, with white skin and plenty of freckles can excel as a delectably slatternly strumpet!

If you are of an ethnic group that is predominated by black-haired people, don't make the mistake of thinking that these rules don't apply to you. The only reason many Black people, Orientals, Latins, etc. don't artificially modify their hair color, is because they feel it would be "wrong" to do so. Such lack of objectivity can also be seen in Scandinavians who have great pride in their blonde hair, but whose appearance might be more effective, in many cases, by *darkening* their hair. I feel sympathy for witches who are of Black or Latin ancestry, who would like to have red hair or blonde hair but feel they "just can't." You can do anything you damn please with your appearance, if by doing so it will create an image that will lead to greater powers of enchantment.

Invariably, somewhere along the path of sorcery, you'll find yourself "selling out" to someone's idea of what you should look like. If your dear old granny liked your soft brown hair and you want to be a blonde, you don't dare bleach your hair, or you'll be "copping out" on granny. If your hair is red and like a Brillo pad, and everybody thinks you're a great pal of an Irish gal, just like Little Orphan Annie, you might want to clap a nice sleek black wig over that fine heritage, but you'll be a "cop-out" to all the folks you've known at the Knights of Columbus dance. If you're Black and you stop traffic with your cat-like movement and you'd look even more exotic with blonde hair, do it!

Pride in what you are doesn't mean you have to squelch your female vanity. In recent years Japan has become loaded with sexy blonde witches, who simply decided they liked blonde hair. Their ancestors might be horrified, but I don't think so. Tinting, bleaching and otherwise modifying hair color is nothing new. It was done in ancient Egypt, Babylonia, India, China, Persia, etc. and many tribes in Africa and the South Pacific have practiced it. Dying and bleaching of the hair was also practiced by many Indian tribes in Central and South America and by natives of New Zealand and Australia. Norsemen died their blonde hair black, put on bearskins, and went forth as berserkers or the original werewolves! So no matter what you do with your hair, you're not making any new modifications, historically speaking.

An unpardonable sin in the make-up of a witch, is a mania for every hair being in place. No man is going to think you are anything other than untouchable if you look the part, and there is no surer method of saying "hands off" than to look like your hair is stamped out of moulded plastic. Most hairdressers will agree that a few hairs straying in the right manner can add rather than detract from an attractive coiffure. If you have known enough men, you'll be aware of the preoccupation many have for mussing a woman's hair. The idea is that it looks like she has been making love, and men hate chaste women (unless, of course, it's their mother, daughter, sister . . . or wife). Anything that makes a woman look a little shopworn, will turn a man on, so muss that hair accordingly. This means that your hair must be styled, though, to really be effective when slightly disarrayed. If you go about with straggly locks it will look as though you don't give a damn, whereas if it looks like you're a lady who cares about her appearance, but your coiffure is a little mussed—that's a different story!

In the previous chapter on fetish-finding, you will recall my mention of long hair. Exceedingly long tresses represent one of the most commonly encountered fetishes, so every well-stocked witch should have a long hairpiece in her bag of tricks. There's *one* to fall for you in every roomful, and he won't be hard to spot, for his eyes will show you you've hit the jackpot with your Lady Godiva mane. And, yes, there are some guys who like hair so short on a woman that you'd wonder why they'd even bother. Usually, these types would be better off with a nice male roommate, but would punch anybody's nose that dared suggest such a thing. If you need to keep such a man enchanted, maintaining a G.I. haircut isn't as bad as it used to be, thanks to the magic of wigs.

Your Undercoat

In our society underarm hair is a taboo that few other cultures share. In many countries, the absence of underarm adornment is considered decidedly unwomanly. The obsession Americans have about underarm hygiene is considered ridiculous by the majority of the world's peoples. The main reason such a taboo exists in the U.S. is because the armpit has never been considered an erogenous zone.

Like the nape of the neck in Oriental cultures, the armpit holds a high position in European taste. It is easy to understand why, when one considers that the hollow under the arm is a cleft, analogous only to one other on the body in appearance; and like the crevice between the legs, it is normally kept closed and is covered with hair. Many old tales describe how the depth of a woman's sexual part may be measured by the size of her armpit. The whole idea seems so preposterous to most researchers that no one has bothered to explore the armpit for any degree of sexual significance.

The men who get excited over a hairy armpit are usually not impressed by the "naturalness" of it, but rather because of its "nastiness." For every man who likes his women's skin smooth and hairless, there are always those who like them just a little bit hirsute.*

Any violation of a taboo is sexually appealing to most men. Don't expect to hear the low-down from men, concerning their secret likes. Most will never tell. You'll just have to find out for yourself if you don't believe what I tell you. Most French, Italian, Spanish and Greek men like a profuseness of underarm hair, and the bigger the forest the better.

A special item that has been produced in Japan for many years and is listed in early catalogues of sexual implements and aides as "night flower" is nothing more than a patch of hair designed to cover the pubic area. Obviously, where there is an incidence of sparseness of pubic hair, a toupee such as this can add a great deal of erotic stimulation. On the other hand, where pubic hair is usually seen, the shaving of the area is considered the height of enticement.

* Women with an abundance of body and facial hair are supposedly more highly-sexed, because their level of male hormones is much higher, thus producing stronger sex drives.

How much or how little underarm or pubic hair, depends on the situation or environment in which your enchantment is to take place. Underarm hair need not be like a bramble bush, but a little five-o'clock shadow will never hurt, witchery-wise. Your decision in such matters requires a thorough knowledge of the Law of the Forbidden as it applies to your culture.

Pubic hair or lack of same can be a delicate decision to make. Keeping your pubes shaved is a real job, and if you miss a few days, the itching can drive you nuts. There are many men, though, who are tremendously excited by hairless sexual equippage. The greatest advantage of a lack of pubic hair is manifested when there is no covering whatsoever over the area, as in the case of nude models, etc. Under normal circumstances, however, a well-grown foliage can be used to great advantage.

Several years ago, I attended an annual affair in San Francisco, which is held in a beautiful grove, and is dedicated to the pursuit of the photographic arts. Displays of the work of numerous photographers abound, and one of the highlights of the day is a photo session with live pretty girls in swim suits for models. I might add that this is the traditional contest where Miss San Francisco is chosen, who subsequently has a chance for Miss California and, hopefully, Miss America.

I was a police photographer at the time and had a couple of "human interest" type photos on exhibit and wasn't the least bit interested in wasting my time taking pictures of pretty girls. But, because there was all this commotion over by the stage where the girls were lining up for the preliminary judging, I forced myself to take an objective interest. The contestants were radiantly lovely, and Bert Parks would have loved each one. Their new swim suits, generously donated by warm-hearted merchants, accentuated their youthful charms; and photographers of all shapes and sizes were clustered at the rim of the outdoor stage, their shutters clicking frantically.

I noticed one bountiful lass was getting more attention than the rest, so I sidled over to examine her more thoroughly. She was a delightful creature, with honey-blonde hair and had on a one-piece black job that contrasted strikingly with her peaches-and-cream skin. Oh yes —and a few wisps of *darker* honey-blonde pubic hair sprouting out of each side of the "V" between her thighs. The poor girl hadn't shaved enough and didn't think it showed, but all those nice men with their cameras didn't mind. In fact, I don't think a single one wanted to spoil her day by telling her, which was quite chivalrous in this day and age.

The girl with the most popular foliage in the park didn't win a thing, except the undivided attention of many males and a full charge of witch-power. I have since known that pubic hair, like all other aspects of the Law of the Forbidden, is *always* effective when it's not supposed to be seen. Think about that the next time you get out the razor or hair remover the night before you go to the lake or beach or the afternoon prior to the costume party you'll be attending as a stripper or can can dancer!

The Law of the Forbidden

The reason there has always been a fascination for witchcraft and sorcery is because it has consistently been considered taboo. Your first duty as a witch is to your appearance. Men are all voyeurs, and most of what they are attracted to is based on what they see. What they see in you, as a witch, must be fascinating, and *nothing* is so fascinating as that which is not meant to be seen.

Have you ever noticed how people will all jump out of their cars when there is a bad auto accident and stand around and gawk at the victims? Why? It's not just because they're sadistic or getting their blood-lust out of their systems or even because they wish to be shocked. It is usually out of curiosity, and why this curiosity for something which might give them nightmares (or make more careful drivers of them)? Simply because something is happening that is out of context with their everyday lives, something that is *for real,* but not something they can pay a few bucks to see whenever they want. In short, something is happening that shouldn't. An event is transpiring that is alien to the way a straight and proper highway scene should look.

You wouldn't like to be lying on the pavement in pain with everyone looking at you. You, therefore, are subconsciously embarrassed for the injured persons, but don't think about them in that respect nor analyze just why you stare at all. Let's move on to another scene, because there's nothing erotically stimulating to most people about the one we have just discussed, even though it is still a direct manifestation of The Law of the Forbidden.

The scene is a night spot that features topless dancers. The tables in front of the low stage are filled with singles and couples watching the bare-bosomed dancers spasmodically jerk to music which is far too loud to talk over. The decor is garish, the lights not particularly dim and the bar full of people who aren't able to get down closer or who don't want to. Among the people at the bar are seated a man and his pretty young wife, who is perched on her bar stool in a manner that reveals more of her legs than it appears she is aware. She is not wearing a mini-skirt but a dress that normally comes about three inches above her knees, actually quite conservative by today's standards. Many other women who are present are wearing mini and

micro skirts, but nobody's noticing *them*. The girl at the
bar is wearing a wedding band, so it is obvious she's married. Her shapely legs are encased in common, garden
variety, beige-tone nylons, with regular tops, held up by a
plain white garter belt. She is wearing classic, black, three-
inch spike heels, in a room full of fashionable square heeled
clod-hoppers. Even the topless dancers are wearing the
Frankenstein look in footwear as they shake their pendu-
lous globules and thrust their vulvas, which are covered
only by a tiny strip of Scotch tape. The young lady at the
bar has her own audience, though, as several bored men
who have been carefully nursing their drinks are furtively
looking in her direction.

What do they see that is so shocking? What kind of lewd
performance draws their attention away from the flailing
hoofers on the stage? What makes them sneakily glance
over their shoulders in the direction of the bar, while their
wives and dates, who dragged them here, are attentively
picking up some pointers (or so they think!) on titillation
from the girls onstage?

I'll tell you what those dirty-minded little boys see. They
see up a nice lady's dress! They see a *real* woman. Her face
is pretty and proper, but provocative, and her hair is neatly
styled. Her dress has ridden up under her, so the backs of
her bare thighs above her stocking tops are in direct contact with the bar stool. She holds her purse in her lap,
which is also covered by her dress, so it appears as though
she *thinks* her legs are properly covered. Actually, one can
follow (if his eyes are good) one of her garter straps far
enough to see it dimly disappear beneath what surely must
be her panties! "Just imagine!" their little boy minds snap
into awareness, and they are back in their bedrooms when
they are thirteen years old—"You can see all the way up to
her underpants!" Suddenly the eighty-six proof voice of

the M. C. jars them back to reality. Their evocation is over. Candy Bumpstead is about to present her twin forty-four magnums, and get a load of those nipples!

Now let's break down the formula, the results of which we just witnessed. First of all, the gal at the bar was out of context with the rest of the "entertainment"—she wasn't part of the show. She was a married woman, or at least with somebody else, so therefore she was available to at least the man she was with, and didn't look chaste, and everyone who ogled her felt as though he was getting something, even if it was just a good look that belonged to someone else! That's *Forbidden Fruit #1*. She wasn't wearing a skirt that was intended to reveal so much leg (*Forbidden Fruit #2*). She was wearing stockings with tops, which skirts are supposed to cover (*Forbidden Fruit #3*). She was revealing her underwear (*Forbidden Fruit #4*), which was regulation white in color and not something showy that any girl might think it cute to display (*Forbidden Fruit #5*), therefore convincing the viewers that it was an accidental, rather than intentional, exposure (*Forbidden Fruit #6*). The men who furtively stared should have been watching the action on the stage, *not* staring at the other side of the room, as it's considered rude and impolite to turn around in any theatre and look at others while the performance is in progress (*Forbidden Fruit #7*).

Combine all these factors with the compulsive power of each man's E.C.I. (Erotic Crystallization Inertia), which fetishistically saw to it that the woman at the bar should steal the show from the dancers onstage. Add the emotional release device of the liquor, however slight the effect or watered down the drinks, and you have nine good reasons why that girl seated at the bar with her husband was the most potent witch in the place! Through her employment, consciously or otherwise, of the Law of the Forbidden, she stole the show. Remember, NOTHING IS SO FASCINATING AS THAT WHICH IS NOT MEANT TO BE SEEN!

When it comes to bewitching them all men are nasty little boys at heart. When the first sexual feelings and subsequent experimentation occurred in a man's life, he was acting in the capacity of a nasty little boy in ninety-nine percent of all cases, and I don't care who might disagree. We can talk 'til we're hoarse about the beauties of love and the majesty of sexual fulfillment—and I agree these things can come to pass in a man's life. But when a boy becomes a man, it is accompanied by lewd thoughts! This is just as sure and true as the idyllic romance which always blows as a gentle and tender zephyr while a girl becomes a woman.

A boy's sexual awakening is prurient, lascivious and lusty and his romantic emergence is a bitter-sweet dawning and he is randy with the one and anguished with the other; and a compleat witch will know how vast a difference exists between the two. This is why you must appeal to the lust within a man with unholy devices. He may lie and say he has no thoughts of secret vices or furtive pleasures and he may remove himself to monkeries to beat his lusts asunder, but they will be there—they will always be there and caging them will make them roar all the louder.

Secrets of Indecent Exposure

In learning how to properly employ the Law of the Forbidden, you must realize that you, as a woman, are ideally suited for such tactics. A man is limited by his clothing styles and even if he were able, he would find that women are not the voyeurs he is, primarily because of the woman's romantic approach to sex versus man's role as a spectator.

If a man exposes himself by unzipping his trousers from behind a bush or in a doorway or subway, he has silently proclaimed himself an exposer, a pervert, a dirty old man. He will most certainly be arrested if he keeps it up long enough and be considered a social problem. If the same man wishes to remove all of his clothing, as a form of protest, as we see happening in radical groups, he might get away with it, but he must still carry the stigma of the misfit, the social freak. He can always join a nudist camp, but if sexual aims are his purpose, he'd better forget that idea, as he would be expelled at the first sign of an erection. If there is a "free beach" nearby, he can cavort nude, but as in the case of social protest nudism and nudist camps, he must go all the way, thereby labelling himself a rebel.

The woman has no such problems, as her potential avenues of indecent exposure are generally those that will allow her to remain a part of established society. A smart witch need never lack for suitable opportunites to expose herself. Simply exposing oneself is not enough, though. In order to compel and fascinate you must employ the Law of the Forbidden. The biggest hurdle to overcome in applying this principle is the fear of embarrassment. There are two ways to do this, each depending on your personality type. If you are thick-skinned and not naturally timid, you're probably an exhibitionist anyway, so the constant knowledge of what your new-found tricks are causing in the minds of your quarries should give you the necessary confidence you need to overcome the fear of embarrassment. If you are shy and bashful by nature, the best way to cope with this fear of embarrassment is to not even try!

You'll notice I stress the "fear" of embarrassment, rather than embarrassment itself. This is because the idea is not to avoid embarrassment, but to entertain it. If this sounds crazy, consider the very mechanism of embarrassment and you will be able to see its virtue.

When you are embarrassed, you blush—the blood vessels of the face and neck dilate to let in more blood, in a manner similar to the chameleon, who changes color when threatened so that he can match his surroundings and not be seen. This is our natural throw-back to protective coloration. You have probably never realized the significance of this form of camouflage when you've made the comment when telling of an embarrassing situation, "I could have crawled into a hole" or "I felt like crawling into the woodwork." To "hide one's face in shame" is an expression that bears eloquent witness to the natural protective coloration that blushing attempts to supply.

Now, the kind of situation that is engendered when we are embarrassed, and subsequently blush, is the very factor that will produce a total reversal of the supercharging of adrenalin that at times of shock and emotional stress will cause our faces to become whiter. The more we need to defend ourselves, the whiter we get. The more our need to "run away" or are confronted with a feeling of helplessness, the redder we get. Whether a situation will cause an aggressive or defensive reaction (whitening of the face) or a retreating and submissive reaction (blushing) depends on whether the situation calls for fighting or hiding.

Animals that are fighters depend on their claws and fangs for survival. Animals who are hiders depend on being able to crawl into a hole or climb up a tree. In setting up contrived situations of embarrassment you are not fighting nature. You are cleverly employing what normally might be naturally unpleasant reactions towards a positive end.

In the practice of ceremonial magic and one of its principle ingredients, telepathic communication, one must either get his adrenalin up in order to send or his submissiveness perfected in order to receive. Call it what you like, that's the way it works. When you place yourself in an embarrassing situation, you become submissive to your surroundings or else you wouldn't blush! Your very aura becomes one of awareness that everyone is looking at you, directing their interest towards you, and in the case of a sexually stimulating situation, directing their energy towards you. You, then, become the magnet, the flame, the psychic receptacle for all your viewer's lust-energy. The fact that you are forcing and accelerating an intense form of self-conscious submissiveness will produce what hours of meditation would fail to do insofar as your powers of magnetic attraction are concerned.

Through your use of the Law of the Forbidden, you have visually presented an image that will artificially do your "projecting" for you. Your appearance will serve as the out-going force that will snare your quarry, as an angler throws his bait. The self-consciousness of your embarrassment will reel in your line.

We find the same phenomenon occurs in a negative fashion when the typical "victim" walks down the street. Victims, whether they be those of rapists or swindlers, often attract their attackers—not because they subconsciously want to be attacked, as is often assumed, but because of their intense *fear* of attack, which makes them ideal receptors. The man who walks down the dark street with a gun in his pocket just hoping some strong-arm man will try to mug him will probably never meet one. Nor will the gal with the black belt of Judo. Contrary to the usual assumption that when you look for trouble, you'll find it, these types aren't looking so much as they are defensively prepared. The drunk who is just placidly boozed up enough to not give a damn, the sweet little old lady strolling through the park, the naive nature-lover exploring in the most likely murder spots are sometimes attacked, but the odds are with them that they'll keep on sauntering along without harm.

It's the girl who is scared, who throws out the scent of fear, who wants to hide, to run, to crawl into a hole, that has been raised on stories of men attacking her or who purposely goes out of her way to get scared or find "kicks" *while thrilling at her own daring*—these are the "victims." A great lesson can be learned from this sort of phenomenon, and the same basic attraction force can be utilized to your advantage and with your control through the use of feminine sexual magnetism as a result of embarrassment.

Now let's define the difference between the type of embarrassment that you will employ from that which you will discard even though *any* kind of embarrassment will make you feel like you're at the mercy of others. Ideas and thoughts go from our brain to various parts of our bodies via the autonomic nervous system. The kind of embarrassments you should conjure up should be those which directly relate to sexual stimulation in your viewer.

If you are working and make a gross error in your bookkeeping that is discovered just after you have been bragging about what a great office manager you are, you will go around with a red face for the rest of the day. But it's highly unlikely you'll find any guy in the office that can identify your erroneous calculations with his sexual urge unless he's turned on by strings of digits! The fact that you're embarrassed is manifested in your crimson face and perhaps a knot in your stomach and hotness in your ears. Your autonomic nervous system has not sent your embarrassment manifestations to erogenous zones of your body, because there is nothing of a sexual nature, that you know of, concerned.

Supposing, though, the elastic broke and your panties

fell down around your ankles (a popular subject for pin-up pictures). Or when you discovered that the roof of your building wasn't so secluded as you thought when you opened your eyes after momentarily dozing off over the paperback you were reading to see the two men who had come up to fix the TV antenna standing ten feet away and obviously not paying attention to their work. Or when you hung one on at the office party and did a strip number that you don't quite remember, but nobody will let you forget. You can't imagine how you could have ever done that sort of thing, but every time you see certain men who were present and think of how much of you they have seen— well . . .

The three cases of embarrassment I just mentioned had one thing in common—they involved sexual elements that presented pleasure to those who viewed them. No one gets any erotic pleasure out of seeing a person become ill in a restaurant though the situation can be most embarrassing to the person with the belly ache. Conversely, the pretty girl whose skirt is blown up by a gust of wind delights all men present, and the redder her face gets, the more pleasure she gives.

A woman who realizes the implications of a pleasingly embarrassing situation will still be just as embarrassed, but her autonomic nervous system—that which telegraphs from the brain to various parts of the body—will cause her to respond in her erogenous zones. When you know you are exciting a man, you, too, can feel a sexual response in the knowledge of what you are doing.

Anything you can do to provoke an embarrassment (submission) of a sexually provocative nature will cause you to throw off the very scent that can cause men and animals to get horny. Don't worry, as no one will attack you in a public place or at a polite gathering, but the sub-conscious impulse will still be there.

How do you purposely provoke embarrassment? It's easy. Just do something you wouldn't feel right doing! Just make sure it is something that would give sexual stimulation to someone else. If you have ten dresses and can't make up your mind which one to wear, choose the one that's a little too short or too tight—in some way revealing —so that you will be self-conscious while you are wearing it. You say you feel cheap? Good! Remember, "cheap" is just another term for "available," and every successful witch knows that available she is, but not to just anybody, and she seldom comes cheap.

5. Fashion: The Witch's Greatest Friend, The Witch: Fashion's Worst Enemy

WOMEN ALWAYS CONSIDER what is out of fashion at the moment as being uncomfortable or ugly. For example, the biggest objection to wearing nylons is the "discomfort" when compared to panty hose. When any new change in clothing styles comes about, the old style is automatically branded as being uncomfortable, and women wonder how they could have ever worn such torturous garments.

Panty hose are nothing more than glorified trousers. When women had to wear corsets, pantaloons and numerous petticoats, they wouldn't have felt right without them. Corsets gave the "support" that meant security, and only the eccentric and the poor were either unwilling or unable to attire themselves in the sort of accouterments that made a woman *feel* like a woman.

Later on when "emancipation" came from the laces and stays and heavy bloomers, the ladies felt "free" with their shirtwaists and chemises and only wore merry widows beneath their step-ins. Silk stockings were the rage, and what a relief they were from those heavy cotton and lisle things. In fact some "wild" young things even dispensed with the long suspenders that held up their hose and rolled their stockings over elastic bands. They didn't consider that it might cut off the circulation in their legs—only the feeling of freedom it gave them.

When rubber girdles appeared, women rejoiced that they could have the support without the encumbrance of a corset; and garter belts and briefs were very daring when respectable women were wearing undies with at least an inch of leg attached over their elasticized cocoons. Whether you wore your stockings rolled or suspended, you had to make sure your seams were straight, but then the gal that got the stares as being a trifle sleazy was the one with the crooked seams.

Women were women, and damn well knew it and rejoiced that they didn't wear trousers like the poor men. As a woman you had the privilege of wearing a dress with a minimum of undergarments by the time the Second World War started, and the bra made a "sweater girl" out of you and "gave your breasts the healthy support they needed" at the same time. Not too many years earlier your bosom had to flop around, because no self-respecting flapper wore anything under the top of her dress with the exception, perhaps, of a thin chemise. What a wonderful thing the bra was with its healthful respite from all the scary articles you read telling how you were breaking down the tissue in your breasts by going without support. Now the granddaughters of those girls are equally convinced that going braless is the only natural and healthy thing to do.

When women started working in war industries, they couldn't wear their feminine frills and no one could be expected to keep her seams straight while riveting on a ships' bulkhead. So as women became "substitute men," slacks took over. From the women's roles during the war manpower shortage the transition to trousers for women easily took place. A new garment in every woman's wardrobe had come into its own.

Men were no longer poor fools who had to be all bound up in those cumbersome trousers with Scotsmen and Greek soldiers the only lucky fellows who could let it all hang out. The outlook changed insofar as trousers were concerned, and women were wearing them—not out of necessity, but out of choice. Capris were comfortable. Besides, you didn't have to worry that some awful man would look up your dress while you gave the dog a bath and you were free to climb all the trees you wanted to.

But something was lost in the bargain. The baby had gone down the drain with the bathwater. The opportunities, recognition and respect that was becoming possible for women with more to offer than their biological fixtures was a truly admirable change. Unfortunately, it couldn't stop at psychic and social emancipation. The trappings of defeminization had to creep forth in subtle, insidious ways that would be guaranteed to convince women they were doing the right thing. New standards of non-beauty were formulated by those women who couldn't measure up to the old standards or else men who hated women because of what might be called "vagina-envy." These ugly women and vagina-less men didn't need any "secret conspiracy." The burning bitterness seething inside them was enough.

Don't confuse these purveyors of asexualization with the homosexual who loves the imagery of the archetypes of his own sex he seeks. The "butch" lesbian, who would rather be a man tries her damnedest to *look* like a man and goes for the most "femme" type girls. A "femme" lesbian is attracted to another dominant lesbian, who knows why she often favors mannish styles. A homosexual man likes other men and only wants to see women in un-womanly clothes *if* he is unsuccessful in his homophile encounters.

The transsexuals and transvestites, bless them, come closer than anyone else to a complete recognition of the Demonic element within them. These people who, because they truly admire and recognize the sensual qualities of the opposite sex, would do nothing to discourage whatever trappings add to the *difference*. This is why transvestites and transsexuals often are said to "make better women than women." They employ all the devices of overcompensation and frequently come out actually looking more convincing.

But then not everyone with a desire to change his sex can be a Christine Jorgensen, even though, as Miss Jorgensen puts it, "It could be as common as a nose job." It takes a great deal of self-realization and courage to know oneself so well as to decide to turn one's Majority Self into the body it represents if that body happens to be the opposite from that which you wear about.

Fashion designers, it must be realized, are in business to make money. There's nothing wrong with that, and the women who are dupes enough to blindly follow the latest trends, whether flattering or not, desire to have their money taken. I see nothing wrong with trying to make a buck on whatever legal means they can find, and most women have made it very obvious that they're far more concerned with what is stylish, than with what looks the best.

There used to be a slogan, popular with the old patent medicine salesmen, whose nostrums were good for so many ailments that if you got rid of one, there was sure to be a symptom present of another malady that the wonder elixir could cure. The saying went, "You can't make money off a well patient. Keep 'em sick." This very policy applies to the fashion industry in the sense that you can't sell clothes to a woman who has a closet full. And how do you get a girl to give up her favorite garments? Tell her they make her look ugly, which is precisely what you are led to feel if you wear outdated styles.

Just as the hypochrondiac must be told he is sick, the woman who has something lacking in her life must blame her unhappiness on something other than her own inadequacies, so fashion and current clothing styles become both her rejection device ("I haven't got a thing to wear.") and her salvation. This type of woman who is stylishly dressed has bought for herself a form of security that will giver her confidence without the need for beauty, brains, talent, ability or actual respect from others.

Be glad such multitudes of women exist, as they make your role as witch that much easier. However fanatical in their up-to-date appearance the fashion followers are, they have never learned that you can't fight nature, and there are certain standards of female beauty that transcend all clothing style changes.

In order to practice magic, you must follow natural law, not violate it. Certain curves are conducive to consistency in the appearance of a woman—*any woman*. Whatever violates these forms reduces the feminine imagery that a woman should maintain if she is to succeed in enchantments. For example, a woman was not designed to look straight up and down, yet many styles foster this appearance and designers champion it. The so-called "bulges" that a woman shuns in herself are the feminine principle in a curvilinear form. Straight or concave lines are *out* for a witch's wardrobe unless you want to appeal to a man whose Majority Self is that of a woman and doesn't know it.

There are basically three fashion patterns: the straight, concave, and naturally feminine convex configurations. The first pattern dresses in angular garments, which do not emphasize but decrease the curved dimensions synonymous with woman. There is a hint that curves might be there but also an apprehension that they might not be. This girl seems to say: "Maybe yes, maybe no." This is an ideal form to utilize if you are tree trunk straight in the torso, but it would be more effective were you to take a tip from the old-fashioned bustle and pad your hips out a bit so you could project a convex image.

The concave pattern is the complete opposite of the ideal shape though most of my readers will find her the most compatible to their vision. Naturally, you would find her most attractive from a woman's point of view, because she is antithetical to your own Apparent selves. She looks like a boy with long hair, and her clothes would most likely have been designed by a man who liked boys or a woman who resented femininity in women. Every extremity of her outfit is like a barb—totally opposite to the tactile dimensions for which you should strive. It's as if she is saying, "Don't touch me." The human brain responds to what the eyes see, regardless of what the mouth says, and the collective unconscious tells us, "This is not a woman." It also tells us that there is something antagonistic to sexual acceptance, much as the thorns on a pretty rose tell us we'd best be careful not to grab it.

Straight lines, angles of all kinds, zig-zag lightening bolt patterns, saw-tooth designs—all masculine dimensions and concepts—will rob you of your femininity. They should not be employed unless the man you are bewitching is of an extremely submissive nature. The reason prison matrons, deadly female super-spies and science-fiction heroines always appeal so strongly to latent homosexuals is because the formidable take-no-crap-from-any-man attitude these ladies project is reinforced by their severely cut tunics, studded leather, and one piece tantalum commando suits with behavioral control units in each breastplate.

A girl dressed in the last pattern may not appeal to you and shouldn't unless you are a self-aware "butch" lesbian or a man. She is a series of curves, or better yet, circles. Circles, circles everywhere, all corresponding to each other —circles for the breasts, shoulders, thighs, calves, arms, abdomen, even the area of the throat. Circles within circles— the same circles every artist and cartoonist learns are the foundation of the picture of a woman. And the fashion designers actually think they can come up with an act to follow this one?

That is the reason why the convex configuration will always win out, fashion and style be damned—*unless* standards of beauty become so inverted and warped that a "woman" woman is no longer considered desirable but ugly and "Get outta my way, you bastard" becomes the new non-mating call of the woman of the future. I hardly think this will happen, though, for so long as there are real witches abroad and enough underground women who take delight in *being* women, the old rules of the game will apply, and the convex type will always win.

She has, in her curved dimensions, a tactile quality that tells a man's vision, "Hold me, stroke me, squeeze me, feel me, touch me, put your arms around me—in short, try me out for size." In order for anything to be tactile, it must be pleasing to the touch, but first it must invite you to touch it. How does it do that? By conforming in its surfaces to the insides of your hands. After all, you feel with your fingers, and the more surface of your fingers that can be accommodated at one time, the more inclined you are to touch something. If a surface is of a nature that looks as though your whole hand would fit "just right" on it, chances are good, unless there's a "Do Not Touch" sign next to it, you will. Even if there's a sign prohibiting you from feeling the tactile object, if it's compelling enough, you'll touch it anyway. Just go to any museum or art gallery and you'll see plenty of evidence of what I am saying. Convex lines create the tactile impression of such an object, except, of course, being another woman, your inhibitions, if nothing else, will forbid such a response.

You see another woman as something too familiar to yourself—too much like what you carry around with you in the sculptured body of your own. You can feel yourself anytime you want (and probably do!). Why would you want to feel another tactile piece of sculpture so similar to yourself? A *man*, though—that would be different—angles, straight lines, round, but straight—tactile, but straight. Surely you like to feel those convex hand-filling art objects previously mentioned, but not the object of art that is more familiar to you than any other—your own body.

That's why you don't like the final pattern. Because you, too, respond to the Law of the Forbidden, and the grass is, indeed, always greener on the other side of the fence. But let us hope that you can now understand, why a heterosexual male with a functioning sense of touch *would* respond to the visual stimulus provided by it.

Surely, the grand award for fashion designers in the world of witchery must go to Mr. Frederick, of "Frederick's of Hollywood." The enduring styles purveyed by this chain of shops are the only hold-outs in the world of fashion.

Without any periodic style changes of a drastic nature,

"Frederick's" has proven beyond a doubt that money can be made in women's wear, selling clothes that make women look sexually appealing! Despite the fact that to many women, "Frederick's" has become somewhat of a joke, the joke is on *them*, for it is just such women who are the butt of the biggest joke in realm of clothing.

While some of "Frederick's" fabrics and colors are decidedly garish, the proper lines are almost always present. Almost blatantly antagonistic to any attempts at defeminization, "Frederick's" also features such trifles as hip and leg pads, falsies in varying degrees of ebullence, extra-high heels, extra-long falls, and other goodies guaranteed to reserve Mr. Frederick a place before the firing squad, should female liberationists ever take over.

While "Frederick's" sells a certain amount of so-called "stylish" garments, it is readily apparent that these are simply a concession to women who think they're buying something sexy if they carry it out of a "Frederick's" shop, yet don't want to violate any clothing taboos. It is for this reason that panty hose, shapeless dresses, and most of the other accouterments of desexualization can be found sandwiched in between the blow-up bras, spike heels, and tight sheath dresses.

Woman-hating men and man-hating women comprise the largest part of the fashion industry. Be thankful to them for eliminating would-be rivals who allow themselves to be duped.

Cartoon Cuties

Regardless of the attempts made by the fashion industry to foist questionable styles on women, there will always be certain standards of sexiness that prevail. No matter how chunky shoes get or how shapeless dresses become, the basic wardrobe of the witch will remain the same.

I find it amazing that women will live for the attention they receive from men and yet look to the pages of *women's* magazines for the styles to employ in their bewitchments. If a witch is wise, she will refer to men's magazines for her pointers in style. She won't have to buy many such magazines, though, as repetition will set in at an early stage. When you look at a man's magazine to see what the perennial witch is wearing, don't study the big centerfold or the slick photo essays. Chances are good you'll only see bikinis, G-strings, or no clothes at all. Instead turn to the *cartoons.* Yes, the cartoons—especially the ones toward the back of the magazine. The reason for this is because the cartoons contain girls involved in everyday situations, for the most part, and as such, they are clothed. But *how* are they clothed!

Invariably, they will be attired in the standard witch outfit, and I don't mean a black cape and a pointy hat. They will be wearing a rather skimpy dress which looks about two sizes too small and so thin that the lines of the body and sometimes the undergarments are visible. The figure will always be full-blown—a mass of circles, so to speak. The face will always be pert, exotic or provocative. The shoes will be as close as the cartoonist can get to an accurate rendition of a spike heel, and if the girl is not bare-legged, she will be wearing stockings with visible tops and garters!

It seems that these masters of exaggeration—the cartoonists—know what will always catch the eye. They may change the cut of a man's suit from year to year, but a curvy cutie's basic appearance—*never!* There are many periodicals devoted solely to the cartoon art. Within the magical confines of their covers you will find the creations of a thousand Frankensteins—all custom made, not dependent on the right model posing for the right photographer with *her* misguided idea of what to wear for her photo session. Nor will you find any women in the cartoons who are any less pretty than the artist is capable of drawing.

It is true, many "girlie" magazines feature photos of models wearing some of the accouterments of the witch but seldom will perfection be attained. This is due largely to the fact that the photographer often trys to be "up-to-date" more than the cartoonist, as he is not limited to a particular style of drawing to which, once perfected, is most easily adhered. The photographer can do much, but he is still limited to the whims of his model, insofar as he himself doesn't want to impose styles of dress which might brand him as some kind of nut. When a cartoonist draws his women, however, *he* is the Pygmalion, the Creator, and no embarrassment need enter his mind nor inhibition stifle his art. Therefore, he creates the eternal witch, the perennial courtesan, the all-pervading strumpet—in a manner that his artistic unconscious tells him is the way a *real* woman should look.

Of course, the single word that exemplifies a cartoon is "exaggeration." Let us take a very useful clue from this word in the pursuit of practical witchery. The secret of the appeal of the cartoon enchantress lies in overdevelopment. Her breasts are not simply large. They are immense. They are either distended globules threatening to burst the fabric which encases them or dangerously outthrust projections. And the nipples! Not just a subtle termination of the breast, but an outgrowth the size of a large ripe olive! Her hips are like motorcycle saddle bags and her waist must be all of sixteen inches. Her buttocks resemble a pair of overinflated basketballs and her features are those of a two-year-old baby. All in all, a monster, if such a creature could actually exist.

Fortunately, our minds are used to sorting out three di-

mensions, so such grotesqueries are unnecessary for a sexy
appearance, as the girl in the cartoon exists in only two dimension. She therefore must have a little bit more going
for her, to make up for the other one. What we are primarily concerned with here, though, is her style of dress.
Proportions must vary, dependent on the number of dimensions seen, in order that the final observations will
appear standardized.

Style is not in need of such optical manipulation, however, when rendered in a graphic manner. A tight dress is
a tight dress, whether seen on paper or in person. Likewise,
a garter is a garter, a high heel is a style of shoe and a
glimpse of panties is not a rose, and I'm sure Gertrude
Stein, who had her own interests in both, would agree. The
uniform of the sex-type witch will be seen in the clothing
worn by the denizens of the single-panel cartoon, and in
some cases, the comic strips. Don't count on the comic strips
for a guide, though, as their creators pride themselves on
maintaining fashion plate standards, especially in the last
few years. Of course, Blondie's attire will probably never
change much, nor will Olive Oyl's, and Orphan Annie is
not to be trusted much either witchery-wise.

Stockings versus Panty Hose

Throw away your panty hose and forget about them!
They are a curse perpetrated on women by people who
would rather you weren't women. Panty hose are nothing
more than cloth chastity belts that assure the wearer that
nobody's gonna see anything they ain't supposed to. There
goes twenty points for the Law of the Forbidden right
down the drain.

The man who ogles a girl wearing panty hose knows that
he can only see so much, nothing more. There is never the

hope that she might forget the hem of her skirt just long enough to give a flash of bare thigh. "Never worry about those ugly gaps where your thigh bulges (ugh) between your girdle and stockings," cackle the ads, brainwashing women into sensual self-deceit. "No more unsightly hardware ruining the trim lines of today's styles," coo the harbingers of defeminization. "Banishes all snaps, clips and straps, so you'll look as smooth as can be," prattle the merchants of misplaced mannishness.

Panty hose are nothing new. Jacques Leotard, a nineteenth century circus aerialist looked great in them. He even had some with tops sewn on. In fact, he gave his name to the garment worn by ballet artists and trapeze performers. And do you know *why* leotards, tights and pre-panty hose were worn? Because little else was and in the interest of propriety the bare flesh had to be covered. That was seventy-five years ago, and tights were worn as a specialized type of garment by both men and women, who, after the performance was over, got into their respective boy and girl clothes.

I am not going to use much space in a tirade about the desexualization of the American male and the defeminization of the American woman. Many competent researchers, psychologists, sociologists and sexologists have observed the phenomenon. The last ones to notice they are being duped are always the people, however. So instead of trying to change things, I'll just say that the field is wide open for a witch who follows my formulas, thanks to those wonderful folks with their panty hose and starvation diets and chrome sequined jump suits and club foot shoes who have eliminated most of the competition.

Panty hose emphatically let a man know he can't have access to a woman's sexual organs, although the story goes that one gentleman was energetically making love to his

lady friend and noticed that with each new thrust, she reacted by violently curling her toes. After calling her attention to her unique aberration, the man was informed that she
had forgotten to remove her panty hose. This story is not
far from the truth, as some women now wear their nylon
security skins under pantsuits and shorts and even to bed
in a manner not unlike the old farmers who used to sew
their woolen underwear on after harvest and remove it
after the first spring thaw.

Get rid of those panty hose. Only the most desperate of
men will condone them. Wear nylons with tops at least two
inches wide, held up by a garter belt or girdle, depending
on how much you should show your luscious flab.

If you are attempting to bewitch a four to nine o'clock
male, black or darker shade nylons are just the thing, held
up by a black garter belt or longish pantie girdle that will
tend to make your thighs look firm but still let a little bare
flesh peek through. If you are working on men in the ten
to three o'clock range, wear beige, tan and cinnamon tone
nylons suspended by a white or pink garter belt or fairly
short girdle that will allow plenty of thigh to balloon out.
If your garter straps are a little frayed, so much the better.
He'll think he's really seeing something he shouldn't! A
safety pin repair job on a garter strap is a real turn-on too.
Another trick to remember is the run in the stocking. Four
to nine o'clocks won't like it much, but most ten to threes
will find a run in a nylon very appealing, providing it's not
on their own wife!

Of course, you can't wear skirts eight inches above your
knees, if you're going to wear nylons that stop seven inches
above your knees. And you shouldn't wear the type of
nylons that come all the way up to your crotch, as you will
be defeating the whole purpose in wearing them. If your
stockings end mid-way up your thigh, you have a lot of

room to play around with in using the Law of the Forbidden. If your hem is two or three inches above the knee, you can control the amount of leg you display with amazing finesse.

If necessary, you can be prim and proper with no indication of what lies beyond the hem of your skirt as it is tucked neatly under your legs which are closed together. You can cross your legs, allowing the tiniest glimpse of bare thigh to peek out over the tops of your stockings, or you can arrange a brazen display of thigh, which will guarantee the wrath of every other woman present—*especially* those wearing skirts much shorter than yours.

You can use the technique of not knowing anything is wrong while one small area of your thigh is "accidentally" exposed in a manner that is not a question of *how much* is revealed, but rather, *how far up.*

Stockings, garters and skirts with enough leeway in length give you the very magical tools to work with in bewitching through the Law of the Forbidden. I have proven the validity of my formulas many times over by sending my witches "into the field" where there are men who pay lip-service to all the latest fashions, deny the principles I set forth, yet still salivate when the bell rings, when they are actually confronted by a girl who employs these techniques. Always remember that a good old-fashioned pair of nylons will be the best friend a witch ever had.

The High Heel

Another flagrant example of hypocrisy generated by fashion changes is the right-today, wrong-tomorrow paradox of the high-heeled shoe. In the Gay Nineties women wore high-button shoes and boots that came half-way up the leg. As the twentieth century gave women the right to vote, it also took away their heavy leather footwear and gave them the French heel, Cuban heel, wedgie, platform pump and spring-o-lator—all high or moderately high-heeled shoes.

A sort of obsolescence manifested itself through the respective periods of acceptance for all of the type shoes I just mentioned. Like the undergarment situation, what was rationalized as "comfortable" one year, was considered "painful" and "unhealthy" the next.

When women wore the French heel after the First World War, it was considered the height of sexiness with its small wineglass-stem type heel. It was also considered a vast relief from the cumbersome boots of the earlier era with their fat heels that lacked grace. Pretty soon only old ladies were wearing shoes with chunky heels. The slender high heel was here to stay.

A few years later, when heels had grown even higher, a thicker, heavier shoe had a short popularity. Largely inspired by the Latin lover image and the immense popularity of the tango, rhumba and other dances, the Cuban heel of the early Thirties slimmed itself out however; and outside of novelty shoes like the wedgie, by 1940 every woman who had any style was wearing high-heels. The old cry "emancipation" went up, and great thanks were given by countless women that the graceful, feminine, light-weight shoe had arrived.

Reminiscences of grandmother's day, when high-button shoes with low heels were the rage, made every woman grateful that *she* didn't have to wear such monstrosities. Thick, chunky heels were worn by old women and for orthopedic purposes, and boots were for horseback riding. This basic ideal continued for many years, and women's legs never looked so good . . . *until* it was decided they looked *too* good by the woman-haters and the ugly uglies, so back to the old drawing board.

Trousers for women had already gained unanimous acceptance with pedal pushers, toreador pants, capris, etc. running their courses. All that was needed to get rid of the high heel was to start by shortening it so that its wearer appeared to be standing in soft mud. Women blindly accepted the new one and one-and-a-half inch heel as sensible and rationalized it by telling of its comfort in all-day standing sessions.

Then came the boots, and, though some of the first ones had spike heels, they soon disappeared in "favor" of lower and thicker heels. Within a short time the full circle had come about with women wearing low-heeled boots, which rose above their knees in many cases.

Now the fashion slaves were cheering a new age of comfort, as they sipped their scotch and waters in their tight Gay-Nineties boots and full-length drawers (panty hose). They gave few eulogies for the "horrible, uncomfortable," spike heels that a few decades earlier had been hailed as freedom from the "heavy, sweaty, binding, unhealthy, confining, cumbersome" footwear of the Gay Nineties which only "bred germs, raised bunions, and did nothing for a girl's legs!"

Now, as some of you read this, while wearing your Li'l Abner gunboats, you wonder how your mom could possibly have walked in those awful spike heels. It was easy, witches, it was easy.

How sad it is that women have never been taught the *reasons* for the appeal of the high-heeled shoe. By high-heeled, I mean the three-inch spike—not the two-inch, inch-and-a-half or one-inch "high-heel." Nor do I mean the chunky heel, however high, which resembles nothing so much as a handle from a .45 automatic pistol.

Despite recent propaganda to the contrary, high-heels are not extinct. Pick up any men's magazine and glance at the cartoons of sexy girls and you'll find the high-heel is every bit as fashionable as it always was. Cartoons are still exaggerations of reality, and the competent witch must be constantly aware of the importance of properly employed exaggeration. In the casting of spells, exaggeration of the chosen imagery is necessary for the emotions to become worked up to their highest pitch. Sexual fetishes are nothing more than exaggerations of what would be considered normalcy. For this reason, it is easy to pass the whole subject of high-heels off as a simple device for fetishistic activity. Even if this were the case, it would be assumed that high-heels should be a universal article of clothing, basing its popularity on such a commonly encountered fetish.

Why, however, is the high-heel, so prevalent as a sex symbol, synonymous with femininity? The reasons are many. First, the three-inch spike-heel forms a distinct "S" curve from the top of the heel to the point where the spike touches the ground. This "S" curve is a traditional curve of beauty, the serpentine curve of mystery, the epitome of fluidic, feminine contour. No other style of footwear is as flagrant in the portrayal of this emotionally pleasing configuration.

Now, something very magical happens when the foot is placed within the high-heeled shoes and the wearer stands up. The back of the calf is thrown out in an *exaggeration* of its normal plane, creating *another* "S" curve directly above the one formed by the shoe. Still another *exaggeration* is formed above the knee, where we find the buttocks thrown out, along with the hips and thighs, and forming a third "S"—this one starting where the waist nips in, bulging out for hips and buttocks and retreating as the knee is approached. One might call this a very unholy trinity, as it is sure to be the basis for much temptation.

One such parabolic curve is deadly enough as a device employed towards positive attraction, but when *three* such "S" curves are used, one on top to the other, the onslaught is too much to possibly be ignored. No one is immune to these geometries when confronted by them. Whether it be seen in the neck of the swan, as it glides across the lake, or in the elegance of the landau bar, fastened to the rear of a vehicle's passenger compartment, or in the mysteriously compelling beauty of the structure of the roller coaster, the "S" curve will always compel attention.

So much for the effect of the high-heel when the wearer is in a standing position. When the really devastating effect of the high heel comes is when the wearer begins to walk. It is virtually impossible to walk in high-heels without the hips and pelvis reacting in an *exaggerated* manner! Any girl who has ever tried to walk in high-heels without shaking her behind should know that the resultant effect is so ludicrous as to defy description. The fact that the walk has become unnatural only applies when compared to the type of walk produced without high-heels. Once the high-heels are placed on the feet, any attempt to walk *without* the posterior swaying becomes unnatural. In short, one doesn't even have to try to walk in a sexy manner while wearing high-heels—it comes naturally!

The high-heel is *always* in style, at least insofar as the emotional appeal it generates. As a device for separating the sexes, it seems to be the only article of clothing worn by women that men have not been able to incorporate into their wardrobes. It is true that men's shoes have been fashioned in the semi-high-heel style but with a thick heel of the type women used to wear when Cuban heels were in vogue. It is highly unlikely that men will ever take up three inch spike heels. So long as such footwear is restricted to women, the woman who is a holdout for her exclusiveness in being a woman will always have such a "badge of office" at her disposal.

No matter how extreme the juxtaposition between men and women grows fashion-wise, if a man wishes to wear women's high-heels, he will have to own up to his transvestite tendencies, which in itself would be a refreshing display of honesty. Men may dress as women, to all intents and purposes, so long as the clothes they wear are purchased in *men's* shops. This gets the feminized male off the hook and eliminates the stigma accompanying the wearing of women's clothing. So long as a man can go into a fashionable men's shop and purchase an ensemble he saw in the latest *Playboy* or—*Esquire,* he needn't fear anyone referring to him as a "drag queen." Should he find the wearing of women's high-heels appealing, however, he has no choice but to receive the questioning glances of all who see him to say the least!

One thing must be borne in mind and that is that anything which looks freakish can negate the otherwise potent force which exaggeration provides. A good example of this is the style of high-heel seen in journals and cartoons catering to purely fetishistic needs. Often these grotesque styles feature heels five inches or higher, some actually rising to the ludicrous height of nine or ten inches. These specially-made shoes are devoid of the "S" curve, and, in order to allow the wearer to stand, let alone walk, it is necessary to build up the soles so that the shoe resembles a corrective orthopedic device rather than an article of footwear.

The most fool-proof type of high heel for the witch to wear is the classic three-inch pump in whatever material or color is best suited to the occasion. Variations include the open toed sling pump—a slightly more naughty and yielding image with just a hint at sleaziness. Then, of course, there is the backless spring-o-lator or as it used to be called, the "mule." Only the most "daring," "cheap" and "loose" women wear this type of heel, or so the hostile females would claim. It is true that the spring-o-lator's very design suggest a shoe intended to be worn while lying down rather than walking. The element of the high-heel is definitely emphasized while the shoe itself is minimized, thereby flaunting the premise that it is the effect which counts, not the utilitarian aspect. It is for this reason, the spring-o-lator must be considered the most "self-conscious" of the family of high-heels. This, then, is why only the most "thick-skinned" of witches can feel comfortable wearing such a style shoe.

I find it charming that little girls, who have not yet learned to deny their gender take great delight in wearing their mommy's high-heels, even though mommy never wears them anymore herself. So strong is this compulsion in these tiny witches that one wise toy manufacturer has produced a "dress-up" shoe for little girls, which is a replica of the "out-of-date" spring-o-lator and comes complete with "fancy silver clips and a red jewel." And don't forget that all "big lady" dolls, such as "Barbie" have a selection of high-heeled shoes from which our little enchantresses can choose to match any outfit in the doll's wardrobe, whereas the child-type dolls come with flat shoes. To the aspiring witches who try to stay on the good side of me by saying they'd "just love to wear high-heels" but can't because it "hurts their feet" I have a ready answer. I say "it's easy—in fact, it's child's play!"

Little boys seem likewise fascinated with high-heels, most likely because they know it is an article of clothing they are not allowed to wear and is reserved for girls.

The rule every witch should remember concerning high-heels is: It is not what is fashionable but what is sensually attractive that counts; and the high-heel cannot be other than attractive, as it represents the natural line of beauty, combined with the pelvic movement which is the very dance of life. Let the fashion industry argue until they're blue in the face. People may not know what they like when they see it, but they sure respond to it. And, after all, in witchery that's what counts.

On Prostitutes and Pentagrams

Some of the best witches are prostitutes. It's their *job* to attract men! They not only learn the little quirks that other women never see in men, but they must be able to dress, act and think outside their natural role.

Unfortunately, many present-day prostitutes have abandoned their uniforms and gone the way of fashion, and there is nothing so dismal as a stylish prostitute. Of course, the girls who wear the panty hose, bell-bottoms and combat shoes can't understand why they aren't spoken for as much as their high-heeled, stocking-clad, tight skirted sisters. And you can be sure the gals who know what most men prefer are not about to tell them.

The "uniform" of the prostitute is virtually little different than the uniform of the compleat witch. Dresses should be tight enough, if straight, to allow the lines of undergarments to be faintly perceptible through the material. Dresses with full skirts should be nipped in at the waist as much as possible with a belt. Straight dresses may also be worn with a wide belt. Unless you are particularly thin, the belt should never be lighter than the basic color of the dress and generally should be much darker.

Avoid the empire line dresses, despite your passion for them. They violate your true waistline, if you have one, and should only be worn by those who are *fat* in the midriff! All hemlines should be no more than four nor less than one inch above the knee. Belts should also be worn with skirts and blouses or skirts and sweaters. The best neckline is always a "V" but unobtrusive variations may be worn. Avoid huge boat necks. They break up your curvilinear symmetry and make you look like a lighthouse. If you can't wear heels, then wear classic flats or sandals. Avoid novelty shoes unless your feet are so misshapen you want to detract from them by drawing attention to the strangeness of the shoe.

Choose uniform patterns or solid colors (more to come on colors). Suits are fine, if they're figure-revealing—nipped in at the waist and have a straight skirt. Peasant blouses are a standard. Flowered prints are always good as are polka dots, checks, stripes, etc. Avoid "camouflage" prints unless your figure is so bad it needs them. This applies to wild psychedelic prints. These patterns were designed by way of acid-tripping and place the importance on the *fabric* of the dress rather than what's inside.

Wear a bra, unless your garment is thin enough that it's apparent you're not! Otherwise, your nipples won't be seen, and what's the point in going bra-less if they don't show? You've either got to show some breast or else some nipple. A bulky sweater, with no bra, shows neither. If you are one of the big-busted, kindly disregard what I just said.

Wear a slip or a half-slip if you wish, but keep it plain and simple—no layers of ruffles to get in the way when you sit down so your legs will be obscured.

Panties should be plain white or pink (or if you *must* wear brand new ones during an enchantment, a color called "eggshell" is good, as it looks a bit dingy) if you're a four to ten o'clock; black if you're on the top end of the synthesizer, between ten to four o'clock. Undies should look as though you didn't plan on anyone seeing them; then they look more forbidden. If you wear "stage undies," with all kinds of embroidery, lace, fringe, etc., it appears that you give everybody a show, and that's all that can be hoped for—a show. You want to give the impression that you are for real, not an entertainer, and nothing turns a man on more than to think he's seeing something you hadn't planned on him seeing. Get out the old panties you wouldn't want to get in an accident wearing, and you can't go wrong.

Sometimes other back-stabbing women can inadvertently do you a big favor simply because they are laboring under the delusions and follies that have been supplied by sex-haters in general and woman-haters in particular.

An amusing example of such an occurrence is the real-life Cinderella story which follows: It all happened in a large insurance firm in San Francisco. A new girl had been hired in an office staffed by several women and two eligible men. She was unmarried, with a pretty face and was just overweight enough to enhance her basically good figure.

One day, shortly after joining the firm, she was struggling to retrieve a folder which had fallen behind a filing cabinet, and in the process of her unexpected gymnastics, revealed a great deal more than the other women felt was proper. It was awful, and the nasty minded men naturally got a big kick out of it. It wasn't so much the exposure, for short skirts had been in for quite awhile. The other women couldn't even complain about the fact that the newcomer was wearing regular stockings instead of panty hose, though they would have liked to. The charge finally levelled at the violater of office tranquillity was predicated upon hygiene and supplied by the fact that Miss "X" was wearing a pantie-girdle that was rather soiled in a crucial area. The florescent office lights had illuminated her like a filming for a living-girdle TV commercial.

By the next day the whispering-campaign was in full swing and sounded more like an actualization of a soap commercial. "Did you see that girdle she was wearing?" "You should have seen that girl's girdle. How disgusting!" "I'll bet her underwear stands up by itself."—and other colorful praises, were loudly sung by all the harpies present. Before long, word had gotten around to other offices in the building and interest started building concerning this "gal in the next office with the dirty underwear." Slowly, surreptitiously and slyly *men* started developing excuses to talk to the girl—men who didn't even work in the same office.

In fact, the girl was later hired by the regional manager of another firm in the same building and placed into a new branch office in a nearby suburb as a receptionist. Her salary was almost doubled, and, as of this writing, she is still holding off her boss's proposals of marriage, though she says she'll give in soon. The moral of this true story is: Never underestimate the power of a dirty girdle!

Worn clothing is always more sexy than fresh, new clothing, whether in blue denims, Levi's or cocktail dresses. This doesn't mean scroungy and dirty but "broken in" clothes. I've known men who were driven crazy by a soiled bra strap revealed through a sleeve opening. Say I'm daft if you will, but these are the tricks, and potent tricks they are. Don't worry about it if your panties get a little damp. The moister they are, the better men like it.

A very famous movie sex symbol of my acquaintance used to allow herself to dribble enough to get a small wet spot on the back of her skirt, implying to all the stupid men who saw her that she was so excited she couldn't control herself. Maybe she was. At any rate, it certainly achieved the desired reaction.

Other sneaky tricks that are decided turn-ons to many men are "unknown" tears or rips in skirt seams that will reveal a glimpse of underwear. A well-trained zipper can also do wonders. When a nice old lady calls you aside and tells you you're unzipped in back, just blush a little more, thank her while frantically zipping up, wait a few minutes 'til she's gone, then pull the zipper back down, hoping you don't run into her again.

If you must wear pants, the same tricks of "accidental" rips and errant zippers can apply. Especially effective is an opened seam on the upper inside thigh or anywhere along the crotch seam up to the waistband in back. When wearing sleeveless tops, consider not only the opportunities for a peep-show through an extra-wide arm opening, but also the role your armpit can play in visual enchantment.

Accessories

Forget about hats that look like Boer war campaign numbers, Soviet secret police, Anzac and Roman lictor models, not to mention French Foreign Legion kepis. You'll be getting right back into the chrome-plated jump suit image. Instead, try a saucy little number or wide sailor, and watch the reaction. Gloves are another accessory that can add to your allure.

The best kind of jewelry is often the simplest. Flashy rhinestones are fine if you're a dominant personality type. Otherwise, tasteful—even corny—necklaces, bracelets and earrings are in order. Unless you are an exotic type, avoid monstrous earrings and arms full of bracelets. Likewise, ten-pound pendants and yards of beads and necklaces will make you look less like a compleat witch and more like a complete fool.

The jewelry you wear must add to your appearance, by serving as tinsel or frosting on the cake, *not* as a walking museum collection, where the embellishments have their own obvious meaning which will make *them* the point of interest rather than *you*. Edith Head, one of the few designers whose creations could be worn by a compleat witch, maintains that only if a compliment is directed at how lovely *you* look, rather than what a beautiful *dress* you're wearing, can you truly feel flattered. This is one point on which I agree with most notables in the field of fashion. Clothing, jewelry and other accessories should complement you, not outshine you. If they do overshadow you, the whole point is lost. The only exception to this would be if you have nothing to enhance, which is true of the great number of fanatical fashion followers! If you have a small, tasteful pendant or ring or blacelet that has particular significance to you, by all means wear it so long as it doesn't detract from the rest of you.

Concerning amulets, wear only *one* at a time, and tastefully, so it looks like a functional piece of jewelry. Would-be witches are notorious for loading themselves up with so much hardware in the form of amulets and talismans that it's a damn good thing they don't really fly on broomsticks since they'd never make it off the runway.

Witches whom I have personally trained wear a small round amulet bearing the Devil's symbol—an inverted five-pointed star with the head of the Sabbatic goat superimposed within the points of the pentagram and Hebrew characters around the perimeter of the circle spelling out the name, "Leviathan," another manifestation of the name of Satan. Of course, there are times when it is more feasible to conceal such a talisman and confine one's neckwear to pearls or costume jewelry. If you are clever (or rich), it's amazing what can be done, though, and I know witches who have had the above-mentioned amulet wrought in diamonds, rubies and other precious substances so at first glance it would not be interpreted as an amulet.

Just remember, your ability as a witch has nothing to do with how many pounds of amulets you wear. The only purpose an amulet serves is as a reminder of what you want or represent. An amulet can, therefore, give you constant awareness of your role, but constant awareness of your role will not accomplish a thing unless you have whatever other devices and actions necessary to go with it.

Color Clues for Witches

This chapter is not going to attempt to tell, by way of the old school of fortune-telling, what certain color preferences signify in people. The synthesizer clock will take care of color and personality in a manner that allows for the most subtle gradations in both. If you insist upon reading about how people who like red are daring, those who like black are morbid, lovers of yellow are intellectual, etc., etc., buy yourself a copy of dear old Mother Schlocker's *Old Gypsy Dream Book and Oracle* or something. No matter how proficient you are in your choice of clothes, the wrong color can lessen the impact of your bewitchment. Your most helpful device in choosing the proper colors is the color wheel.

Starting with red at twelve o'clock, the corresponding colors of each personality type encircle the synthesizer. If you wish to charm a man, find his position on the circle and choose the color exactly opposite to wear. There are some simple rules which will serve you well if they are observed. The color a man would *least* likely wear on himself is the color he responds to best on a woman. The color a woman hates worst on herself is the color she will like on a man. This formula is so simple to employ that it requires no involved study of the psychology of color, although modern researchers, like Faber Birren, have contributed a great deal towards a comprehensive understanding of the subject.

If you look good in red, you may not like to wear the color, but prefer green. When deciding on the proper color, or combinations of color, you will often encounter situations where the last color you would ever choose to wear can be the best for the role you are to play. The vast difference in your Apparent type that a simple change from your usual color choice can produce is truly remarkable. Of course, your skin tone and hair color must be taken into consideration. If you have a pinkish complexion, purple is the worst color possible for you, and if your skin has a yellowish caste, stay away from greens.

If you are not actually fat, light colors are always sexier than dark ones, as they show more of the contours of your body. Most witches make the mistake of assuming black to be the standard for all clothing. Black can be very effective, but must be used with discretion. The color pink is always sure to work magic, as it is the color of feminine intimacy. Likewise, white is always good for a witch who is in doubt as to the best color. If white clothes are worn in an enticing manner, they will often steal the show from all other colors. The erotic stimulation many men derive from nurses stems from the fact that a nurse's uniform is usually figure-revealing, very sound in its basic design and white. Even the pale blue and green uniforms worn by nurses have the waists where waists should be, a smooth (and thereby tactile) finish and a fitted line. If nurses and waitresses get more than their share of attention from men it's only because they're often the only women around who wear clothes that make them look like women.

Bright colors of any kind are best worn by witches of a more dominant personality type, although, as with a red hair dye job, a loud colored dress on a usually mild mannered girl will often do wonders to change her personality. When you wear loud colors, you automatically place yourself in a position to attract men from the lower half of the synthesizer clock. When you dress in pastels, muted or toned down colors, you will appeal to the males on the top half of the clock.

Owing to the fact that, as far as their ECI (Erotic Crystallization Inertia) is concerned, men are still young boys, they will most often pick bright red as a preference. Every witch that isn't a bonafide fatty should have at least one bright red dress, whether she can stand it or not. Also a pink and a white. If you have these basics, you need never worry about not having a thing to wear witchery-wise. Then if you wish to get mysterious you can always wear black, but don't say I didn't tell you, when you find out that the pink, white or red dresses did what the black one couldn't. Of course if you're really overweight, black is best. It's a shame that certain colors are almost sure to steal the show, but being realistic is a large part of being a compleat witch.

Don't think for one moment, though, that the color of your dress is more important than the Law of the Forbidden. Sexual compulsions will invariably win out if a contest is at hand. Don't delude yourself that by donning a scarlet minidress over your panty hose and chunky shoes you'll be any competition for a gal of equal looks who is using "the formula" and wearing a beige suit. Color is important but must be employed as a *single ingredient*—not as the sole magical weapon.

You probably wonder where browns and grays fit in on the color wheel. Browns, beiges, tans, etc. are all variants of the yellows, golds, orange-yellows and oranges that make up the "earth" section of the clock and are harmonious with all of the colors on the left side. For example, everything from green at six o'clock to red at twelve o'clock can be mixed with browns and remain compatible colorwise. Try and mix violet or blue, from the other side, and you get an ugly mess. The same formula applies to gray on the right side of the clock. All colors in this section are compatible with gray from red to green. Add blue to gray and it works fine. Likewise, green or violet. Just try mixing yellow or orange with gray and see the awful results.

Those occupying a six or twelve o'clock position can easily go in either direction; however, neither grays nor browns will be quite as effective as on those to the far right or left of the circle.

A good clue to a man's position on the synthesizer may be given by the color he chooses in clothing. If he wears a necktie, the one that appears to be his favorite should tell you to wear the color directly opposite on the color wheel.

Many witches think that to get on the good side of a man it helps to wear matched outfits and nothing could be more ill-advised. Girls who go out and buy a red sweater to match their boyfriends red shirt give a Bobbsey Twins ring to the whole affair and unwittingly encourage a platonic relationship. I have had numerous would-be witches come to me for tuition wearing slinky black outfits, assuming I will be impressed, because they might have seen me on a TV show or in a magazine wearing black. I do appreciate their thoughtfulness but hasten to inform them that a man who goes around wearing black clothes all the time, of his own choice, would prefer to see women wearing light or pastel colors.

Most businessmen who *must* wear black or gray suits, however, respond strongest to girls in loud, bright colors. This illustrates why subjective/objective preferences must be taken into consideration in a person's choice of clothing colors. For example, a person who wears a lot of black objectively such as a waiter, priest, musician, concert artist, etc. cannot be typed accurately, but one who wears black because he loves it is a different story. I have found that people who prefer to wear black actually favor the color red, but refrain from wearing it because they are often introverted. The man who wears black clothing of his own choice will seldom respond to loud colors on a woman, but the wearer of black who *must* can be judged by the color of his car.

Unless he had no choice in the matter, his car color will tell you a lot. Again, just consult the synthesizer, and appear in the opposite color from his car. If his car is a drab or nondescript color or one of the "practical" colors, such as light green, pale blue, beige or tan, he needs a gaudy wench, so bedazzle him with your color. If his automobile is bright red, black, white or some exotic color, *don't* think you need to compete and wear your loudest colors. There is good reason for this. If his car represents his Apparent self's color choice, he wants his woman to be the opposite. If his car represents his Demonic self, then it'll take a lot more than a crimson dress to woo him away from his red fiberglass lover. No matter what, it's bad witchery to dress in the color of his car!

The same factors apply concerning living quarters. It might look good in the movies to see a gal in her all-white bedroom, wearing white, but it just doesn't work that way and is limited to publicity photos. No man wants to be overwhelmed by the room around him when he's trying to get to first base with a woman. And having the room in identical colors to what its occupant is wearing does just that. It fairly yells at him, "You'd better please *me* too!" or like a chaperone, "Just what do you think you're going to do to *us*?".

When decorating a room in the right color is an issue, the ideal witching-room would be one with revolving or changeable walls of different colors. If one is to really explore the potential effects color can produce, opportunity and facility for quick changes must be present, which is often easier said than done. The simplest means to attain such color modifications is through the use of lighting. A small spotlight against the base of one wall, mounted in a housing which will hold removable colored filters, is the ideal arrangement. Then, if you want a blue wall one night, you can change it to pink the next.

Despite what you may think, black is an ideal color for a witch's den of iniquity, as any color accessory can be used, any color clothing can be worn, and *you* will be the star performer at all times. Black is limitless in its perspectives, and a small room can lose any confining quality it might have if painted another color. It used to be thought that a black room would be restrictive, depressing and morbid, but if there are highlights of any sort in furnishings, art, rugs or draperies, you can't go wrong with black walls.

In addition to its adaptability for decorating, a black room is the most restful when the lights are off and totally devoid of distraction when you want to read or work; not to mention it makes an ideal ceremonial chamber for your magical rituals.

Another tip: Red carpeting has proven itself to be the most conducive to keeping people in a room, so don't use it if you want a fast turnover of visitors. People naturally linger on red carpet, and restaurants and bars that want to keep their places full have found it to be one of great assistance. I have found that a room with black walls and ceiling with bright red carpeting will make people lose track of time completely, especially if the room is rather long and narrow.

If you want to use mirrored walls in your room, be extremely careful that you don't have more than one wall so covered. You know how distracting the mirrors in a beauty shop can be when one mirrored wall is opposite another, especially if one wall is slightly off parallel from the other. With certain colors and the proper deviations in the placement of mirrors the most horrible crimes and raging madness can transpire, and *you* don't want to be the loser in such cases.

6. Bitchcraft

Virtue is its own punishment—"nice girls" lose—and one of the surest signs of potential proficiency in witchcraft is an inability to get along with other women.

This doesn't mean that you should not *know how* to get along with members of your own sex, because a successful witch can. It simply implies that you are certain to meet with disapproval from many women when you are not purposely trying to gain their approval.

If you go around worrying about impressing women (who, of course, love nothing better than to know you care about what they think) that automatically places you at their mercy. Outside of an admittedly homosexual group, all social circles that are composed of exclusively men or women serve as retreats rathers than boosts. To a group of highly successful businessmen, an exclusively male organization can serve as either a retreat or contact ground for further business goals. This, in many ways, makes sense. But for women (who are for better or worse ninety-nine percent dependent upon the support of men) to congregate together, seeking each other's approval, it is at best commiseration—at worst, ego shattering delusion and at all times indicative that something is missing in the way of erotic or emotional fulfillment.

Every witch needs a friend, just as anybody else, but unless *you* can be the leader in a group of women, forget it! No other gal is going to lead you down the path of success unless there's something in it for her—romantically, financially or vicariously; and for that matter, neither are very many men. At least when pleasing a man, you possess that little "something different," which makes all the difference—the representation of his Demonic self!

I have found that the most proficient witches are those who prefer the company of men to that of women. I'm sure everyone reading this has lost out at one time or another simply because she was only concerned with her responsibility to another girl. Chances are good that other girl planned and plotted very carefully whatever move it was that led to your romantic or domestic failure yet was never once looked upon as a villain by anyone else. If you will think back on your own personal situation, the other girl involved was one who didn't quite have the things going for her that you did.

Maybe she was single and you were married, and she envied you for your smooth-running marriage or handsome husband. Or possibly she was married to a real churl while your husband was a prize. Maybe it was an economic jealousy or one inflamed by your talents or knowledge—or possibly, *looks*? "Wait a minute," you say, "the woman I have in mind was very good looking and *I* should look that good. It couldn't be *that*!" Don't forget what you've read earlier in this book. *Your* standards of female beauty *don't count*! Naturally, you will think a gal is a real doll, who looks like you would like to look, and invariably she will be your complete opposite type.

A girl's worst enemy is always one who is the same physical type as herself, with slight modifications, and her best friend is the complete opposite of herself. If you are tall, with an angular face, your best friend will be short with a round face. If you are fair skinned and blue eyed, your best friend will be olive skinned with dark eyes. These are not oversimplifications but excellent examples. The similarity in appearance between you and your worst enemy is an important factor in the ability a witch can have to predict those who will bear watching. Therefore, there are two types of women to watch out for and who will take away what you have or at least spoil your happiness if given half a chance. The first is the girl who is similar in appearance to yourself but not quite as pretty. The second is the one who is totally opposite in appearance but not quite as pretty.

If it sounds as though I'm contradicting myself, consider this: It's easy enough to pass judgment on a girl who looks like she might be your sister, finding all kinds of faults in her appearance. For this reason, an objective physical evaluation is seldom made of a woman who resembles in any way the person who is passing judgment. Two girls of identical appearance would be certain to find many flaws in the physical makeup of each other that would be lacking in whoever was speaking. Therefore, the old cliche must be considered before negative judgment is passed: What does she have that I lack appearance-wise? If you cannot find anything, then you'll find her to be no real threat but one who *would like to be!*

Concerning other women of totally opposite types, the reverse is true when it comes to evaluating beauty. If a girl who looks like you will invariably get a non-objective and critical evaluation, your female opposite will receive plaudits on her good looks, even though she might be sadly wanting for allure. Here is where the lurking menace lies. Because your opposite, and often best friend, is seen in a non-threatening light, you are willing to credit her with a degree of beauty she very often lacks. While you tell others of her beauty, they listen, and they look and possibly they are not impressed, and *she* knows it, but *you,* you fool, *don't!* Resentment builds, and, out of resentment, however deeply buried, will come outlets for it. Little plots are hatched, and soon you find yourself saddled with a genuine psychic vampire, who will drain you of your vital energy and actually weep and moan (and not out of happiness!) whenever something nice happens to you. And you—sweet, nice, virtuous, understanding thing that you are—pick right up on those vibrations, those feelings that there's something wrong. You concern yourself all the more with your friend and her welfare, as by now she is bound to have developed several problems.

Make a little test, and tell a "friend" you suspect of being a rival of some wonderful thing that has just happened or is about to happen, even if you have to invent it. Then watch her problems begin. Observe how her illness flares up or financial problems suddenly appear or she bangs her car up or her child's tonsils become infected—*right now!* If she shows her hand after three such tests, you can be sure you don't need her for a friend. I have written in my *Satanic Bible:* "Thrice-cursed are the weak, whose insecurity makes them vile. . . ." And these types can be very vile indeed yet hide their viciousness admirably. All this falls into the classification of resentment, and resentment and disapproval go hand in hand.

To be a resourceful witch, you must be able to see the bitchiness in other women for exactly what it is, then in your own way, beat them at their own game. You must learn to be a worse bitch than they.

It is more difficult for many women to be a bitch than a witch, and the nice gal that everyone likes so well, usually winds up on the short end unless she has already attained a position of real security. In the business world, the most successful women are those who have used their feminine wiles in reaching the top, not really concerning themselves about the other woman's approval but concentrating on bewitching men. Then, once they have reached the top, they can easily charm other women. They have become strong enough so that other women, knowing themselves to be in a much lesser position, either refrain from venting their envy, refuse to entertain it in the first place or, if they are stupid enough to try, make fools of themselves.

Nice girls *do* lose in most cases. A girl who is every other girl's big buddy is a drag to most men. Nothing bores a man more than to hear about all the wonderful qualities of female friends. Listening to a girl talk about other men might make the man angry, but hearing all about your sweet and harmonious friendships with other women will sicken and bore him. If you start to talk about your hostile feelings towards another woman, though, his ears will perk up. A man won't like you as a bitch if your bitchiness is directed towards him, nor will he cater to it if it endangers his profession or the feelings of people for whom he is concerned. Otherwise, he will usually be quite titillated by your bitchiness toward other women.

As a test, voice your wrath for another woman (even if non-existent) in the presence of a man you know, calling her every name in the book. He'll be all ears, and probably ask you to describe your foe's appearance. Describe her as being built about the same as yourself and in a manner that will convey the idea that she is attractive without your actually saying so. Your listener will be supplied with vicarious fantasies, associations and projections, the complexities of which need not be understood in order to be brought forth.

The main thing you will prove by his interest and attention is that men *like* bitches! They find them scintillating and sexually stimulating, and it doesn't matter whether you are dominant or passive by nature.

Taking Advantage of Men Who Think They're Taking Advantage of You

I mentioned earlier in the book that even the most worthless male can be employed by a witch if for no other reason than to increase her power. Whether or not you wish to attract undesirable males for sexual purposes is your own business, for it can not only be risky but also a nuisance. Still, the psychic energy the panting suitor, creep and pest pour out to you can be a readily available source of power. If these types have nothing else to offer, they have their enthusiasm, which equals the most unbridled form of lust.

Let's compare them to a twenty-five watt light bulb, which is bright enough to read by in a small room but could hardly illuminate a ball park. The world is full of these twenty-five watt types, who have nothing really to offer a girl yet think they are entitled to the best. They won't do anything to improve themselves, and, even if they wanted to, their little twenty-five watt brains, emotions and limits of responsibility couldn't take the extra charge. The filament would simply give out.

Whenever such a man succeeds in landing a desirable woman, who might be equivalent to say one hundred watts, he can't expect to "light her bulb" single-handedly. He might give her enough of a glow to take him home, but it will take three more like him to keep her happy. If he is as

wise as most twenty-five watters, he will be deceived by
the woman of his fancy and either not even know it or go
out and get into fights over her, much to her delight. If he's
a rare exception who knows he is limited to twenty-five
watts of power, he'll keep her a lot longer (maybe even
permanently), realizing that it's better to have twenty-five
percent of a good thing than a hundred percent of nothing.

This same analogy applies to women of low wattage who
desire high voltage males. An example is the counter girl
who rings the door bell of the movie star and practically
rapes him in his home then complains six months later that
that lousy actor is a big phoney who makes love to a girl
until he's tired of her and then gives her the boot. Instead
of reflecting upon the hundred watts of power the actor
jolted into her twenty-five watt psyche and rejoicing for
the experience, she goes away assuming *she* gave *him*
something special! She did, in a way, but so do millions of
other women who go to sleep with the actor's picture under
their pillows! And that is precisely why *he* is one-hundred
watts and she is twenty-five!

What you, as a witch, accumulate in the way of lust-
power from others will in turn give you greater magnetic
power *over* others. This is why, as the witch declared while
she pee'd in the ocean, "every little bit helps." In some
cases, the brightness from a person of greater magnitude
can "rub off" on one who is of lower intensity and cause an
increase in wattage in the low wattage person. Suffice it
to say, in such cases a magical technique is employed that
would assume the equivalent of a rewiring job.

Under most circumstances, the kind of man you wouldn't
want to know, who practically drools over you and makes
a pest of himself and can't understand why he can't have
you, is a pretty hopeless case. He could buy every meta-
physical course that was available, burn candles, study the

black arts and burst his pea-pod brain trying to figure out what is wrong with himself, never realizing that he might need a shave or the front of his trousers cleaned or something more flattering than that nice old windbreaker jacket. Aleister Crowley used to say that every man and woman is a star, which is very true. What some of the most involved occult scholars often fail to realize, however, is that stars are of varying magnitudes.

Don't refrain from displaying your witchy charms, thinking you already receive enough attention. Each twenty-five watt man who sees you and goes home and masturbates with you in mind is unknowingly performing a magical ritual which will, for at least a second or two, throw every one of his entire twenty-five watts of power into your very being, and you, in turn, will become even more desirable. It doesn't matter that he is unintelligent, gross, coarse, unkempt or in any other way undesirable. His whole will, borne of his animal lust, is throwing a small charge into your battery and therefore making it stronger. As I have previously stated, movie goddesses don't go to bed with the men that actually keep them on their pedestals. They don't need to.

There are many men who will think you're fair game, just because you may have let slip that you're a witch. Right away, they'll ask you to "prove it" or assume you're ready to violate a few taboos by climbing directly into the sack. Or else they'll ask you to tell their fortune, feigning a great interest in the occult, invariably bringing astrology and ESP into the conversation. They will be so-o-o-o serious with you and your art and nod understandingly as you describe spells and charms. They will also suggest that you help them in their search for esoteric wisdom and teach them the ropes. Some will tell you they are warlocks and the only thing to do is to get together for some kind of ritual, i.e., go to bed.

Every witch soon learns the thousand and one approaches of the man who thinks he is taking advantage of her. Remember, what I told you earlier. The most frantic men are the ones who want the slap in the face from a woman they can "respect."

Here is how you do it. Here is how you can have your cake and eat it too. As long as they are so intent on using *your* witchiness as *their* seduction device, take advantage of it. Tell them yes, you can teach them all of these things. You can explain the type of magic in which they seem so interested. Yes, you can even practice sex magic with them —you'd be delighted to. All the while you are employing the Law of the Forbidden—getting your quarry all fired up, his head nodding in agreement to everything you tell him. Of course you don't really tell him anything of the *real* magic. Just the hackneyed old crap that he expects to hear, about tannis root and High John the Conquerer and your magic circle you stand within and how you gave that old biddy at the office a boil on her bottom. After enough of this, explain that you feel he has a great deal of psychic force that you'd like to use, but it will require something of a sexual nature. At this point you can be *sure* he'll still be with you, and you won't really be lying either.

Continue, describing how the only way you can be sure of his latent power is through the use of a special ESP sex ritual. He must, for a period of one month, each time a specified night of the week rolls around and at a precise time light a red candle, place it over a piece of parchment bearing your name and for one hour think of you as hard as he can, allowing himself to become excited to the point of an orgasm.

Explain that he is *not*, under any circumstances, to attempt to contact you in the meantime or it will show his inability to follow the instructions which will be necessary when you "later get together for closer contact," and you will have to forget you ever met him. At the end of one month, you explain, you will notify him as to where he should meet you for further instructions. Of course, he will follow your instructions if he is frantic for you. He will also supply you with some witch-power in the bargain. And you will never call him. In fact, you will do your best to forget about him, thus insuring his added fervor.

If he is just playing the field and doesn't care that much about you, chances are good he won't bother doing what you tell him, but then he wouldn't have been compelled enough to do you any good magically, anyway, so you're not out anything. Don't let your conscience bother you about taking the poor guy's magical energy and not even thinking about him. He would have taken *your* sexual favors had he the chance and most likely thought you just another conquest.

If you live in a town where everybody knows everybody else, and you can't disappear, or if you ever run into the guy again, act very disappointed in him, telling him you didn't receive a thing in the way of vibrations but adding that maybe if he tries some more he will improve. If he isn't sufficiently insulted by all this, it's because you have placed everything on an occult basis—the very same basis upon which he first approached you.

If you were to tell a man to get lost, after flirting with him or giving him a leg show, he would simply call you an insulting term, implying that you were a tempter of men's sexual parts and go away in a huff. In this case you're not telling him to get lost but to go home and jack off in such a manner that for him to become offended, he would have to deny all his previous "deep interest" in learning what you could impart of witchery. His meaningful search for the hidden secrets would be exposed as a sham. He has no choice but to follow your instructions. If he, by some chance, really *is* versed in the magical arts, he cannot be offended, as he will know that what you are telling him to do is magically valid and credit you with knowing your trade.

How and When to Lie

It has often been stated, "The truth hurts." If the truth were known to people concerning the whys and wherefores of their own actions, very few situations would be entered into. The wile and guile of the proficient witch will never be resented, because she knows how to pet, flatter and butter up her quarry. You can tell anyone anything and he will accept it, so long as enough flattery accompanies it. Even though what you say may be preposterous, if you can compel a man's sexual interest, he will go along with whatever you say.

The only thing holding people back from doing things they would like is the lack of an excuse. The reason "white" witchcraft is so appealing to people is because it gives them an excuse to practice the black arts by calling them "white." If a man wants to look at prostitutes and shady characters, yet maintain his respectability, he can be a sociologist. If he likes to hear lurid, sordid or spicy stories, he can be a priest, psychiatrist or guidance counsellor. If he likes to look at dead bodies, a mortician or embalmer; women's vaginas, a gynecologist; women's feet, a shoe salesman. If he likes to eat, he can be a chef. If he wants to wield power over others, he will practice hypnotism. I'm sure you can supply many other examples.

This doesn't mean that everyone enters a profession or

trade simply to legitimize their fascinations and compulsions. There are many who do, however, and for these, socially acceptable outlets allow them to indulge their passions. You, as a witch, must know how to *allow* others to do what they really want. You don't have to make most people do what you want of them. Just find a way of making it fit into their natural interests, then supply a rationale.

Innumerable accounts have been related about ministers who consorted with women of loose morals in order to "save them," and as many jokes tell of the clever "holy" substitutions in nomenclature in order to justify sexual acts. To many persons, hypnosis is an outlet for erotic gratification, in that it allows the subject to engage in acts that would normally be repressed. One of the most common fallacies about hypnosis is that the subject will not engage in any act that he would not mormally do. If a girl with sex on her mind goes to a fairly desirable hypnotist for her nail-biting, and the hypnotist regresses her, causing her to become convinced she is in a previous incarnation, she will gladly and without guilt sexually submit to the hypnotist, even though she may be married at the time. The hypnotist merely needs to place her in a period in history where she wouldn't be married to her present husband, and everything will be okay. All she needed was an excuse to which she could attach significance. Of course, she will *never* be able to question a belief in reincarnation, no matter how logical the argument against it might seem. To do so would place her conscience in jeopardy, so objectivity is out of the question.

I have seen many examples of sexual feelings being interpreted as other phenomena. For example, when a pattern has been established of religious fervor accompanied by strong sexual feeling, the believer can never allow herself (for this phenomenon is most prevalent in females) to recognize such feelings for what they really are. So long as she is experiencing joy or suffering, agony or ecstasy, on a religious level, the orgasms can come by the dozen. But just let anyone place her in a position where she will need to re-interpret her experiences, and you're in trouble.

Don't ever take away a convenient falsehood. If you remove certain conventional lies, you will be hated for it. Most people need lies. This is one of the most important reasons why you, as a witch, must learn to lie when it is expected of you. The consistency of your image depends upon it. So long as *you* know the truth, that's all that matters.

There are two kinds of lie. The first is the lie that people want to hear. If you have ascertained that your quarry expects to hear certain things, you must tell him what he wants to hear, no matter how far-fetched or unable you are to back up what you say. You will encounter the need for this type of lie regularly in fetish-finding and in your public relations as a witch. The second type of lie is the one that will gain you credit and recognition, whether others want to hear it or not. This is the kind of lie you must be careful with. This is the sort of lie that causes failure to almost everyone who practices it. This is the type of idle boasting that places your foot firmly into your mouth and causes no one to take you seriously *after* they get to know you.

Remember, a smart witch may not be taken seriously at first, but later will be viewed with seriousness. The failure might convince his audience of his depth, in the beginning, but soon he is exposed as a fool when his false front disappears. And just *how* is his phoney facade exposed in such a devastating manner? Because he never mastered the fine art of lying.

In order to master the art of lying, you must first master

a few other things. The Great Imposter, Fred De Mara, will always command a certain degree of respect, because *he could actually do the things for which he claimed legitimate standing!* There is nothing wrong with saying you sang at Carnegie Hall and you *could* have stood in the doorway at midnight and hummed a few measures, but if you open your mouth to sing at the next party and it sounds rotten, you have just, as they say, blown it. If, however, you have sung the lead in your local civic light opera production of *Naughty Marietta* and were acclaimed as an exceptionally talented singer, and you happen to be at an affair where your quarry will be suitably impressed and possibly arrange for you to go on tour with an important new show, a Type II lie is in order. Tell him you have sung wherever you'd like—before crowned heads, etc., because when he asks you to sing, if you can back your contrived pedigree up with action, those very lies you told will not be questioned and will pay off. If you hadn't told them, he might never have asked to listen to you.

If it is subsequently discovered that you made up the whole story, yet you are fulfilling your role as a singer, the people who count won't care one bit about your little sham. The only ones who will get up in arms, demand your removal (yet secretly gloat over your exposure) will be those who are your inferiors in the first place. Study, hard work, perseverence and conscientiousness should be rewarded, and if you have gone out of your way to excell at something, use it as a credibility device. Don't tell lies about your achievements unless you can produce if the tools are placed into your hands.

Don't tell people about the movie contract you passed up, if your appearance is less than stunning, without expecting a few questioning glances. If you are an absolute knock-out, and say the same thing, people might not believe you, but at least they'll think, "Well, if she hasn't been spotted by a director, she sure *ought* to be!" If you proclaim yourself a great enchantress and then proceed to tell everyone in the room all your problems, you're no witch! If you sit down to advise another woman about her domestic situation and have gone through a succession of four bum marriages, could you really expect anyone to attach much validity to your advice? Would you be foolish enough to counsel a friend on child-raising if your three children had been living with their grandma for all but one year of their lives?

Self-aggrandizing lies must always be consistent with your actual abilities. Don't employ them unless you can back them up with action. If you want to lie, you'll get more than enough practice on individuals who *demand* that you lie to them in order that their own interpretations, delusions, preconceptions and moralisms will not be offended. In this way, you will be able to lie with a light heart, knowing you are being kind to others and giving them the opportunities to do things and think things that they crave. It is the only humane thing to do.

Lie and give pleasure. Lie and soothe consciences. Lie and supply the food for the ego that truth can seldom provide. Lie and become a hero, for whatever lies are popular will always win votes. Lie, but be not *yourself* deluded by your lies, lest you lose control, for he who loses control over his own motivations can never progress to a proficiency in sorcery.

Learn to Be Stupid

It has been said that a donkey should never be sent to college, because nobody likes a smart ass. Very few men like a woman who asserts her intelligence, and the truly smart witch will *demonstrate* how intelligent she is rather than pay lip service to her mental prowess through the use of an awesome vocabulary. Of course nothing turns a man off more than an utterly stupid woman, *except* one whose speech is laced with highly technical, analytical and clinical expressions when they are not needed.

Countless comedy characterizations have been based on the pseudo-intellectual woman, yet there are plenty of them in our midst. With these types, words become a substitute for sex appeal, for these women hate the fact that they were born as women and want to be accepted on a basis other than femininity. There is nothing wrong with this, so long as there is no desire to practice applied witchery, as sex, sentiment or wonder must accompany such a pursuit.

Intellectualism for its own sake seldom has any place in the behavior pattern of the witch, unless one can cleverly combine it with sex and wonder themes. This would produce a glamorous lady mad-doctor, wearing a skimpy laboratory smock and working amidst the surroundings and equipment of Frankenstein's workshop. Such a woman would be expected to be highly articulate, as it would be consistent with her image. Undoubtedly, she would find many men that would gladly submit to her "experiments." It should be obvious that in such a case, even pseudo-intellectualism is in order, as it is all part of the game.

If you find yourself inclined towards placing verbosity above your physical attributes, you must learn how to act stupid, especially if your physical attributes are lavish. When I say stupid, I mean *stupid*! Overcompensation is the only means that can be employed to artificially bring an overbalanced situation back to a central balance point. This is one law that applies in all phases of magic. If you are a nut on using big words, you'll have to force yourself to check your speech. Don't worry that you'll make a fool of yourself, even if you throw in a few genuinely ignorant comments. If all else fails, you might try gum-chewing. It's pretty hard to be an intellectual with a mouth full of gum.

The girl who *is* in trouble is the one who is *not* very bright in the first place and trys to play the cute-but-dumb seductress. She is simply making the worst of an already-bad situation! The girl who is really intelligent can *always* afford to act less so; but the girl who tries to act and talk in an intellectual manner but who lacks common sense will *always* fail. Any dumb belle can learn a mouthful of big words, yet be at a loss when it comes to thinking anything out for herself. Such people are educated morons, and if they could be shrunk down and feathers glued on them, would out-sell parrots, hands down.

Men *do* appreciate women with brains, but don't ever kid yourself for one minute that you can use a totally intellectual approach as a magical weapon when bewitching a man. His first thoughts will always be based on your appearance. Once you have bedazzled him, you may allow him to realize you are intelligent as well. Then he will think he hit the jackpot when he met you.

Intelligence is always of secondary importance in enchanting men, although it should eventually be apparent to any man who is himself intelligent. No girl likes to be thought of as stupid, yet there is a vast difference between real stupidity and a sensible restraint from the use of over-bearing and high-flown pseudo-intellectualism. If such tasteful restraint from unnecessary technical and scholarly verbosity is what you would consider stupidity, then you'd best study stupidity and learn it well!

How to Charm a Married Man

In bewitching a married man, the most important thing to consider is his potential guilt at entering into a relationship with you. Most men have such guilt although they seldom admit it even to themselves. In order to avoid the conscience problem, it is necessary to apply certain rules of witchery. You must consider *your* purpose in bewitching him. Are you in love with him? Are you searching for *the* man and feel you have found it in him? Does he appeal mainly from a sexual urge? Are you chiefly interested in him for a playmate? Do you wish to get married? Are you looking for a sugar-daddy? All these questions must be considered.

If you are in love, or think you are, and you have marriage in the back of your mind, then he must be dissatisfied to a great extent with his present wife before you will stand the slightest chance of gaining your ultimate goal. He must theoretically still be "searching" for the right woman, and his present marriage, though perhaps pleasant, still leaves him unfulfilled. If you can see the earmarks of such a situation, you stand a chance of success. Don't ever make the mistake of going by what he tells you though. Base your analysis of his marital situation on the information you can gain from other sources, as he will invariably tell you everything is bleak if he wants to get you in the sack badly enough.

If he appeals to you primarily because you have a yen for his body, seduction is duck soup. A married playmate is usually the safest kind, and you have the knowledge at all times that he must be desirable to someone else or he wouldn't be married! If your motivations are mostly sexual, a great deal as to his desirability can be fortold by checking out his wife. If she is sadly lacking in female attributes and is dull, stupid, plain and without personality, he probably won't be much better once you get to know him. If a couple, who are attracted to each other in the beginning as a result of opposite natures, live together for any length of time, each is bound to pick up qualities and traits of the other. If his wife is utterly devoid of any quality, he probably is too, unless, as previously mentioned, it is a mismatch.

When shopping for a lover, however, don't concentrate on men whom you must "rescue" but on those who have made it obvious that they can get a desirable woman but might want to sample what you have to offer as an addition to what they already have. Remember, it's better to share a good thing than to have the whole pie if it's mouldy.

If you're looking for a sugar-daddy, married men are usually your best bet, for their unconscious need to assuage their guilt will make them much more generous than the single man, who not only lacks the "habit" of obligation and responsibility towards a woman but often actually does whatever he can to avoid it, hence his single status. It is a fact that the man with responsibilities will always take on more, but the shirker of responsibility will fight hardest to avoid it. The confirmed bachelor wants the fun of marriage but not the responsibility.

When I speak of marriage, I mean "committed cohabitation," where two people are living with each other as man and wife even if no formal marriage has taken place. This is a very important factor to consider in the light of present social mores. Any marriage is only as valid as its solidity, and if all you are interested in is a certificate and you've chosen a man who is already married as a means to obtain it, you might as well forget it. The odds are against you and you'd best do your diploma hunting with single guys as your quarries.

There are still plenty of choice specimens who have been so anesthetized by swarms of defeminized women that they appear heterosexually defunct. The proper use of the Law of the Forbidden will often awaken lustful thoughts in men you would think "don't care," thereby rousing them from their torpor. If formalized marriage is utmost in your mind, this type of single man is best, as he hasn't had much experience fighting off nuptually-minded females mainly because he hasn't allowed himself to show the slightest romantic interest in the sterile slaves to fashion that have crept round him.

Regardless of what your motivations might be, the first trick to learn when bewitching a married man is to let him think *you* are married too. This will relieve him of much of that unconscious guilt of consorting with you, in the first place. Buy yourself a cheap wedding ring or engagement/wedding set. These are easily obtained in dime stores. Be sure you have pictures in your purse of your kids too. Of course, if you really *are* married, you'll already have these accouterments. Make sure the pictures of "your children" fit your image. Use your nieces' or nephews' or cousins' photos.

The more convincing you can be as a love-starved, frustrated married woman, the easier it will be. You will ease his conscience on one hand and employ the Law of the Forbidden on the other. No married man likes to hear about how wonderful your "husband" is, so play the misunderstood wife bit to the hilt. As an alternative, you can use the story that your husband is a nice guy but he has his activities on the side, so he lets you have yours.

Whatever you do, though, don't make it appear as though your husband is a pathetically devoted man who is waiting up for you, who is playing him for the fool. Men have a way of feeling sorry for that type, probably because they can often identify themselves with them, and you'll find he won't be so quick to get involved if it means contributing to the hurt of "such a nice guy." In reality, these "nice guys" are often getting quite a sexual kick out of their wives making it with other men while they sit home and read the funnypapers. Your quarry won't stop and think of it in that light, however, should you hit him with the "poor sap at home" story.

Instead, make your husband out as either a nice guy but a swinger or a callous jerk who goes out with the boys, stays late at the office, insults you in front of your friends, never so much as kisses you, drinks up his salary, doesn't give a damn when you try to look nice for him and only cares if you're not home in time to fix his dinner.

Concerning your appearance, try to get a look at his wife. If it is apparent that she is, or at least once was, his ideal physical type, you have a sound basis on which to establish your appearance. Take whatever physical factors in his wife's appearance that are possible for you to emulate and do them one better. If his wife is skinny, get a little bit skinnier than she. If she is plump, gain weight. If she is quiet, be quiet. Don't think that by showing him something his wife isn't he'll necessarily get enthused. More often than not he'll only feel uncomfortable around you, because you are too alien.

A man doesn't really want the opposite of his wife in another woman. The fact that she *is* another woman is usually variety enough. Any similarities to his wife will make him more at ease with the feeling that he's known you much longer than he has. There is a certain vicariousness a married man often feels in knowing that the ostensibly married woman with whom he is cavorting could well be his own wife. He knows it isn't his wife, but the fact that she *could* be also acts as a conscience-easer for his own actions.

Many single girls who want to charm their married bosses will find it impossible to play the role of a married woman, as their true status will be known to their employers. If you are one of these, don't despair, as you have a good chance to employ a full-time barrage of flattery, thereby building up his ego sufficiently to compensate for the guilt he might feel in getting to know you better. Since you're in a position to be near him eight hours a day, five days a week, you have a monopoly on him over his wife already. No matter how devoted she might be, he still sees more of you.

If he is an office manager, impress upon him your feelings that he should be the big boss. If he *is* the big boss, tell him how much of a responsibility he has working with others who don't seem to have the sense of responsibility that they should. Make him feel that it is only through his fortitude and benign understanding that things keep going. Convince him that you *want* to help him, and it's not just because it's a job. Be sexy, but *humble*. Be humble at all times. Don't play the role of the efficiency expert who has all the answers and knows his business better than he. If such is the case, *he* should be the one to discover it and solicit your advice. If you have buttered him up enough, he *will* come to you for advice; but you must demonstrate humility at all times.

Instead of criticizing other women in the office, be more humble than they, show respect for their positions if they have seniority, yet do a better job. In short, don't start inter-office friction that will make *his* job more difficult. It's your job to make his day run smoothly, so he won't wish he were at home with his wife instead of on the job with you! You'll find that you won't have to criticize the other women—he'll do it for you! He'll start drawing comparisons and feeling *you* should have seniority over *them*. You will have pumped his old ego up like a Goodyear blimp, and the bigger a man's ego is, the less guilt he will feel at having a good time.

Above all, when charming a married man, strip him of as much guilt as is possible, while maintaining enough vicariousness to add spice to your relationship.

If your affair is to be a lasting one or you feel you have a good candidate for divorce and remarriage, be very cautious about breaking the news that you aren't really married. If you merely want to maintain a meaningful but unmarried relationship, it won't usually matter, for once you have established your beachhead, the truth can come out concerning your single status. Ninety percent of all married men will quickly shy from the idea, however, of dumping their present wife to acquire a new one, unless the present wife is obviously not for them.

Any single woman who takes up with a man who has been married for many years, with children whom he loves, stands little chance of breaking up the marriage. She is deluded if she thinks the answer lies in throwing a curse on his wife, so she will die and leave the way clear for a new marriage. I have seen so many examples of this type of situation that I wonder at its prevalence.

The typical story is the single woman in her thirties, who has never been married and is desperately in love with a man who is older by several years. The object of her love has been married to the same woman for twenty or more years, with children and possibly grandchildren. Our would-be seductress often has remained a virgin until well into her late twenties or thirties and may have even had her first affair with the man whom she now wishes to marry. Invariably, the married man's wife is as sound as any woman can be who has been married to the same man this long. In other words, the married couple know each other pretty well! The glamour has settled, but a strong bond exists.

What is Miss Desperate to do? How will she pry her stolid lover away from the woman that is anathema to her? The first thing that crosses her mind is to get rid of the wife. If only something could happen to the old biddy. (Of course, the "old biddy" was *never* a "young biddy" while in her twenties and thirties like her unmarried rival was for so many years; and if there is anything more pathetic than an old biddy, it's a young one!) Naturally, murder is not the answer, though you can be sure it has crossed Miss Desperate's mind. A CURSE! That's the answer! Curse the wife that she should drop dead, and everything will be coming up roses.

If Miss Desperate were to seek my help in the matter, I would tell her to concentrate on getting more passion out of the man and quit thinking about cursing a woman who has done nothing but make a good home for a man and his children for many years. I would recommend a love spell to maintain a fulfilling relationship between her and the man for whom she claims soul-searing love. *no!* Nothing doing! Miss Desperate doesn't want that kind of relationship. She wants to get rid of the Missus. She wants to then get married. By this time the crystal becomes clear. Miss Desperate is *not* in love with the man. If she was, she wouldn't care if his wife was alive or not so long as she could be assured of many years of romance and security (for in most of these cases the guilt-stricken husband would gladly support the girlfriend, and it is "quite strange" how many such cases involve men who are well-to-do).

In so many words, Miss Desperate has shown her hand.

She has been trying to get him to dump his wife (the worst possible thing to do), thereby adding to his guilts at being with her under the quilts. Even if the Missus should oblige Miss Desperate and graciously drop dead, a phenomenon would develop that would almost seem poetic justice. Hubby would grieve terribly at the loss of his dear wife and companion. Conscience-stricken at all the horsing around he had done with Miss Desperate, he would avoid seeing her. Contrary to the role into which she would like to be placed—a devoted love who stuck by him and who now would be needed by one who could at last avail himself of her—Miss Desperate now finds herself a pariah, a scarlet woman who wished his dear wife dead.

Six months pass and the lonely widower is consoled by his children, goes off to Europe or their cabin at the lake, buries himself in his business and . . . meets a sweet young thing somewhere along the way! A breath of freshness is she, this pretty thing of nineteen or twenty—in fact, a great deal like his wife was when he met her; and with tenderness and grace he takes her, for she *does* love him, not just out of pity, but out of respect; and they are married and his children are a little perplexed but happy that he is happy.

This is why I would never throw a curse under such circumstances, though I have no compunction when the vicious cry out to be destroyed. If you are one of the many Miss Desperates, consider how real your love for him is. Do you really want him out of choice? Or is your pride in grave danger of destruction, because you can't afford to lose that which came too little and too late? Pride is a wonderful thing, but it must be properly exercised, like anything else, and prudery is not the best exercise, as it often atrophies more than it strengthens.

Giving In

Women assume themselves to be the ultimate romanticists. They feel that any man to whom they sexually succumb must surely be forgotten insofar as any lasting romance is concerned. If a man is to be landed, it is thought, a girl must keep him in abeyance until his commitment has been made. This common type of Victorian behavior still seems to serve as the standard.

The fallacy of such an inhibiting form of conduct can easily be discovered by any witch who is willing to objectively experiment. In reality, it is the man who carefully plans his campaign to snare the woman of his choice, and when that woman finally responds to his manuevers, his ego will not let him readily discard that for which he has so strenuously labored. The woman who thinks that she will easily lose a man whom she has inspired to pursue her will actually find that she has to work at rejecting him, more often than not.

The surest way to lose a man whom you have bewitched —using sex or otherwise—is to worry about it. It is not the act of sexual submission that causes a man to leave you, but the desperation you project at the fear of losing him. Practically every case of outright rejection I've encountered is engendered by women who have only themselves to blame. These girls place a man in such a defensive role at having "ruined" them, that even those who might otherwise have sold their souls for the women in question wind up sneaking out while the gettin's good.

Why do so many women play the game of "If you're gonna play with me, it's got to be for keeps?" Simply because they have been so brainwashed by dubious moralisms that they would rather be stuck with a man who turns out to be a complete washout and retain their "honor," than to realize that sex to a man does not necessarily mean "love." The male romantic prognosis is exactly the reverse of the female, and every witch should learn this rule well.

Most women must first feel "romantic" stirrings, which, if strong enough, can lead to sexual encounters. In males, however, the most lasting loves start with sexual activity. If a man has an opportunity to "skip the bullshit" and sexually release himself with a woman whom he desires, shortly after meeting her, any real feelings of romantic love which might exist will subsequently be able to be seen in their true light. The idyllic yearnings of the young man who demands not sex of his beloved will seldom result in any mature and lasting relationship.

Men *can* be trapped, using sex as a weapon. It's done every day. Very few meaningful and lasting romances or marriages have ever been attained as a result of a *deliberate denial* of courtship sex, however. True, some have succeeded *in spite* of sexual denial, but hardly ever because of it!

If a woman can free herself of the desperation she often feels for a man to whom she has given herself, his very pride will prohibit him from hastily rejecting what he considers to be his conquest, unless he is one of the earlier-mentioned types who only respect a woman who is tougher than he and who, by her denials and assorted kicks to the groin, gains his "respect." If this is the kind of man you want, you must do more than simply deny him sexually, though. You must literally treat him like a worm.

The Folly in Trying to Charm a Self-Aware Homosexual

You won't have to do too much to charm a homophile who is firmly ensconced in exclusively masculine relationships except to treat him in as *non*-sexual a manner as possible! In this instance, I mean "charm" as it refers to befriending, influencing and ingratiating—*not* seducing! And in those areas, you would proceed in much the same way as you would when dealing with other women, which will be explained a little later.

If you want to seduce a well-adjusted homosexual man (and there are plenty), you'll most likely wind up as one big fool. Some gals just can't get it through their thick skulls that there *are* men who won't succumb to their charms, no matter what they do in the way of enticement.

I have known would-be witches to get their sights set on a handsome man whom they know to be homosexual, fuss over him, cook for him, smother him with kisses, among other things, all to no avail. Actually, such frantic antics are nothing more than attempts to "reform" the homosexual, usually conducted by girls who are lesbians but don't know it. In their sexual uncertainty, they see a man's body, but a non-aggressive, "safe" man, who isn't about to "outdo" her own need to dominate the situation. Hence, she is the "rapist," acting against a man who is powerless to resist. There is only one problem. She has nothing to put inside him, and he hasn't the enthusiasm to attain the erection necessary to "praise" her as a woman nor anything but revulsion at the thought of performing orally upon her, as girls just aren't his thing.

The whole business winds up in utter frustration. For what she *really* would like to do, she hasn't the proper sexual equipment. If she had such equipment, she would be another man and everything would be hunky dory. The fact that it isn't unconsciously motivates her desire to "reform" him in order to "get even." One such deeply frustrating experience can lead to a veritable "crusade," in which no eligible homosexual is safe from her massive doses of pulchritude, should he cross her path.

If you have any designs on any of those "beautiful" gay men, you'd best study the entire spectrum of the gay world. And while you're at it, delve a little into yourself!

The Lesbian Witch

Lesbians often make very capable witches, for they can attract men, bewitch them and accomplish whatever their ends might be without allowing themselves to be drawn into emotional involvements with them. If a lesbian has the guile to employ the most flagrant external devices of the heterosexual witch without resorting to clothes and hair styles that will give her away, she can go the limit of enchantment.

Because she is built the way she is, she can still employ her body as any other woman should the need arise. She is not dependent on an erection in order to function sexually which is the pitfall of the homosexual male who may be required to play a heterosexual role. The lesbian will find that the men who are most naturally attracted to her will occupy the lower half of the synthesizer clock. Hence, because she is often lusted after as a dominant female, she is not expected to readily succumb sexually.

Another factor in the lesbian witch's favor is the fact that lesbianism has become an increasingly popular fetish, and if a man is turned on by lesbians, it doesn't matter much what you look like or anything else! You'll find a type of phenomenon occurs that I mentioned in the previous section, except with the sexes reversed. The male lesbian-lover is usually a homosexual who doesn't know it; but unlike the female lover of male homosexuals, who is unaware of her lesbian tendencies, the male lover of lesbians fares much "better" at the hands of his beloved. Any suffering on his part is welcome, and the wise lesbian witch will always bear this in mind. He doesn't really *want* to win, but to be placed at your mercy, and the bitchier you act towards a lesbian-loving male, the more frantic he'll get. These men are the exception to the rule concerning bitchiness toward men. You can insult them without mercy and they'll eat it up, and if they start to become surly, all that is necessary is one cheerful word from you. If you are a lesbian, take full advantage of the compulsion you will often encounter if your fetish-finder smokes it out.

Lesbians, like redheads, are usually either loved or hated, and this is one of the pitfalls of the lesbian witch should she show her hand to the lesbian-hater she may wish to charm. It is for this reason that you should move on swiftly to an apparent heterosexual image, should your fetish-finder not get the violently positive reaction it will if he is hung up on lesbians.

Another pitfall, and a much graver one, is the prospect of an emotional reaction to the girlfriend or wife of the man you set out to bewitch. This can often touch off an unconscious resentment towards the very person you wish to enchant, and try as you may, those old vibrations will come through loud and clear, signalling to the man that he'd better keep his eye on you and not because he finds you attractive! If this sort of situation occurs in connection with one of the previously mentioned lesbian-loving males, it's not so bad, and who knows, you might even develop a threesome! But if your quarry is one of those other types and you get a yen for his lady, your chances are about as slim as a nineteen cent hamburger.

Insofar as your "in-group" activities are concerned, the same rules of personality typing apply as with male/female classifying. Just find your position on the synthesizer and proceed with whatever relative evaluation applies to the other gal.

Gestures, Mannerisms, Toilet Habits and Assorted Ploys

An abundance of masculine development manifests itself in anything symbolically aggressive. Hence the dominant male will blow his nose and the feminine or passive male will sniffle or draw in. Through the mannerisms of the nose and its functions much can be told. The male trait is that of ejaculation, the female of drawing in—the penis as opposed to the vagina.

The more masculine one is, the more inclined he is to blow out through the nostrils. Men use more handkerchiefs for nose-blowing than do women for this reason. A predominantly "female" woman uses a hankerchief primarily for dabbing and will only blow her nose if she has a severe cold and then infrequently. A woman may shed tears profusely, but have to be told by her man to blow her nose, as she will sniffle until a hankerchief is proffered.

The term "snivelling" has long been associated with weakness, and the occasional misnomer, "weaker sex," as applied to women, is immediately brought to mind. Actually, the "passive resistance" required to retain bodily waste requires more control, more constraint, and hence more work than the masculine trait of expulsion or ejaculation of excreta.

The more masculine traits a woman has, the more she

blows her nose. A feminine man will sniffle and rarely use a handkerchief. This has nothing to do with homosexuality but with male/female principles and how they are balanced in the individual. Retention of bodily fluids is a female trait. This includes withholding nasal mucus, feces, urine—anything involving the carrying of or bearing of body wastes. Constipation is more common in women than in men, and during pregnancy, with its added factor of retention, constipation becomes even more frequent a problem.

Watch a man's toilet habits. Does he make sure he relieves himself immediately before retiring to bed or embarking on a situation where retention and subsequent discomfort will ensue? Does he go to the bathroom even though it is not yet absolutely necessary "just in case" he might have to go a short while later? If so, his "retention-feminine" traits are in the minority.

All acts of "carrying" represent a woman's "duty." A common example of this is in the woman who will retain her urine to the point of impending incontinence suddenly hastening to a rest-room barely in time to avoid wetting herself. A further development of this phenomenon is the woman who, possibly inebriated, has become incontinent and in so doing loses her sense of "duty" and becomes easy sexual prey for the first man to come along. Incontinence of urine during intense sexual excitement has proven embarrassing to many women, but is completely understandable when one considers the parallels in the act of at first holding in then giving way to sexual abandon with its ensuing "release of duty."

While we're on the subject of masculine/feminine counterparts, let's take basic sitting habits into consideration. A man with an abundance of male traits will "make room" for his genitals at every opportunity and so will sit with

his legs either apart, sprawled out, one ankle resting on the
other knee, etc. The masculinely libidoed female will also
be inclined to sit in this fashion. The man with a basically
feminine makeup will sit with his legs close together, and
if they are crossed the genitals will be tightly tucked between them (drawing in) and one knee resting tightly on
top of the other.

Using a variant of a previous example then, the un-
ladylike exposing of the area of the crotch, whether accidentally or intentional, by a normally feminine woman is
an inclination towards sexual abandon. Whenever you see
a man sitting with his legs crossed tightly, one over the
other, you may be sure he is "guarding himself," quite
possibly resents women (for obvious reasons) and if outwardly heterosexual, limits his romantic adventures to the
nearest whorehouse. You will seldom be able to change
this type of man, as he is unconsciously guarding his "virginity" and will most likely remain a small boy when it
comes to sex and consciously perform sexual functions only
to "be one of the fellows." Actually, he considers girls
"sissy stuff," little realizing his own sissified manifestations.
This type can be seen running the gamut from the Casper
Milquetoast, who unconsciously hates women, to Clark
Kent in *Superman*.

Insofar as your own sitting habits are concerned, disregard completely any charm school training you might have
had that tells you to sit with your legs together and your
feet tucked neatly under your chair. You'll be pegged for a
prude. Crossing your legs at the ankle and sitting with
them off at an angle will give you a clinically supercilious
look that always appeals to masochistic males. Unless you
want to appear both frightened and frigid, don't sit with
your legs pressed tightly together and your hands on both
thighs. If you do, you might as well wind some rope around

your knees while you're at it. Crossing your legs at the knee, resting one on the other, and entwining them like a pretzel is a definite "come-on" for many men as is crossing your legs at the knees and swinging the crossed leg as you talk. When facing your quarry while seated with your legs crossed, make sure you are at a slight angle and not directly facing him. It also helps when sitting with crossed legs to tilt your hips, sitting on one cheek more than the other, with the hip closest to him higher than the other.

When you are playing the bitch game, don't forget that putting your arms akimbo while sitting and especially while standing will always look sexy to a man. In this posture, the hands are placed on the hips, either open or making a fist and the legs pressed firmly to the ground and slightly apart. An alternative position for the legs is with one thrust forward, bent at the knee, while the other is stiffened, thereby throwing one hip out in back and to the side. A good figure can be displayed to very good advantage with the hands on the hips but don't overdo it and make sure it is accompanied by the proper demeanor and dialogue.

Use your tongue as a means of expression. It is much more sensually stimulating to a man to see an occasional tip of the tongue flashing than a whole mouthful of twenty-percent-less-cavities. Because the tongue is normally hidden, like the genitals, its exposure on a pretty girl is a very stimulating thing to behold.

Certain movements in the course of everyday activities can easily be employed as bewitchment devices. A simple act like alighting from an automobile is a good example. A girl can follow all the prescribed rules of ladylike conduct when leaving her car seat, maintaining a firm grip on the hem of her skirt, her legs tightly together as she gingerly tries to extricate herself in a manner reminiscent of Harry

Houdini escaping from a padlocked milk can. *Or* she can get more mileage from the Law of the Forbidden than she can from the compact she's driving. All it requires is the right audience, and you'll be running neck and neck with the girl in the topless club we discussed earlier. You'll be sure to give some poor (lucky) man a vision that will stay with him and insure you of added witch-power.

After opening the car door to get out, swing your legs outside as you normally would, with a cursory tug at your hem to establish the fact that you are proper and to supply a fertile ground for the Law of the Forbidden. Then, as you are almost ready to stand up, "suddenly remember" that you left your keys in the ignition or purse on the seat. For a longer opportunity, you can use the ploy of suddenly remembering the need to find something in your purse or a package that you almost forgot to remove. Rummaging among several packages on the seat next to you is ideal. Keep the car door open, "forgetting" all about it, as you whirl around to attend to your almost-neglected parcel on the seat. With one leg outside the car, pull the other in, as you twist your body. If you maneuver correctly and employ the right body English, that nice man trying to put the bicycle in the back of his station wagon will get a better look at your panties than your husband has in the last five years!

After you have finished the task on the seat next to you that has so thoroughly absorbed your interest for the last several seconds, straighten around in your seat to once again alight from the car. When you notice where your skirt has crept, act *very* concerned and quickly and embarrassedly pull it down as far as it will go, primly clamping your legs together, of course. Oh yes, in the interest of safe driving it is not recommended that this be practiced on freeways or wherever a heavy flow of traffic is present.

If you have small children, while tending your toddlers at play you have dozens of opportunities to employ the Law of the Forbidden, and the psychological implications in looking up a pretty momma's dress are too obvious to even mention.

Slightly less Freudian, but nonetheless effective, are little doggies that need lots of untangling and attention when they are out for walks. A frisky poodle on the end of a leash is good for more ups and downs than a game of squat tag. Big doggies can have their advantages, too, when it comes to making a spectacle of a perfectly respectable girl. I have a large Doberman who has a penchant for putting his big nose under lady's dresses and lifting them up; and whether you believe it or not, I did *not* teach him to do such a thing!

Of course, there is the old trick of dropping your groceries and having to retrieve them. This is similar to the automobile bedazzler, in that it enables you to start out with an absolutely irreproachable modelling school crouch which can develop, through twisting around to collect all the stuff, into a real eye-opener for any males present. I know one witch who can drop groceries so they land in perfect formation. As a little girl she was the jacks champion of her block, little realizing it would lead to bigger things.

Since women started wearing pants, one of the finest institutions for learning the Law of the Forbidden—the carnival and amusement park—has all but bitten the dust. The various rides supplied opportunities for proper ladies to expose their charms in a manner far superior to leaping on a chair and shrieking, *"eeek!, a mouse!,"* while hoisting the skirt. As a girl was spun, pummelled, whirled, turned upside down and every other way, knowledge of many of the tricks this chapter contains was unnecessary as the machines did it all for you. The fun house supplied slides, barrels, rocking horses and the music that was to become the anthem of the Law of the Forbidden—the sound of the compressed air as it shot through what is called in carnival-ese, the "blow hole." Steeplechase Park at Coney Island had a special section of seats for spectators to sit and watch the girls' dresses blow up. The shrill screams and wild shrieks of the women whose underwear was revealed by the blast of air were the songs of the Sirens to the many voyeurs who would come early, find a good seat and stay late.

When I worked around amusement parks and carnivals it didn't surprise me to see the compulsion this spectacle produced in men, who would linger longer before the blow hole than they would before the "pros" who shook and shimmied on the platform of the girlie show and wore con-siderably less. What *did* fascinate me, however, were the women who would go through the fun house with their escorts, squealing loudly each time a jet of air would send their skirts up, acting all the while as though they wished they had never consented to submit themselves to such indignities. Occasionally, the next night one would return, with a different man, or perhaps alone and perhaps dressed just a little sexier, with her make-up a little heavier and go through the same "ordeal" as she had the night previous.

Another thing that impressed me was how the women who were being attacked by that apparently searing blast from out the flames of Hell would often become helpless, immobile. They remind me of nothing so much as a deer caught in a spotlight which knows it is completely exposed, yet does not move in its fascination for the situation. One would think the sound was the hissing of thousands of ser-pents or a cataract or the maelstrom, judging from its effect on some of the girls. Now scientists have a name for that kind of noise. They call it "white sound."

7. Means of Divination

How to Tell Fortunes with No Previous Experience

EVERY WITCH should be able to hold her own when it comes to divination, fortune-telling and popular application of the Black Arts. Unfortunately, altogether too much time is spent in studying occultism and far too little energy is expended in learning the practical side of human behavior. The would-be witch who thinks she will become a wonder-worker by studying cards or star charts had better spend a bit more time studying people, lest she become the victim of her own folly.

In order to know man well enough to manipulate him, we must be aware of the forces that motivate him, and it becomes increasingly apparent that the psychic sciences have become a formidable motivating force, actually supplanting traditional religions in many instances. You'll notice that I treat the psychic sciences as a motivating factor in man's behavior. By this, I do not mean to imply that psychic "forces" are at work impelling man to do their bidding. I *do* mean, however, that the techniques of the individual divinatory arts are but misdirection devices for the competent witch to *use* as she sees fit.

Let's start with the most popular of the means of divination—astrology. Why astrology? What has insured its popularity? It loses its continuity when any attempt is made to correlate its findings to the synthesizer, which seems to fit everything in the Apparent/Demonic/Core range of personalities into perfect position, however subtle the gradation may be. Astrologers will argue that their art is not, nor was it ever intended to type human beings, but merely to relate events to the movements of heavenly bodies.

My answer to this is that *people* make events, and if the solar system doesn't have any bearing on people's activities, then a lot of astrology magazines are sold under false pretenses to millions of people who believe, to a greater or lesser degree, what they read. Before one even attempts to understand astrology, or any of the occult arts, he should ask himself "Why?" Usually, the answer will be: "Because I want to learn what others have not learned."

Next, it is automatically assumed that to learn what others do not fully know, one must study that which is not fully known or at least that which is shrouded in mystery. Again, the Law of the Forbidden is seen in action. The assumption is always that if there is anything important to be discovered, it will require a long, hard, esoteric search. Actually, all great discoveries are made when they are practically tripped over, stumbled upon and "accidentally" uncovered. Despite all the physical evidence of the usual non-esoteric means of discovery in the mundane sphere of our existence, seekers after magical and occult discoveries persist in refusing to overturn the rock which lies at their very feet to observe what might hide beneath. It's too simple. And the mania for the forbidden will not allow it.

The greatest mistake any witch can make is to think that

to accept and practice the force known as "magic" it will be necessary to study great amounts of occult literature. The reason so few competent magicians exist, is because most persons who seek magical wisdom approach it from an occultist's point of view. The main reason for this is because what is forbidden is always more fun, and the unknown is about as forbidden as you can get or it wouldn't be unknown.

Anyone can crack a book about the history of Rome, how to make fireworks, flower arrangements, human anatomy, the effect of music in Russian nationalism or why people commit suicide. "What the Hell does it matter why people commit suicide or how people behave in nudist camps," thinks the would-be witch or warlock. "That kind of book isn't going to tell me anything I want to know about casting spells!" The simple facts of the matter are that such study material is too easily accessible, too mundane, too close to home and, therefore, it is not only uninteresting but also assumed to be worthless from a magical point of view.

There *are* some subjects that have validity, which are pursued by occult scholars, but unfortunately precious few. One example is handwriting analysis. If, however, many handwriting analysts would discard the occult sciences as a supplement to graphology, they would be far more capable. Instead of learning the fine points of astrology, numerology, palmistry, etc.—thinking them to be a worthwhile extension of graphology—it is far wiser to move in the other direction away from esoteric ramblings.

Well, a study of the stars and their relation to human affairs is about as esoteric as you can get, so a great many people feel that it's an ideal place to start! But why not start at man and work *outward* utilizing what we know best as a basis? The astrologer studies far-removed heavenly bodies, then attempts to correlate human activities, behavior and physical appearance with the distant planets.

Why not start with man, the best known and most readily observable phenomenon? Man is the only thing in our known universe with which we can irrevocably identify ourselves. Therefore, it is not correct to assume that *all* evaluation of personality types and behavior must evolve from a study of man himself? We do not know how other things in our solar system feel. We know how man feels, but do we want to admit to *feelings*? I say we do not, so we exteriorize them at every opportunity, even insofar as our studies of ourselves are concerned as witness astrology. Instead of typing the known universe, using ourselves as a base of operations, with gradations carefully selected, we seek to discover the nature of ourselves through distant examples.

Can man ever really know himself? I say yes! But first he must study himself and others of his species. And even before he studies himself, he must start small. He must study animals that walk on all-fours, then graduate to the parallels he can find in himself. This is why I have based so much on our synthesizer, because it measures man and his predilections; and once this subject is known well, the bigger things start snapping into focus. Sometimes these revelations appear frighteningly, other times joyously, but at *all* times accompanied by that unique thrill that comes with discovery.

When one considers the reasons, it becomes easy to understand why astrology has become the most popular of all divinitory sciences. Of course, a wise witch "believes" in astrology, because she knows that most everyone else does! If enough people believe in something, then the successful manipulator will find a way to capitalize on such a belief. Like it or not, that's the way it is. If the competent witch knows where the stars will supposedly lead a person, she can be waiting, first in line.

Belief in astrology *on the part of others* is one of the best magical weapons upon which any witch can rely. Even the most skeptical will enjoy and emotionally accept what astrology has to tell them, because anything concerning one's self is always more interesting to hear about than anything else. Instead of telling you all about the methods of using astrology, I'll tell you *why* you should employ it. There are numerous books available on the subject, as simple or as intricate as you wish in their teachings. If you learn to cast horoscopes, thereby assuming the role of astrological seer, you will find yourself able to set up and arrange self-fulfilling prophecies with a remarkable degree of certainty.

The stars may affect no one at all, but astrology affects everyone! Here are a few reasons why:

1. It is based on a "scientific" principle—the solar system, mathematics, time, biology, endocrinology and who knows what all—are incorporated into astrology.

2. It is a consistently available shot in the arm for the ego.

3. It is esoteric. It is easy enough, in its daily horoscope fashion, for anyone even of the simplest mind to understand; yet it will allow those who wish to go deeper into its theology the opportunity for endless study.

4. It is a socially acceptable conversation piece which will allow gossip a fertile playground in that it permits people to talk about others in an analytical way under the guise of "studying" them astrologically. This is done in much the same way as *some* psychologists, social workers, marriage counselors, sexologists, etc. will "study" their clients or patients—secretly for prurient rather than clinical reasons, except the astrology buff needs no credentials to

do the same thing. Neither does a bartender, but then he does not claim knowledge of an esoteric nature.

5. It is a much more scintillating conversation opener and sustainer than any other popular religion as it is ego based. One will find few listeners at a social gathering if he approaches the person he wishes to meet with "What have you done lately to please Jesus?" or "Where were you baptized?" On the other hand, "Under what sign were you born?" or "You must be a Scorpio," is almost sure to elicit a reply.

6. It is "safe" in that it is compatible with other religions. One can go to church on Sunday after reading his daily horoscope without fear of even a gentle roasting.

7. It allows man freedom from having to make his own decisions. It has been said by almost all astrologers that the stars impel, rather than compel. This means that unlike other gods of other religions (for that is what astrology has become to many), there is no inflexible, whip-cracking, stern-faced Jehovah but a rather benign guidance from the solar system that allows for human modification by those who are "aware." Certainly a much more easy-going way of having someone or something else make decisions for you and guide your destiny.

8. It is flexible in its application. There are no absolutes. Its ambiguity makes it difficult to totally discredit its message. The findings of one astrologer can always be contradicted by another—the second astrologer taking other factors into consideration that the first missed.

9. It has been around long enough to emboss itself on the collective unconscious so that even if we *could* ignore it, some of our forebearers most likely *could not*.

10. It can gain substance by pointing at the moon and its obvious influence and announcing that if the moon can influence the tides, behavior, etc., then so can planets,

stars, etc. likewise influence earthly situations. This is the very successful trick used by stage magicians; if one sword can be thrust through a previously inspected object which rests within a cabinet, and afterwards the object is removed and shown to have been speared through by the sword, it is thereby assumed by the audience that the pretty girl who then gets into the cabinet will be thoroughly impaled by the succession of numerous swords in addition to the first one. We must not forget that at one time it was proclaimed that the moon contained lunar armies, strange ships sailing on lunar seas and was even made of green cheese—while the *same* "experts" also knew the subtle influences of distant planets upon the earth!

11. It can appear valid in that people *do* act the way their astrological signs imply they must. It is a fine case of the tail wagging the dogma, the planets having nothing to do except provide a rationale for the dogma of astrology—the dogma acting as the controlling factor—*not the stars!*

"Cold Reading" and "Casing the Mark"

Cold reading is the old carnival method of telling fortunes, which is not much different from the "psychic" method of telling fortunes, except it is more accurate and strips away most elements of self-deceit from the fortune-teller herself. As a resourceful witch, you should be able to tell fortunes by whatever system you choose to employ. You can be a "gifted" reader and prophet with no previous experience. It's simple. All you need are a few simple hints about human nature, and a good credibility device. Contrary to the great racket raised by various con artists in astrology, tarot reading, and the like, it doesn't matter in the least *which* means you use in your readings. It is your own insight on which you will actually be depending. The most successful seers are usually those who have the least knowledge of occultism.

You too can predict the future happenings of your friends' lives just by the application of an easily learned formula. First, if you have no reputation as a seer or prophet, you must obtain a device which does! This will make up for your lack of ability as a convincing witch or warlock. This device we will call the "credibility factor." It is sometimes known in Satanic magic as the "convincer." Many such convincers exist, such as palmistry, tarot cards, tea leaves, crystal balls, astrology, numerology, etc.

After you have chosen the convincer you are going to use, you must spend enough time familiarizing yourself with the basics of your device. This is more important in the case of astrology, numerology and tarot than it is with palmistry, crystal gazing, the Ouija board and other less involved credibility factors. It is for reasons of simplification that I recommend the less complex convincers to the beginner.*

The next step is to make up your mind whether you are going to use your new-found powers on your friends and acquaintances or confine your wonders to strangers and new-found friends. If it is a circle of established friends that you wish to mystify, you must tell them that you have been studying with a witch or warlock, whom you cannot name, but has recently bestowed great wisdom upon you. This will give your supposed new knowledge substance when combined with the convincer you have chosen by adding to the convincer another credibility factor—experience, not yours in this case, but someone else's.

* The Ouija board, because of its extreme popularity and ease of use, will be found to make an ideal convincer. Just move the planchette so it answers in the way most conducive to your reading. If the board says it's so, *it must be.*

If your soothsaying is to be purveyed to total strangers or recently-met friends, then it is duck soup. You need only hang out your shingle as a "gifted" reader or psychic, who has been at it all your life! If your subjects consist of both types, then use both methods respectively but don't get your signals or your subjects crossed.

Now, let us assume you are "reading" your first subject. Possibly you are using a crystal ball, or instead, a table full of tarot cards might be spread before you. Whichever convincer you use must be made to be the very focal point, the object of intense concentration, the most important factor in your reading. It must never appear that you are studying the person sitting before you, even though you are. After all, *you* are not telling them anything—the cards are!

It is a brutally hard fact that humans will not have faith in another human being that bears no credentials, and those silly little tea leaves in the cup give what you say more credence than any amount of true insight you might have.

After you have gazed thoughtfully at the palm of his hand, or whatever, then you look up into his eyes, take a deep breath and heavy-handedly prepare to give him the first profound revelation. What is this first great proclamation to be? Simple. The same as most of the statements you will be making throughout the entire reading or at least *half* of the reading. You tell him something nice about himself—something he wants to hear. This opens up the gate of emotional acceptance, so immediately he becomes your friend! Therefore, he will be inclined to believe anything you tell him, because he believes so strongly in what you have started with—nice things about himself!

After you have told him a few nice things, you cloud your face all up and get a worried look in your eyes. Now you hit him with the "evil forces" pitch. Tell him something bad has, is, or is going to happen. If you tell him something bad has happened, and there are certain forces working against him, he will be more grateful than ever when you imply that you are the person who has been chosen to help him. He will go away feeling that he's finally met someone who "understands" his problem.*

If you want to play the evil witch, you can tell him that something bad is *about* to happen or is going to happen in the distant future. Chances are, your suggestion will be followed through, and what you suggest *will* actually happen—truly prophesy! He has already accepted your words as nice to listen to, so the unconscious is wide open for suggestion when you hit him with a "curse," which in reality, it is. Don't be a real villain, though, and leave him with nothing but misery to look forward to. See to it that there is always an "out" to the mishap you predict. Tell him that everything will resolve itself, and things will work out all right. Fortune tellers can be terribly dangerous, because in telling a "bad" fortune, they can actually cause bad things to happen that might not otherwise occur.

The most successful readers make the good outweigh

---

* This technique of sending the customer out of the fortune-teller's with more problems than he came in with, is called "casing the mark." Unscrupulous fortune-tellers who specialize in this technique usually make their biggest money on the candles and charms that are sold as protective measures against the very "evil forces" they have supplied. The fortune teller is often not to blame for this sort of action, however, as many "clients" will become very upset if they are not told about the "forces" that are working against them. They will insist that "something will be done" by the fortune-teller, who, in order to add tangible credence to the customer's dependence upon her, will load the customer up with enough candles to convincingly flatten his wallet. You will find the "evil forces" pitch will always work with those who are not too capable as individuals. You will actually do your quarry a big favor if he or she is somewhat of a loser by employing this device. By telling him that he has forces working against him, whether human or otherwise, you are taking him off the hook. You give him a rationale for not succeeding and therefore are the best friend he's found in a long time. Here again we find the ego sop working like a charm.

the bad in their readings and you should too—if for no other reason than to keep your subjects as friends! What you actually tell them is not nearly so important as how well you flatter them even making their faults flattering—such as: "Many people think of you as rather irritable, but you only appear that way because you have helped people so much who have kicked you in return that it has become hard for you to go around with a great big smile." Using this technique, it will be unnecessary to tell your subjects any real information about themselves, as they will read all manner of "accuracy" into your reading just from the authentic bits and pieces you might have said which they have picked up out of context.

Whatever you do, don't neglect your convincer for any length of time! That deck of cards, lined palm, string of numbers, birthdate or crystal ball is your passport to success. *After* you develop a reputation for having great psychic powers, then you can rely less and less on the convincer, as your personal "powers" will become the convincer.

It has often been said that the device employed by the reader only acts as a means of diverting the reader's conscious thoughts and thereby opening up the unconscious so that he might "pick up" the unspoken message from his subject. This is certainly true, but it leaves half the story untold. The other half is the diverting of doubt on the part of the subject to total belief as a result of the credibility of the convincer. Here is a little Satanic secret. If you use this "diabolical" method of fortune-telling—this apparently "phoney" means—without self-deceit knowing full well what you are doing, you will be startled and perhaps even frightened at the *amazingly accurate things you will come up with!* Try it and see.

Prophesy

Anyone who is aware of what is going on now as well as what has happened in the past can reasonably predict what will occur in the future. This, of course, applies to world affairs as well as events on a much smaller scale. To be in tune with the world around you is all that is necessary to predict what will happen next. The only fly in the ointment is: how many people *are* actually attuned to the world around them?

One must be in touch with reality at all times in order to successfully predict the future. The only other alternative is to fake it. There are several good methods of faking predictions. You'd be amazed at the way some of the most famous seers arrive at their conclusions. The easiest way of doing this is to use two sets of predictions. This is especially simple if you are dependent on news services to broadcast your prophecies.

Let's assume you give a great yearly prophesy, telling all important events that will transpire in the year to come. Your proclamations appear in hundreds or even thousands of newspapers. Well, some newspapers might receive one set of predictions to print, obtaining the article from one news service, while other newspapers receive a totally different set of predictions, sent them from another news service. Each of the two sets of predictions are completely different, yet touch upon the same topics. The millions of people who read the set of predictions that happen to be accurate are sure to remember the miraculous workings of whoever happened to be the prophet whose words they read earlier in the year.

One of the finest old carnival techniques of prediction is to announce the winner of an election in one town or county, then to announce the opposing candidate as the winner in the next county that the show plays. You can easily see how the seer is bound to be correct—at least *half* of the time! It is in the towns where he has made the correct prediction that the *next* season around he reminds all the people of his accurate prediction in the event that they may have forgotten. In this way it is easy to build up a strong reputation as a prophet.

All it takes is *one* profoundly accurate prediction to start you on the road to fame, and if you make a hundred predictions, *ten* of them will probably turn out right. This is especially true when it applies to births, marriages, divorces, deaths, etc. involving public figures of great magnitude. Of course, if you can get another person to go around telling of your wonderful predictions, especially if that person happens to be a well established commentator, writer or journalist, you have it made!

The only thing I find distasteful about many people in the prediction business is their sanctimonious attitude, leaning on the respectability of religion and using it to give themselves a holier-than-thou image. If these types could only free themselves from the guilts inspired by the biblical warnings against the practice of soothsaying, they wouldn't have to overcompensate in such a simpering manner in order to "atone for their sin" of making predictions. This applies to all fortune-tellers, mediums, psychics, pseudo-mystics and magicians, etc. who have to hang the walls of their consultation rooms with plaster saints, mouth platitudes about the great gift that God has given them and in general, cloak their Black Art with sanctimonious white light! These people are playing the Devil's game, but refusing to use the Devil's name, and their hypocrisy is bound to annoy the old Prince of Darkness!

8. Ceremonial Magic

Sex Magic without Sanctimony

WE'VE COVERED the spectrum of what the well-dressed witch should wear, but what about the well *un-dressed* enchantress? Here we must return to the elemental principles of the Law of the Forbidden. Sheer nudity in itself is usually not nearly as stimulating as a glimpse of the forbidden. Going about topless won't accomplish a thing unless you radiate the feeling of embarrassment it could bring.

Place a nude model on a platform in an art class, who does that sort of thing every day, and only the most inexperienced males will find any erotic stimulation present. The types that go to museums and masturbate in front of a Titian or Renoir when nobody's looking are getting scarce. It takes a great deal more than nudity nowadays to compel sensual stimulation.

Topless clubs get boring, because the dancers are blasé about their exposure. They cannot radiate the powerful magic that comes with embarrassment, even though the first five times they might have (which might have been why they got the job in the first place). The greater success of "amateur" strip and topless performances attests to the fact that men want to see a secretary, schoolteacher or another guy's wife any day. Even though most "amateur" topless contests are fixed, with obviously experienced girls working the show, the audience *wants* to believe the contestants are all terribly naughty, apprehensive and embarrassed ladies. The girl who says "I could *never* do that" is the one who would cause the greatest sensation if she were to do a strip tease or appear at a cocktail party in a topless dress. Her red face would insure her success rather than the size or shape of her breasts.

One of the most magically depleating things that can happen, yet one that most witches would surely believe to be in their favor, is for the girl who doesn't think she could ever take her clothes off or go topless in front of others to discover that after the "initial shock wore off after a few minutes it didn't seem so bad." The real secret, of course, is to *maintain* your self-consciousness realizing it to be a positive factor.

When you adjust to a situation that would be sexually provocative to others and becomes blasé, you have literally cut off your magnetic pull. The most highly successful and truly charismatic glamour goddesses never become blasé or lack self-consciousness of their sexuality.

Most women know the old trick of unbuttoning one of the middle buttons of a blouse so that it will appear as though it accidentally became unfastened. This is always good for a sneaky peak at what lies beneath as you move about. In utilizing the Law of the Forbidden, you can make many of the things you do appear as though you were unaware of them happening. Thus, you will be employing a double threat by your proper and conducive choice of garments and also by your apparent lack of knowledge of your exposure.

So many opportunities present themselves that an entire volume could be written on the subject; and the most effective turn ons will never look staged. These are "exercises" you should practice that will allow you to develop a hyper-awareness of your own sexuality while remaining safe from any stigma of social rejection. Rather than call these "exercises in embarrassment," I prefer to label them exactly what they are intended to be—Magical Rituals.

It has been stated that all women are exhibitionists to a certain extent. The thrill that any healthy woman obtains when she knows she is exciting a desirable male is the most natural thing in the world. So far I have attempted to clarify many of the misconceptions about what men are turned on and off by. My findings are the results of many hours of listening to the experiences of women whose business it is to please men and have them come back for more. Besides prostitutes, there are ten times as many "average" women who have told me tales in great confidence that they invariably think will place each of them or the men they describe in a singularly freakish light. When you hear enough of such "singular" experiences, it becomes apparent that they are not so singular after all and are only thought to be by the individual.

The only thing you must realize, when performing little rituals in sexual self-consciousness, is the *positive* value of such an experience. That there can be a secret thrill connected with each exercise there is little doubt. What is important, however, is that you make a *ritual* of the experience. In order to be a powerful witch, you must learn the meaning of ritual in its most magical sense.

A ritual is an act, or series of acts, that are entered into with complete and total awareness of one's actions, plans, feelings and purpose. All rituals do not take place in a specially designed chamber as you shall see. If you want to be a witch, you'd best learn the first three dimensions before you concern yourself with the fourth. The only way to start is to become aware of your own existence—*super aware!* Then, in what will appear to be the most subtle and non-esoteric ways, *make others who will increase your witch-power aware of your existence!*

Because their sexual energy is potential magical energy and nature intended that they be attracted to you, *men* are your best source of witch-power. Therefore, by your own sexual self-consciousness, you can draw this power from the men who need only to be placed within your magnetic field. Remember, the purpose of a ritual such as the one I'm about to describe is *not* to pick up men but to produce within yourself an accelerated charge of sexual self-consciousness.*

While performing your ritual, remain as aware as possible that you are doing something naughty, forbidden, possibly even nasty. This is not the time to try to scrape your psyche clean with thoughts of breaking inhibitions and false guilts. This is the time to turn unfounded guilts and inhibitions into an *advantage!* Allow yourself to feel as self-conscious as you can. You may find that some rituals are more subjective than others and consist of situations of which *you* alone are aware. Naturally, these will supply a great deal of sexual stimulation for yourself but not for

*As with so many commonly-used terms, the literal meaning of "self-consciousness" is often forgotten, whereas the popular usage, e.g., ill at ease, embarrassed, etc. is most frequently brought to mind when the term is used. In the context of ritualistic self-consciousness, I intend to imply *both* the literal or semantic: conscious of yourself, hyper-aware of your own sensations and being *and* the popular: embarrassment felt by you resulting from another person's awareness of you in a particular situation.

others. The main advantage of such rituals is to generate
sexual self-awareness in a highly intensified manner—infinitely more than simply standing nude before the mirror
and chanting as practiced by some witches. Here is one
magical working any girl can perform with no equipment
other than her own body, a mirror and her normal clothes.

Undoubtedly, there are some of you who have already
tried this, as it falls into the same category as undressing
in front of a window with the shade pulled up but is decidedly safer and much more stimulating. Apply your
make-up so you feel as though you look as seductive as
possible. Fix your hair in an attractive manner. Take off
all your clothes and step into the sexiest pair of high-heels
you own. Now you are glamorously decked out at your
highest and lowest extremities, head to toe. If you wish to
add an extra fillip, put on some of your favorite accessories
—hat, gloves, jewelry. Now you're all set. Get a good look
at yourself in a full-length mirror, visualizing what you see
as exactly how men will soon be looking at you. Go to your
closet and get your coat—*only your coat* and put it on and
button it. Now go out.

Go where there will be people, especially men. If you
are driving, stop in a gas station to use the rest room, so
the attendants can see you. Go into a newsstand for a pack
of cigarettes, where men are playing the pinball machines.
Walk around. Go up to street repairmen or construction
workers and ask directions. At all times consider yourself
to be stark naked! Imagine that every man you encounter
who looks at you is studying each contour of your luscious,
ripe body—savoring the sight of your nipples and scrutiniz-
ing the shadow between your legs.

Remember, you need not speak to anyone unless you
want to. If you feel daring, go into a bar and have a drink.
If it is feasible, when in a place that you're sure is tempo-

rarily deserted, as when you are alone in an elevator, museum or art gallery, hotel or motel corridor, etc., open your coat all the way up and stand in the nude, momentarily caressing yourself if you wish. Walk around until you have almost exhausted the time you have set aside for your ritual, then go home.

As soon as you get in your room, remove your coat and stand before the mirror. Imagine that you see yourself as a desirable man would see you, perhaps one you encountered during your walk. Look at yourself from an imaginary man's body, allowing yourself to feel as sexually excited as you might, were you a man. As you gaze at yourself in the mirror, picture yourself as being in one of the places you were prior to returning home. Imagine that you are one of the men that were looking at you and how he must have felt being able to see you as you look now (for you must *assume* that he could see you nude).

Didn't you look absolutely shocking, your lovely body completely exposed as you shamefully flaunted yourself. Feel as though you have a male sexual response as you study your reflection—*you* are not yourself, as you stand before the mirror. Your reflection is really you. The body you feel around you is that of a handsome man, terribly aroused and excited at the outrageous display of the sensual naked body of the girl who is exposing herself. Allow yourself to build to as high a peak of sexual excitement as possible, masturbating yourself to a climax, attempting to feel as the man would as he watched the girl (you) perform such an act in public.

As you are overcome by your sensual responses, close your eyes, fall to the floor, thrash about in wild abandon— or do whatever will contribute to the most intense orgasm. *Now* is a very important time from a magical standpoint. As you are coming down from your climax, say to yourself:

"I am a witch; I have power over men!—I am a witch; I have power over men!" Repeat this over and over, as your climactic recedes. Keep saying it to yourself, moving your lips and speaking as loudly or softly or inaudibly as conditions will permit.

Then, either slip into your clothes and pursue your normal activities as though nothing had happened, or if it is late, slide into bed and go to sleep. The first time you perform this ritual, you might want to go easy, and just walk around the block or go to the laundromat, possibly spending only a few minutes in public. You'll find at least an hour is best, though. After the first ritual, you should notice an immediate increase in your powers of attraction, and you will know that you are accumulating some real witch-power.

This ritual is truly discreet and is virtually fool-proof insofar as your personal safety is concerned, providing you don't go wandering in disreputable areas or senselessly throw open your coat in an indiscriminate fashion.

The actual mechanics of the ritual just described serve to bring about many vitally important ingredients towards your success as a witch. The emphasis on the power of strong contrasts is supplied by the fact that you are "dressed up" in all the readily visible areas of your body while totally naked under your coat. The same element is present in the incongruity of mingling with people who are clothed while you are naked in an unstaged environment. If this does not present a feeling of self-consciousness, you'll never make it as a witch, for you lack the emotional response of the individuals on whom you would be working your magic. If you are so alien to other's emotional responses, I would recommend you give up on trying to be a witch or else take a few lessons from a Martian or Venusian who has learned to "pass."

The Law of the Forbidden is subjectively practiced in your constant awareness of your outrageous behavior. Any embarrassment you develop while walking around will cause you to be noticed by men who normally might not pay any attention to you simply because you are radiating "that feeling," *not* because anyone actually knows you are naked. Momentarily exposing yourself completely, as in an elevator, etc. will give you an added thrill in knowing you are getting away with something, thereby adding to your accumulation of secret accomplishments and subsequent power. Even though your objective mind might not consider such an act an accomplishment, in your highly-charged state, it will subconsciously go on record as such! *

When you return home from your walk, you begin an exercise in ego-circuitry, allowing both your Apparent and Demonic elements to manifest themselves. The mirror has long been utilized for magical purposes, though few practitioners actually realize the fantastic potential and myriad uses of reflective planes. During the detumescence period, your self-proclamation will retain its substance, as your mind and body are unwinding and opening and are like a yawning chasm just waiting for suggestions. This is the time a woman wants to be told she is loved more than any other, because the reinforcement to her psyche that such an admission brings is worth a thousand hugs and kisses at any other time. When you tell yourself exactly what you are at this point and that you have power over men, you are accomplishing far more than a simple exercise in positive thinking.

* This is the type of ritual that could well be practiced by girls and women who are addicted to shoplifting, as it is well known that such behavior is often of a sexual nature. The thrill and subsequent accomplishment of stealing an un-needed or worthless article serves to accumulate a secret sort of prowess. In training witches-to-be, I have found that many girls who have had compulsions to shoplift, once put on this ritualistic "prescription," lose all such desires to steal.

When you resume your normal activities, after getting dressed, you have symbolically closed your ritual chamber behind you, thereby isolating your previous act and making it a ritual in the truest sense of the word.* The combination of all the elements we have discussed cannot help but have an accumulative side-effect in the awareness you have of your own powers of seduction and the aura which will surround you.

Casting a Spell

Before you consider spell-casting, you must be totally aware of yourself as a veritable dynamo of desire. You cannot be half-hearted when you attempt to throw a spell or curse. You must know what you want and be fully prepared to take advantage of it when it comes to you.

Magic depends on an emotional response rather than an intellectual approach. When you are spell-casting, you must be prepared to throw all emotional repressions and inhibitions to the wind. This is why the casting of a spell is best performed in the sanctity of your home or a place where you can be alone. Group rituals are seldom as effective for the actual throwing of a curse or charm unless each one of the participants is fully in sympathy for whatever the ceremony is to attain. Otherwise, group ceremonies are best employed as statements of faith, dedication and homage to the Dark Forces, much as a church service would be, but to different gods. You don't have to be Satanic to enjoy a nude altar, but apparently it helps if you're a man. There is no doubt, though, that the solemnity and Gothic awesomeness of a good Satanic Mass would warm the heart of Barnabas Collins!

---

* I have expanded on the mechanics of the ritual chamber and its magical importance as an isolation device in my *Satanic Bible*.

For your personal ceremonies you'll need privacy, a good imagination, some creative ability and the proper time slot. Time-wise, it's always best to attack your victim while he sleeps, vampire-style. The reason so many traditional witches and sorcerers are nocturnal is because it's the best time to do such dirty work. When a person is asleep, his defenses are down, his subconscious up and his brain is receptive to whatever strong impulses you can throw his way. The ideal state for the witch who is "sending" is one of highly charged emotion, while the best condition for the recipient to be in is as passive and dormant as possible. Take a nap, if need be, and wake up in the wee small hours to perform your spell.

There are many ways to curse an enemy, using the powers of ceremonial magic, but the main difference in any of them is in the device employed to approximate or imitate the victim. Pictures, photos, wax or clay models, among other things can be created of your intended victim, but the device that I would recommend best is a hand-made doll similar in construction to those used in the practice of voodoo magic. The voodoo doll has become synonymous with cursing, and if for no other reason than this ready-made association, should such an effigy be used.

The importance of making your own voodoo doll can not be minimized, as the creative energy you expend in fashioning the doll will definitely add to the effectiveness of your ritual. Adherence to the prescribed method of making the doll requires that you use plain material for the outside and stuff the inside with feathers or cotton. Despite what you might hear to the contrary, the best color is the basic color of the victim's skin. You may make a very effective doll from a pair of new socks, which are readily obtainable. *IMPORTANT!:* Whatever you do, *don't* use material that you have worn from which to fashion the doll nor salvage material from clothing worn by anyone for whom you care.

Use one of the socks, slitting the ankle part in half to the heel, for the body of the doll. Fill the sock with feathers until you reach the back of the heel where the slit you have just made ends. Now sew up the slit so the two halves form the legs. Fill each leg with feathers and sew up the ends, forming feet. Next, take a piece of string and tie it tightly around the toe of the sock about two inches from the end, forming the neck which separates the head from the torso. If you have done all of this correctly, the toe of the sock should form the head, the foot part will become the body, and the ankle or leg section of the sock will be transformed into the two legs. The second sock may now be cut up for use in making the two arms of the doll, which after being stuffed with the feathers, are sewn to the body.

The doll should be sewn by hand for best results as a sewing machine for such a small item will most certainly eliminate the personal touch you supply by hand-stitching. Each stitch should be drawn with tender loving hate, thinking of your enemy with each thrust of the needle!

Next, you must supply the head of the doll with the face of your enemy or at least a reasonable facsimile. If you are talented at drawing, you can sketch a likeness, cut it out and paste or glue it on the doll's head. If you are fortunate enough to have a photograph of your enemy, so much the better—especially if, when trimmed down, the photo will fit in the place where the face should be.

Now the doll must be dressed. If you can obtain an article or a portion of your enemy's clothing, utilize it, as it will add to the imagery. It helps to dress the doll in a way that resembles the style of the person to be cursed, as regards to color, material, etc. If the victim has a particular habit, such as carrying a cane, umbrella or briefcase—or uses a certain type of tool regularly—it should be incorporated into the doll by placing a miniature of the implement in the hand. By the time you have finished, the doll should be a vivid representation, carefully constructed, of your enemy.

Put the finished doll aside for twenty-four hours, if possible in a place where you cannot fail to see it. This will allow the anticipation of what you are about to do to become intensified by the anger engendered by being confronted with your enemy.

After twenty-four hours have elapsed enough of a presence has been developed in the doll. Have your pins or nails ready to stick into the doll. The use of nails, rather than pins, is recommended, but other implements, such as knives, daggers, ice picks, etc. may be used. It is wise to ascertain the victim's "weak spots" health-wise. The reason for this is that the curse will work much better and faster if the victim has been known to have stomach trouble and the nails are thrust in the vicinity of the doll's stomach. If the person to be cursed is known to have migraine headaches, concentrate the nails in the doll's head. If there is a history of arthritis or aching joints, poke your nails where the knees, elbows, spine, shoulders, wrists and hips would be. When you push the nails into the doll, do it with great deliberation, feeling as though each twist and jab is actually penetrating your victim's body. Use as many nails as you wish until you have gotten all the hatred out of your system.

Once this is done, put the doll away in a place where it will be out of sight and, hopefully, out of mind. It is best to perform this ritual in complete privacy as it is serious business.

If done properly, it is *not* necessary that your victim have any knowledge of your curse. If no results are obtained it is *not* because magic doesn't work. One reason might lie in the fact that your victim is not really deserving of such treatment and *you* are the wrongdoer! It is best to fully and honestly evaluate a situation before indiscriminately throwing a curse. The best protection against any curse is the admiration and love bestowed upon you by others.

Another reason a curse will sometimes fail is anxiety. If you sit around waiting on pins and needles for your victim to fall and break a leg after performing your ritual, it is unlikely anything will happen. So once your ritual has been performed, be satisfied that you have performed a powerful and well-planned working and have confidence that it will work. Then just sit back and wait for the results, without continually thinking about when and how it will happen.

A third, and very important reason for failure is guilt. The person doing the cursing must feel no guilty conscience at having performed the ceremony, or the ensuing apprehension at what she has done will surely consume her while her intended victim gets away scot free! This is why "white" witches stupidly say that if you curse a person it will return three-fold. If you are so sanctimonious that you have to impress others that you are a "white" (good) witch, it's a cinch that you would feel such guilt after throwing a curse that it *would* bounce back and harm you!

One thing stands sure, though: even if your intended victim is protected from your curse and not harmed, you will have released a lot of anxiety and hostility from your system and will be able to carry on your everyday activities with much greater ease. If everybody were sticking pins in dolls instead of irritating others, driving recklessly, starting fights and insulting their friends, things might actually be running a lot smoother!

Hate can be a good thing, if properly directed and

honestly admitted. When hate is bottled up, however, and attempts are made to twist it into love, it is still *hate*—just with sugar-coating added! Then, instead of being able to come out in one fell swoop, that hate just sits there, oozing out in disguised, syrupy-sweet viciousness or irrational acts!

How to Protect Yourself from Another Witch's Curse

There is no need to fear another's curse unless you are a deserving victim. Naturally, no one would consider themselves a deserving victim any more than the so-called "white" witch thinks she practices magic for other than "good" purposes. This is why it is often wisest to assume that even if we are minding our own business and not bothering anybody, *somebody's* going to hate us, sooner or later.

There are people who will take offense no matter what you do to please them, and if they know how to throw a curse, they will. These are the truly wretched individuals who usually are so miserable that they are the victims of a far worse curse than any they can throw your way. Assuming you are an undeserving victim of such an unscrupulous individual, your *fear* of that person or his curse is often enough to make life miserable for you. This is especially true of extremely sensitive would-be victims of curses. If your fears of being cursed by such a person are bad enough to affect your everyday life, then in effect you *are* being cursed.

In order to protect yourself from a curse or the fear of a curse, you must meet it head on, confronting it with more than a simple defense. In this case the best means of defense is offense, and the only way to prove to yourself that you are stronger than the curse is to literally consume your fear of it rather than be consumed by it. An old and secret means of doing this is to fashion a likeness of the person who has cursed you from some edible substance if you know who that person is. You can use a fruit or vegetable carved in the form of the person or bake a cookie after having moulded the dough so it represents the curser or witch.

The origin of the gingerbread man, as described in an earlier chapter, is simply the casting of a likeness of the man the witch wishes to enslave and after eating it gaining control over him. Make your likeness of the person who has cursed you as realistic as possible, considering the material you have to work with.

After you have completed the likeness, place it in a darkened room on a table with only one white candle illuminating it from behind. Then sit or stand directly in front of where you have placed your carving or cake, feeling as much intense fear as possible. Allow your thoughts to dwell on whatever it is that your attacker has used to torment you. Tremble and shake in terror. Get it all out of your system in one fell swoop. *Then*—say, in words to this effect, "All right you rotten bitch, you've had your little curse . . . now it's *my* turn to show you *my* power over *you*! Advance slowly toward the likeness as a tiger stalking its prey. Pick up the representation deliberately and methodically, studying it with great disdain and contempt. Prod it with your fingers as you hold it, almost feeling it squirm in your hand. Pinch it, tweak it, torment it—imagining it as *your* victim, now, helpless and mute. Lick your chops ghoulishly. Talk to it insultingly, call it by name. Torment and torture it, knowing it has been recently doing the same to you. Then, slowly and with fiendish delight, *bite the head off*! Chew it thoroughly, smacking your lips, and swallow it. Then proceed to gnaw off the arms, legs, and finish up with the body.

When you have finished, lick the crumbs from your lips, wipe your mouth, blow out the candle and walk out of the room.

An interesting variant of this procedure is to spit out the pieces you bite off, having chewed each piece thoroughly. Gather the pieces you have spit out and throw them down the toilet! Of course, if you eat the likeness, it'll wind up there anyway, but your system might benefit from some part of it.

Choose whichever means is most emotionally appealing to you.

How to Become a Succubus and Attack the Man of Your Choice While He Sleeps

A succubus is an evil female demon who visits men in the night and, while they are sleeping, has sexual intercourse with them. A man knows he has been attacked by a succubus when he wakes up in the morning and his night shirt is stiff with dried semen. He is likely to go about all the following day with lewd thoughts in his mind, generally of a woman, the appearance of whom was the image taken by the succubus who attacked him.

If he is a good man, and holy, he will not let this thing pass unattended. He will seek out his priest, telling him of his nightmarish experience and produce his rigid nightgown as proof. He will describe the dream which accompanied his monstrous visitation, recalling to the best of his ability the details of his encounter. The priest, a wise man, will understand, as he knows such evil does exist and has heard many such accounts and inspected many semen-encrusted nightshirts. The fact that many of the succubi described to him match the faces and bodies of some of the women of the town concerns him no small amount as well it should. Something must be done.

A great deal was done, for several centuries. Now at last it is safe to become a succubus and enter the dreams of the man you desire. All you need is an indelible image of his physical attributes in your mind, a burning lust, a place to work it out, and some help from other men!

Choose a time when he has been asleep for at least four hours. Exercise your sensuality by going forth earlier in a manner to excite other men, even if only visually, employing the Law of the Forbidden and the Virtues of Embarrassment. Do not depend upon your strong desire for the man you wish to summon, as it alone is not enough. It is important that you engender the lust-energy from *other* men, as they will be supplying, through their sexual fantasies of you this night, the proper balance—the completed circuit of needed magical energy.

Enter your chamber at the prescribed hour and start to masturbate. If you can force his image into your mind at the exact moment of climax, it is highly likely he will receive your visitation. If a man who is masturbating with your image in his mind or who is having intercourse with you should reach climax, and at that time you envision the object of your desire and you yourself reach a climax while thinking of your quarry, you will be sure to reach him as he sleeps.

If you wish, add some incantations or burn some incense or candles to make your charm more "magical." Women are romantic; and witches are, after all, women, so such devices will always be popular. In the way of accouterments, whatever makes *you* feel like a witch, who is casting a powerful spell, will make your magic stronger. If the man you have visited does not come to you, it is only because he needs to be summoned, not because you are not in his mind.

As a succubus, the purpose of your working is to enter his mind and body as he sleeps, although such things often prohibit sleep and cause him to lie awake with a knot in his solar plexus. Once you have visited him in this manner and caused his mind to dwell upon you, you must summon him.

The reason lust spells seldom work for would-be witches is because the victim has not been softened up properly, prior to the ritual, which is actually a summons. For the actual summoning, many rituals can be employed. Here is one example.

A few days after your visit as a succubus, or even the next day if you're anxious, perform the ritual as described in the chapter on "Sex Magic." Instead of envisioning the excitement of the men you have encountered during your "outing," as you stand before the mirror, imagine yourself as the man you wish to summon and talk to him from the mirror. As he stands in your body he hears *you* command him to come to you. Make it as convincing as you can, using the same procedure and reaching your climax as you would if you were practicing this ritual as a "strengthening" rather than a summoning.

Perform the succubus and summoning ritual as often as you feel the desire. If you persevere, your "dream lover" will become a physical reality. Unless you learn well the "lesser" magic contained herein, however, you have no right to complain if your summoning is short-lived. Always remember, there is far more magic to witchery than that which takes place during a ceremony.

On Choosing a Familiar or a Demon

Every witch should have a familiar or a demon. If you have a pet of any kind that is totally dependent upon you, it is more protection from the destructive thoughts of others than you can imagine. Love is dependence, and a creature who depends on you might just be the one ingredient you lack to safeguard yourself.

You need not fear your familiar or demon will tell any tales about your activities, nor will it complicate your life by burdening you with its problems other than to expect food and care. In choosing a pet, care should be taken to ascertain whether it will occupy the role of your Demonic or Core personality. If it is representative of your Demonic self, it will be exactly the opposite of yourself. Some such combinations are easily defined, like the slender girl with sleek hair and delicate features with the bulldog or turtle; the rotund man with the greyhounds or the excessively large woman with the chihuahua. Examples of the Core personality manifested in a familiar are observed in the talkative little woman with the house full of canaries, the outdoors type with the Irish setter and the exotic type with the ocelot.

In choosing a familiar, make sure it will act as an extension of your Apparent/Core personality. In this choice, you will be able to intensify the strength of your existing personality, by the addition of another creature's magical energy, which is already close to you. If you are *satisfied* with what you are, who you are and what you can do, then choose this type of familiar. If, however, you want to modify your personality, temper it or otherwise mutate it, the choice of a Demonic pet (which is as close in appearance as *you* will ever envision an actual demon) is your best bet.

When people look like their pets, their relationship is definitely that of witch/familiar. The magical end result of such a relationship is a lycanthropic state, where the person becomes the animal and the animal becomes the person. In the theoretical manifestation of this phenomenon, the inactive, often sleeping person's psyche roams abroad inside the animal and acts are performed by the animal with or without direction by the human.

When people are extreme opposites of their pets, the pet must *not* be handled, fondled or cuddled by anyone other than its owner. Unlike the owner of the familiar, who thrives on people making a fuss over her pet (for they're indirectly making a fuss over *her*!), the demon's owner makes people keep their distance.

Let's review the types we just observed in this light. The sylph-like girl will be very guarded, lest anyone attempt to handle her prize bulldog, even though he may be snorting his head off with enthusiasm. The corpulent man with his greyhounds will warn those who come too close that they may snap and the buxom dowager will have a fit if anyone pokes his finger too close to her little darling's nose.

On the other hand, the chatty bird lady will fairly trap you into staying in her living room until you have the opportunity to personally commune with each of her canaries and hear the subtleties in each's voice. The man with the setter will hold court for hours on his dog's merits, all the while eating it up as you stroke its ears. And the gal in the gold lamé pantsuit will wind up with a law suit for sure the way she lets everyone pet her ocelot.

Whatever your choice will be—familiar or demon—the love and devotion engendered by it will carry you through many a magical predicament. And don't think that the cat is the *only* animal that can supply such power. I've had cats all my life—both big and little—and I love them dearly; but I've also had dogs, snakes, iguanas, crocodiles, rabbits, a capybara and a tarantula named Bruno, who died of old age, and they gave me more than I can ever repay.

9. Public Relations for Witches

As a practicing witch, you must decide whether to make it known or to work your wonders while people think of you as a woman but not a witch. There are advantages and disadvantages to each approach.

The disadvantages are thus: If you call yourself a witch, then your moves will be suspect and your motivations will be analyzed. You will let yourself in for a lot more side activity, such as telling fortunes, making predictions, giving advice to friends and being invited to parties to sing for your supper. You will be asked by local reporters and columnists for interviews, once it is discovered there is a "real" witch in town.

If you choose to keep your witch-power secret, you will lose some of the ego gratification that is gained in making your occult pursuits known to others. You will have to swallow your assertiveness when you are forced to listen to other and perhaps much less magically endowed gals boast of their witchiness. You will often be condemned as simply a "bitch," rather than a witch for your actions. Were you to be known as a witch, any violation of taboos could be more readily expected and therefore accepted.

If one is to consider the advantages of each approach to witchery, the self-proclaimed witch has the opportunity to bask in the light of an immensely popular topic. She will be the center of attention wherever she goes, and her ego will be well fed. She will find many men approaching her as some sort of sexually promiscuous bawd who is possessed of the Devil, so if sex is what she is after, she'll have every opportunity thrust at her. If she likes to talk, this is her best approach, for she will be expected to give a lecture on the Black Arts wherever she goes. Unless you are a good talker, this may not be your best bet. If you are the quiet type, it is still possible to advertise the fact that you're a witch, but your actions will have to speak louder than your words. The most bungling and incompetent witches are those with the biggest speaking tubes, and like it or not, you'll often have to temporarily play second fiddle to them. Don't worry about them presenting any threat to your schemes or plans, though, as they usually burn themselves out after their knowledge of occultism is exhausted, leaving them with little or no knowledge of the very real world around them.

If you are asked, as a self-proclaimed witch, to give an interview to a reporter or journalist, make damn sure he is for real. There are more people doing "research" on witchcraft now than you would imagine, but then just hang out your shingle and you'll find out fast. The majority of people who will want to interview you are only using it as an excuse for their own prurient interests and seldom will an interview given to one of these types ever appear in print. If you are certain that the reporter who is interviewing you is legitimate, tell him what he wants to know, providing it does not violate any secrets you would be better off keeping to yourself.

Whatever you do, don't pull the old ploy of acting noncommunicative with the explanation that witches don't want any publicity or that you can't give an interview because all witches want to be left alone or any other of the nauseous hypocrisies spouted by so many "public" witches. If you don't want publicity, don't tell people you're a witch. In case you don't realize it, the witch has become a minor celebrity and you must expect to be approached by the curious if you have proclaimed your witchhood.

It is assumed by most self-proclaimed witches that it is all right to talk up one's occult ability at a cocktail party or neighborhood gathering but where perhaps thousands of people will know about it—*never!* The reasons for this phenomenon are all too obvious to a psychologist or sociologist. The neighborhood witch can feel security in her own little world, knowing all the answers she must and keeping her Black Arts confined to her peer group, where she can come forth or retreat as she so pleases. Once she has stuck her neck out and been recognized as a witch by multitudes of people, she is suddenly on stage and knows she'd better give a good performance or her name will be mud.

The hostility of many "underground" witches to "public" witches, like Sybil Leek, Louise Huebner, et al, is not based on differences of occult opinion so much as resentment that the public witches are doing what they (the underground witches) would like to do, had they the opportunity. With the cocktail party witch, fear of failure plays a large part in the reluctance to become famous. Witches who loudly proclaim their prowess to all within earshot, yet become very reticent to talk when an interviewer is trying to get material for a story, are much like the regular customer in the bar who sings, and badly, the same two or three songs nightly, much to the sorrow of the bartender, customers and especially the piano player, whose noxious task is to accompany the "great voice."

If one night a grandiose announcement was made about the treat that was in store for the customers, a build-up of the "singer's" vocal achievements was given, a spotlight played upon him where he sat, a microphone placed before him and a nice round of applause made, the singer would probably disappear and never been seen again. If you ever want an incompetent person to stop doing something, just put him on stage.

Another giveaway of the incompetent witch that is common only to those who make known their art is the "I can't do it for money" routine. You will find many of the would-be witches who nobly proclaim their disdain for worldly compensation for their services are like the person who can perform well as long as he's not getting paid for it, but when offered the opportunity to do the same thing for pay, will refuse. The reason for this type of behavior is that the person who is not charging for a service places the other person in a beholden position, thereby allowing the giver to call the shots. The receiver *must* be nice to the giver and not expect too much.

If you are about to tell someone's fortune and precede your reading with the information that you cannot charge money for your services, as your "gift" would then be made commercial, you need not worry about goofing up, as whatever you say will be a favor. It is always more difficult to succeed in business, thereby making a profit, than it is to give things away. Certainly, this doesn't mean that you must charge for your services as a witch, but if you do, it will at least be assumed that your abilities are greater.

The only reason I mention all this is because the admitted

witch will be confronted by people who seek out her help for problems of all kinds. If you agree to assist those who seek your aid, you won't have time for your own enchantments. The greatest advantage in being an unknown witch is the opportunity to perform for yourself, without psychic drainage from others who expect you to work on their behalf. The above-ground witch is plagued by such requests. If she acts the least bit charitable, she will be vampirized by everyone she knows, to work charms for them. If she decides to capitalize on her new-found talents, figuring she'll earn a little extra money for goodies, and charges a small fee, she will be expected to produce a two-dollar miracle, complete with money back guarantee!

The best way to handle these pitfalls if you are known to others as a witch is, first and foremost, *don't perform magic for others!* Instruct or teach them, if you must, but unless you can really feel sympathy and compassion for the other person, don't undertake a magical ritual on their behalf! Ninety percent of the success of any magical ceremony is based on the genuine desire and emotion of the practitioner, and if your friend can work up enough of it for what she wants, let her learn to work her own magic. If she can't get worked up enough over that which she would like you to obtain for her, she has no business having it in the first place!

Tell your friends' fortunes, make predictions by the dozen and be known as the girl who knows the real secrets, but don't be drained of your vital magical energy by someone who is too lazy to learn to do it herself. If anyone tells you they can't practice witchcraft, because it is incompatible with their religion, yet wants you to use the "Devil's" power to help them, tell them to pray to their god, whoever he may be, but not to expect to reject Satan with one hand yet expect a big handout from him in the other! These hypocrites are usually the type that wouldn't make good Christians, because they have no faith in prayer, nor would the Devil want them because they refuse to commit themselves.

If you pride yourself on being a compleat witch and don't care who knows it—*bravo!* You'll undoubtedly be asked to elucidate on your witchery, by those who are genuinely interested. If you are legitimately approached and asked for a statement that may appear on the air or in print, be gracious and give whatever kind of interview the sincerity of the reporter commands. If he is a boor, treat him to a large serving of misinformation, so far fetched that it will be apparent to anyone with intelligence that you are putting him on. If your interviewer is objective and sincere in his approach, treat him the same way— graciously, that is—avoiding any of the aforementioned sanctimony about "we witches don't want publicity." If you are antagonistic to publicity, don't ever place yourself in a publicity-oriented situation where you have to say so. We see altogether too many of these "publicity shy" types being interviewed, and it is safe to assume that no one had to bind and gag them to get them to the TV studio or hold a gun at their head to get them to open the door for the reporter.

You must expect to run into scoffers. If they're worth bothering with, just size them up according to their position on the synthesizer, use a little of the Law of the Forbidden, flatter them a bit, and you'll have them eating out of your hand. People often scoff because they don't understand. If they scoff and know nothing about what constitutes magic and witchcraft, you *know* it's because they don't understand. Those that understand a subject and still scoff may have something worthwhile to say, but he who is ignorant of the subject and scoffs is like the rustic who saw

the giraffe and said "There ain't no such animal." Scoffers
are always the easiest to bewitch, just as they are the
easiest marks on the carnival lot, once you learn how to
handle them. Just remember the line in *Dracula*, where
Professor Van Helsing says: "The power of the vampire
lies in that no one believes in him."

How to Break the News

How do you break the news to your family, friends and
associates that you are a witch? Start out kidding. Very
few people will get angry if they think you're not serious,
unless they're right out of the Middle Ages in their thinking and be warned there are still some around. The majority, however, will accept you as a witch, so long as you
keep light-hearted about it. It will be easy enough to spot
those who *want* to take you more seriously and subsequently admit your sincerity to them.

You won't run into any static from men, as a rule, but
women must be handled carefully, especially mothers and
mothers-in-law. Just because I said earlier in the book that
a potentially compleat witch usually has difficulty getting
along with women, I didn't mean that she shouldn't *be able*
to get on well with women should it be necessary. If you
can charm another woman, you can charm her man and
at times that may be necessary.

If you happen to be thrown into a situation whereby
another woman's husband indicates that he is strongly
attracted to you, and you *want* to keep them both as
friends, a degree of tact is necessary. This is all too common an occurrence, which can develop into a decidedly
sticky mess. There are definitely times when it pays *not*
to try and charm another woman's husband, especially

in what purports to be an extremely rewarding friendship between couples.

It would be unfair to you to have to stifle your charms in order to keep things harmonious, yet any display of seductiveness on your part can give the most platonic relationship a hint of more carnal pursuits.

Many married persons will actually do all they can to encourage an illicit relationship for their spouse, who thinking themselves dutiful, unknowingly avoid any such encounters their mates might set up. I wish I had a dollar for each time I've encountered such a situation.

The husband who finds the idea of his wife dallying with other men stimulating is far more common than would ever be thought. This phenomenon occurs with the greatest frequency in marriages of ten years or over. Consider this, when your husband leaves you "wide open" for seduction: it doesn't mean he doesn't love you anymore, but that he is vicariously acting out his Demonic in *your* body!

Before you consider how *not* to charm another woman's husband, first consider, if you are married, whether *your* husband consciously or otherwise really *wants* you to charm the other guy. Don't readily expect an honest answer, though, should you come out flat-footed and ask hubby. Few men want to admit to such planned cuckoldry, should they be so inclined. There are those who become swingers, not really getting much out of their affairs with other women, simply as an excuse and encouragement for their wives to consort with other men, which produces for them much more erotic gratification than their own liaisons. If you have such a husband, remember: he is placing his Demonic in your body, and therefore assumes your sexual response to be as surface as his own. When you make it with another man, don't make the hearts-and-flowers scene, as well, but limit it to how he wants to see you—a sex-crazy spouse with hot pants. If he demands to hear the gory details, as so many do, tell him exactly what he would like to hear, knowing his predilections, fetishes, etc., as you do. *Don't* let him think you are in love with anyone other than him, though, nor indicate that you cannot cool off, once your cravings are spent.

If you see that it is imperative to keep another woman's husband at bay, the best thing to do, rather than stifle your witchiness, is to spend more time ingratiating yourself with the wife and less with the husband. Get her so convinced that you couldn't care less about her husband, that she will almost feel sad that she is married to such an unattractive creep. If you do this well enough—praising her husband for all of his fine qualities, yet making it obvious that he is sexually unappetizing—you'll find *she* will be the one whose Demonic will be hurt at your rejection of her hubby. Then, as hubby champs at the bit over you, she'll find herself almost encouraging you to turn on the charm in a way that will surprise you. It will be as though she wants assurance that her husband can attract you, by making it appear as though you are playing up to her husband. No woman likes to think that no one else wants her husband, but her pride insists that she calls the shots insofar as when, how and where.

The formula, therefore, is to concentrate on befriending the wife, acknowledging the husband's many non-sexual attributes, act as though you aren't the least bit interested in anything other than a platonic relationship, and you'll soon have the most possessive wife practically throwing her husband at you! The issue is not: How *not* to charm another woman's husband, but: How to charm another woman's husband and make *her* love every minute of it!

The truly successful witch is the gal who you've heard discussed by other women, who say good-naturedly, (and right in front of their embarrassed husbands) "You ought to meet her, what a doll, and what Frank here wouldn't do to have a fling with *her!*"

The best witches are those who have had to go through their lives getting along with women, and then, having learned well that lesson, start learning the tricks in this book. The witch who can charm men well, but falls to pieces if called to task in a group of women, cannot call herself a compleat witch! For most of you charming women should be duck soup. You've probably been concentrating on it all your lives without knowing it. If the occasion arises where you must ingratiate yourself with another of your own sex, just see to it that you present *no* apparent competition, sweep the Law of the Forbidden temporarily under the carpet and get out your most sexless clothes. You can't lose—unless she's a lesbian or a guy in drag.

Breaking the news to your children is easy, without the need to be dishonest. Small children are always fascinated with the strange, fantastic and magical, and to have a mommie who is the personification of all that is indeed a wonderful thing. Young children do not have to be taught to accept the magic in life. They know it exists. They are already witches and warlocks. You will just be rejoining them.

When the rain is softly beating on the windows you can tell them of your craft, embellishing the starkness of manipulation with the faerie lore that will never die, and they will be your guides as you soar forth upon the night-wind.

What of those who read these words and take these secrets with them. What if all the carnal world should reel with compleat witches plying their art. Who, then, would be their quarry? Fear not. You cannot battle nature and win, though it would appear transitionally to be so. Even the men who read this book and think they know all the tricks will still tumble as they always have.

You can't erase millions of years of human response, simply by knowing why you do the things you do. Not if they concern the Rules of the Chase. Religions and ideologies will come and go, and the Games will begin and end, but man's basic nature will remain the same. Yet only through understanding himself will he be able to embrace and cherish the demon within him. Then he can revel in his nature and feeling glad, move on to the Final Solution.

Answers: 1. yes; 2. invalid; 3. yes; 4. no; 5. invalid; 6. yes; 7. yes; 8. yes; 9. no; 10. yes; 11. invalid; 12. yes; 13. invalid; 14. yes; 15. no; 16. yes; 17. invalid; 18. no; 19. invalid; 20. invalid.

Select Bibliography

Anonymous, *Chorus Queens, Or The Private Lives of Broadway Hotcha Chorus Girls*. Detroit: Johnson Smith & Co., 1937.

Anonymous, *The Confessions of a Taxi-Dancer*. Detroit: Johnson Smith & Co., 1938.

Anonymous, edited by Robert Kramer, *The Horn Book*. North Hollywood: Brandon House, 1967.

Arthur, Gavin, *The Circle of Sex*. San Francisco: Pan Graphic Press, 1962.

Baines, Anthony, *Musical Instruments Through the Ages*. Baltimore, Md.: Penguin Books, Inc., 1961.

Barker, J. C., *Scared to Death*. New York: Dell Publishing Co., Inc., 1969.

Bauer, W. W., *Potions, Remedies and Old Wives Tales*. New York: Doubleday & Co., Inc., 1969.

Becker, Stephen, *Comic Art in America*. New York: Simon & Schuster, 1959.

Bedichek, Roy, *The Sense of Smell*. New York: Doubleday & Co., Inc., 1960.

Berman, Louis, *New Creations in Human Beings*. New York: Doubleday, Doran & Co., Inc., 1938.

Bessy, Maurice, *Pictorial History of Magic and the Supernatural*. London: Spring Books, 1964.

Birnbaum, Henri, *Love and Love's Philosophy*. New York: Pageant Press, Inc., 1955.

Birren, Faber, *Color: A Survey in Words and Pictures*. New York: University Books, Inc., 1963.

————, *Color in Your World*. New York: Crowell-Collier Publishing Co., 1962.

————, *Color Psychology and Color Therapy*. New York: University Books, Inc., 1950-1961.

Blackford, Katherine M. H., *Reading Character at Sight*. New York: Independent Corporation, 1918.

Bloch, Iwan, *Odoratus Sexualis*. North Hollywood: Brandon House, 1967.

————, *The Sexual Life of Our Time*. New York: Allied Book Co., 1926.

Bodin, Walter and Hershey, Burnet, *It's a Small World*. New York: Coward-McCann, Inc., 1934.

Boss, Medard, *The Analysis of Dreams*. London, Rider, 1957.

Bourke, John G., *Scatalogic Rites of All Nations*. Washington, D.C.: W. H. Lowdermilk & Co., 1891.

Brick, Hans, *The Nature of the Beast*. New York: Crown Publishers, Inc., 1960.

Budge, E. A. Wallis, *Amulets and Talismans*. New York: University Books, 1961.

Bulliet, C. J., *Venus Castina*. New York: Bonanza Books, 1928 and 1956.

Bunker, M. N., *Handwriting Analysis: The Art and Science of Reading Character by Grapho Analysis*. Chicago: Nelson-Hall Company, Publishers, 1959.

Byfield, Barbara Ninde, *The Glass Harmonica*. New York: Macmillan Co., 1967.

Cameron, Ian and Elisabeth, *Dames*. New York: Frederick A. Praeger, Inc., 1969.

Carrington, Hereward, *The Physical Phenomena of Spiritualism*. New York: Dodd, Mead & Co., 1920.

Carson, Gerald, *One for a Man, Two for a Horse*. New York: Doubleday & Co., Inc., 1961.

Cauldwell, David O., *Transvestism—Men in Female Dress*. New York: Sexology Corp., 1956.

Cavendish, Richard, *The Black Arts*. New York: Capricorn Books, 1968.

Clarens, Carlos, *An Illustrated History of the Horror Film*. New York: G. P. Putnam's Sons, 1967.

Cohen, Daniel, *Myths of the Space Age*. New York: Dodd, Mead & Co., 1965.

Collyer, Martin, *Burlesque*. New York: Lancer Books, Inc., 1964.

Corinda, *Thirteen Steps to Mentalism*. New York: Louis Tannen, 1968.

Crow, W. B., A History of Magic, Witchcraft and Occultism. North Hollywood: Wilshire Book Co., 1970.

Dannett, Sylvia G. L. and Rachel, Frank R., Down Memory Lane. New York: Greenberg Publisher, 1954.

Darwin, Charles, The Expressions of the Emotions in Man and in Animals. London: Murray, 1873.

Davenport, John, Aphrodisiacs and Love Stimulants. London: Luxor Press, 1965.

de Leeuw, Hendrik, Women—the Dominant Sex. New York: Thomas Yoseloff, 1957.

Deren, Maya, Divine Horsemen: The Voodoo Gods of Haiti. New York: Chelsea House Publishers, 1970.

Deutsch, Helene, The Psychology of Women. New York: Grune & Stratton, 1944.

Dingwall, Eric John, The American Woman—A Historical Study. New York: Rinehart & Co., Inc., 1956.

Durant, John and Alice, A Pictorial History of the American Circus. New York: A. S. Barnes & Co., 1957.

Efron, David, Gesture and Environment. London: King's Crown Press, 1941.

Eisler, Robert, Man into Wolf. London: Routledge & Kegan Paul Ltd., 1951.

Ellis, Albert, The Folklore of Sex. New York: Charles Boni, 1951.

Ellis, Havelock, Psychology of Sex. New York: Emerson Books, Inc., 1946.

Ellis, Julie, Revolt of the Second Sex. New York: Lancer Books, Inc., 1970.

Elworthy, Frederick Thomas, The Evil Eye. New York: The Julian Press, Inc., Publishers, 1958.

Evans, Bergen, The Natural History of Nonsense. New York: Alfred A. Knopf, Inc., 1946.

Feldman, Sandor S., Mannerisms of Speech and Gestures in Everyday Life. New York: International Universities Press, 1959.

Fe're, Charles Samson, The Sexual Urge—How it Grows or Wanes. New York: Falstaff Press, Inc., 1932.

Ferenczi, Sandor, Further Contributions to the Theory and Technique of Psycho-Analysis. London: Hogarth Press, 1926.

———, Sex in Psycho-Analysis. New York: Dover, 1956.

Fielding, William J., Strange Superstitions and Magical Practices. Philadelphia: The Blakiston Company, 1945.

Fiske, John, Myths and Myth-Makers. Boston and New York: Houghton, Mifflin & Co., 1897.

Flugel, J. C., The Psychology of Clothes. New York: International Universities Press, Inc., 1969.

Freud, Sigmund, *A General Introduction to Psychoanalysis*. New York: Liveright Publishing Co., 1935.

Fosbroke, Gerald Elton, *Character Reading through Analysis of the Features*. New York: G. P. Putnam's Sons, 1933.

Garland, Madge, *The Changing Face of Beauty*. New York: M. Barrows & Co., Inc., 1957.

Gibson, Walter B. and Litzka, R., *The Complete Illustrated Book of the Psychic Sciences*. New York: Doubleday & Co., Inc., 1966.

Gifford, Edward S., Jr., *The Charms of Love*. New York: Doubleday & Co., Inc., 1962.

———, *The Evil Eye*. New York: Macmillan Co., 1958.

Gindes, Bernard C., *New Concepts of Hypnosis*. New York: The Julian Press, Inc., 1951.

Goffman, Erving, *Behavior in Public Places*. New York: The Free Press, 1963.

———, *Interaction Ritual*. New York: Anchor Books-Doubleday & Co., Inc., 1967.

———, *Stigma*. Englewood Cliffs, N.J.: Prentice-Hall, Inc., 1963.

Gould, George M. and Pyle, Walter L., *Anomalies and Curiosities of Medicine*. New York: The Julian Press, Inc., 1956.

Gowland, Peter, *How to Photograph Women*. New York: Crown Publishers, Inc., 1953.

Gray, Frank, *Scoremanship*. New York: Bantam Books, Inc., 1969.

Gresham, William Lindsay, *Monster Midway*. New York: Rinehart & Co., Inc., 1948.

Grollman, Arthur, *Essentials of Endocrinology*. Philadelphia: J. B. Lippincott Co., 1941.

Habenstein, Robert W. and Lamers, William M., *Funeral Customs the World Over*. Milwaukee, Bulfin Printers, Inc., 1960.

Hadfield, J. A., *Dreams and Nightmares*. Baltimore: Penguin Books, Inc., 1954.

Hall, Edward T., *The Silent Language*. New York: Doubleday & Company, Inc., 1959.

Hall, Edward T., *The Hidden Dimension*. New York: Doubleday & Co., Inc., 1966.

Herman, Lewis and Marguerite Shalett, *Foreign Dialects*. New York: Theatre Arts Book, 1943.

Holder, Robert, *You Can Analyze Handwriting*. Englewood Cliffs, N.J.: Prentice-Hall, Inc., 1958.

Hoskins, R. G., *Endocrinology—The Glands and their Functions*. New York: W. W. Norton & Co., Inc., 1941.

Hunt, Morton M., *The Natural History of Love*. New York: Alfred A. Knopf, 1959.

Keats, John, *The Insolent Chariots*. Philadelphia: J. B. Lippincott
   Company, 1958.
Klapp, Orrin E., *Collective Search for Identity*. New York: Holt,
   Rinehart & Winston, Inc., 1969.
――――, *Heroes, Villains and Fools*. Englewood Cliffs, N.J.:
   Prentice-Hall, Inc., 1962.
――――, *Symbolic Leaders*. Chicago: Aldine Publishing Company,
   1964.
Köhler, Carl, *A History of Costume*. New York: Dover Publications,
   Inc., 1963.
Kretschmer, E., *Physique and Character*. New York: Harcourt,
   Brace & Co., 1925.
Lariar, Lawrence, *Cartooning for Everybody*. New York: Crown
   Publishers, 1941.
Laurent, Emile and Nagour, Paul, *Magica Sexualis*. North Holly-
   wood: Brandon House, 1966.
La Vey, Anton Szandor, *The Satanic Bible*. New York: Avon Books,
   1969.
Legman, Gershon, *The Horn Book*. New York: University Books,
   1964.
Leigh, Michael, *The Velvet Underground*. New York: ·Macfadden-
   Bartell Corp., 1963.
Lofland, John, *Deviance and Identity*. Englewood Cliffs, N.J.:
   Prentice-Hall, Inc., 1969.
London, Perry, *Behavior Control*. New York: Harper & Row, Pub-
   lishers, Inc., 1969.
Luckiesh, M., *Visual Illusions—Their Cause, Characteristics and
   Applications*. New York: Dover Publications, Inc., 1965.
Mangels, William F., *The Outdoor Amusement Industry*. New York:
   Vantage Press, Inc., 1952.
Mannix, Dan, *Step Right Up!* New York: Harper & Brothers, Pub-
   lishers, 1950.
Maslow, Abraham H., *Motivation and Personality*. New York:
   Harper & Row, Publishers, Inc., 1954.
Masters, R. E. L., *Eros and Evil*. New York: Matrix House Pub-
   lishers, 1966.
McCullough, Edo, *Good Old Coney Island*. New York: Charles
   Scribner's Sons, 1957.
McGrady, Patrick M., Jr., *The Youth Doctors*. New York: Ace Pub-
   lishing Corp., 1969.
McLuhan, Herbert Marshall, *The Mechanical Bride*. New York:
   The Vanguard Press, Inc., 1951.
Meerloo, Joost A., *The Dance*. Philadelphia: Chilton Company,
   1960.

Milner, Michael, *Sex on Celluloid*. New York: Macfadden-Bartell Corp., 1964.

Möbius, Felix, *Zauberei Geräuschen*. Leipzig: Koehler, 1936.

Morris, Desmond, *The Naked Ape*. New York: McGraw-Hill Book Co., 1967.

Mortensen, William, *The Command to Look*. San Francisco: Camera Craft Publishing Co., 1937.

Nelms, Henning, *Magic and Showmanship*. New York: Dover Publications, Inc., 1969.

Němĕcek, Otto Kar, *Virginity, Pre-Nuptial Rites and Rituals*. New York: Philosophical Library, 1958.

Nierenburg, Gerald I., *The Art of Negotiating*. New York: Hawthorn Books, Inc., 1968.

Ostow, Mortimer and Scharfstein, Ben-Ami, *The Need to Believe*. New York: International Universities Press, Inc., 1954.

Packard, Vance, *The Hidden Persuaders*. New York: David McKay Company, Inc., 1957.

Pauwels, Louis and Bergier, Jacques, *The Morning of the Magicians*. New York: Stein & Day, 1964.

Pilat, Oliver and Ranson, Jo, *Sodom by the Sea*. Garden City, N.Y.: Garden City Publishing Co., Inc., 1943.

Podolski, Edward, *Music Therapy*. New York: Philosophical Library, 1954.

Poinsot, M. C., *The Encyclopedia of Occult Sciences*. New York: Robert McBride & Company, 1939.

Priestly, J. B., *Man and Time*. New York: Crescent Books, 1964.

Quinsel, Reinhart, *Sexual Exhibitionism*. New York: Award Books, 1968.

Rawcliffe, D. H., *The Psychology of the Occult*. London: Derricke Ridgway Publishing Co. Ltd., 1952.

Reich, Wilhelm, *Character Analysis*. New York: Orgone Institute Press, 1949.

————, *The Function of the Orgasm*. New York: Orgone Institute Press, 1942.

Rhodes, H. T. F., *The Satanic Mass*. New York: Citadel Press, 1955.

Riordan, Judson, *Peeping Tom*. New York: Venice Publishing Corp., 1967.

Robbins, Rossell Hope, *The Encyclopedia of Witchcraft and Demonology*. New York: Crown Publishers, Inc., 1963.

Rogers, Agnes, *Women are Here to Stay*. New York: Harper & Brothers, Publishers, 1949.

Rogers, J. A., *Sex and Race (Vol. I and II)*. New York: J. A. Rogers Publications, Vol. I: 1940, Vol. II: 1942.

Rose, Elliot, *A Razor for a Goat*. Canada: University of Toronto Press, 1962.

Rosenteur, Phyllis I., *Morpheus and Me*. New York: Funk & Wagnalls Company, 1957.

Rubington, Earl and Weinberg, Martin S., *Deviance—the Interactionist Perspective*. New York: Macmillan Co., 1968.

Rule, Lareina, *Name your Baby*. New York: Bantam Books, 1963.

Sagarin, Edward, *The Anatomy of Dirty Words*. New York: Lyle Stuart, Publisher, 1962.

———, *The Science and Art of Perfumery*. New York: McGraw-Hill Book Co., 1945.

Samstag, Nicholas, *The Uses of Ineptitude or How not to want to do Better*. New York: Ivan Obolensky, Inc., 1962.

Scheimann, Eugene & Neimark, Paul, *Sex and the Overweight Woman*. New York: Signet Books-The New American Library, Inc., 1970.

Seabrook, William, *Witchcraft, Its Power in the World Today*. New York: Harcourt, Brace & Co., 1940.

Sheldon, W. H., *Atlas of Men*. New York: Harper & Brothers, Publishers, 1954.

———, *The Varieties of Human Physique*. New York: Harper & Brothers, Publishers, 1940.

———, *The Varieties of Temperament*. New York: Harper & Brothers, Publishers, 1942.

Sigaud, C., *La Forme Humaine*. Paris: A. Maloine, 1914.

Sobel, Bernard, *A Pictorial History of Burlesque*. New York: Bonanza Books, 1956.

Sprenger, Jakob and Kramer, Heinrich, translated by Montague Summers, *Malleus Maleficarum*. London: The Pushkin Press, 1948.

Stanislavski, Constantin, translated by Elizabeth Reynolds Hapgood, *An Actor Prepares*. New York: Theatre Arts, Inc., 1936.

Steinach, Eugen, *Sex and Life*. New York: The Viking Press, 1940.

Stekel, Wilhelm, *Bi-Sexual Love*. New York: Emerson Books, Inc., 1945.

———, *The Interpretation of Dreams*. New York: Liveright Publishing Corp., 1943.

———, *Patterns of Psychosexual Infantilism*. New York: Liveright Publishing Corp., 1952.

Szasz, Kathleen, *Petishism—Pets and their People in the Western World*. New York: Holt, Rinehart & Winston, Inc., 1968.

Tabori, Paul, *The Art of Folly*. New York: Chilton Company, 1961.

———, *The Book of the Hand*. New York: Chilton Company, 1962.

————, *The Natural Science of Stupidity*. New York: Chilton Company, 1959.

The'tard, Henry, *La Merveilleuse Histoire Du Cirque*. Paris: S. Guida-Prisma, 1947.

Thigpen, Corbett H., *The Three Faces of Eve*. New York: McGraw-Hill Book Co., 1957.

Thompson, C. J. S., *The Mystery and Lore of Monsters*. New York: The Macmillan Company, 1931.

Thouless, Robert H., *Straight and Crooked Thinking*. London: Hodder & Stoughton, Ltd., 1930.

Tridon, Andre, *Psychoanalysis and Love*. New York: Permabooks, 1949.

Truzzi, Marcello, *Caldron Cookery*. New York: Meredith Press, 1969.

————, *Sociology and Everyday Life*. Englewood Cliffs, N.J.: Prentice-Hall, Inc., 1968.

Turner, E. S., *A History of Courting*. New York: E. P. Dutton & Co., Inc., 1954.

Vernon, Jack, *Inside the Black Room*. New York: Clarkson N. Potter, Inc., 1963.

Volta, Ornella, *The Vampire*. London: Tandem Books Ltd., 1965.

Wagner, Geoffrey, *Parade of Pleasure*. London: Derek Verschoyle, 1954.

Wall, O. A., *Sex and Sex Worship (Phallic Worship)*. St. Louis: C. V. Mosby Co., 1922.

Walton, Alan Hull, *Aphrodisiacs—from Legend to Prescription*. New York: Associated Booksellers, 1958.

Waterman, Philip F., *The Story of Superstition*. New York: Alfred A. Knopf, 1929.

Wedeck, Harry E., *Dictionary of Aphrodisiacs*. New York: Philosophical Library, 1961.

————, *Treasury of Witchcraft*. New York: Philosophical Library, 1961.

Weidenreich, F., *Rasse und Körperbau*. Berlin: Springer, 1926.

Winick, Charles, *The New People*. New York: Pegasus, 1968.

Wright, Lawrence, *Clean and Decent*. Canada: University of Toronto Press, 1967.

X, Dr. Jacobus, *Untrodden Fields of Anthropology*. New York: American Anthropological Society. Privately Re-issued.

AFTERWORD

By Blanche Barton

One might wonder what manner of man would write a book like *The Satanic Witch*. Only the founder of the Church of Satan could take such delight in identifying human manipulation games, and amplifying them hundred-fold. Another man, upon discovering how devious and naughty certain women can be, might be resentful. Not Anton LaVey. He recognized from a young age why women have always been regarded with suspicion in the Christian church (sometimes expressed in mass burnings), and that they've always had a much more appreciative ally in the Devil. As LaVey writes in his prologue, *The Satanic Witch* should not be dismissed as a "treatise on man-catching." The High Priest devised a system of sorcery that emphasizes equally "Lesser Magic" (basic psychology, glamour, non-ritual manipulative magic) and "Greater Magic" (ritual, ceremonial magic). Both types of magic depend on the manipulation of the intellect and the emotions using various means to create a desired effect. While LaVey's *Satanic Rituals* deals almost exclusively with Greater Magic, *The Satanic Witch* is THE workbook for Lesser Magic, for both sexes. Many of the principles LaVey developed as basic to his Satanic philosophy are contained in this book. When you know what the roots of his blasphemy were, you see how inevitable it was that Anton LaVey write *The Satanic Witch*, along with his founding book, The Satanic Bible.

Since Anton Szandor LaVey was born on April 11th, 1930, his "E.C.I." (as he calls it) was the War Years—when men were men and women were desperate. With so many boyfriends and husbands away fighting the Axis of Evil, women yearned for masculine attention. Since most of them were "good" girls, they resorted to sly techniques of subtle (or not so subtle) exposure in order to fulfill their erotic needs. The music and fashions of that period remained the most sexually evocative for Anton throughout his life. A couple of years after the war, LaVey ran away to join the circus. Though he signed on with Clyde Beatty Circus mid-season as a roustabout and cage boy, he was already an accomplished musician. His talents weren't overlooked. When the regular calliope player showed up drunk for his performance one too many times, LaVey volunteered to step in. His performance delighted the crowd and he stayed through the end of the season. During that time, along with training lions and tigers, he learned about the use of music, lighting and costuming to dazzle and manipulate an audience.

But Anton's education in the uses of female pulchritude really began when the season was over and he got off-season work on several carnival lots. There were the girlie shows (traveling strip shows), the sex shows (disguised as educational hygiene lectures, warning against the dangers of V.D.), and there were the corn-fed lovelies who sashayed around the midway dressed in their Sunday best, giddy and blushing from the contact with show folk. The carnival was still a much-anticipated event in some parts of America; many girls in the rural towns LaVey passed through dreamed of being movie stars. Dancing in the girlie shows seemed glamorous and reckless, and the midway impresarios wooed them with spotlight promises. The girls would sign on, then give up by the time they reached the next town.

Anton really enjoyed working the Mitt Camp—the area of the carnival where the fortune-tellers and gifted psychics, hypnotists and magicians plied their trade. It was here that he was initiated into the still-secret techniques of "cold reading"—sizing up a customer in order to tell him exactly what he wants to hear. The Romany trade had been refining these subtle perceptions for generations, passing on cues of smell, body language, face reading and acute listening in order to divine people's deepest fears and desires, and then "see" it in the cards or palms. Evaluating the individual's facial structure and body type, the seer could tell what kind of future the customer really wanted to know about, and could feed back appropriately. When he eventually sat down to write this book, much of that occult knowledge LaVey had learned on the carnival backlots found its way into these pages.

The next course Destiny planned in Anton LaVey's Satanic education was in the burlesque houses of Los Angeles. By the time the carnival season ended in the fall, LaVey had earned a reputation as a flamboyant character and a reliable musician—always a rare and successful combination. Claiming he was 25, he found work at the popular Mayan Burlesque Theater, the Burbank, and at Zucca's in Culver City. While he watched reactions to the bumps and grinds onstage, he also saw how much attention the more demurely-dressed girls perched on the barstools got in that sexually charged atmosphere if they "accidentally" showed too much leg above their hemlines. Once in a while one of the female customers would be overcome by exhibitionism and jump onstage, starting her own show. That's when the men would sit up and take notice. She was embarrassed, flushed, drunk, but compelled beyond her will (apparently). The poor dear. She was usually "helped" home by her husband or boyfriend. One can only imagine the measures that had to be taken to calm her down once they got home (or down the alley). It was when he was working at the Mayan that Anton had a brief affair with Marilyn Monroe, who blended elements of vulnerability and sexuality to her benefit.

In September, 1949, Anton LaVey enrolled in San Francisco City College as a criminology major. Since childhood, LaVey had been drawn to horror novels, to the occult, aberrant psychology, to the abnormalities of mind, body and spirit. Criminology seemed an obvious expression of those interests. During his studies at City College, he came across a concept of criminal profiling that was developed by Cesare Lombroso in the late 1800s. Though discredited now, Lombroso claimed he had identified certain facial features that could denote a specific criminal type. He collected hundreds of early photographs of criminals, correlating facial elements to the crimes he or she had committed. This intriguing theory led LaVey to the works of W.H. Sheldon and E. Kretschmer (cited in *The Satanic Witch* bibliography) who also had written books linking physique and character traits. This merged neatly with the skills he had already learned in the carny Mitt Camp, and what he was discovering on his own through his keen observation.

While he was taking classes, Anton was earning money as a musician in burlesque houses and night spots around the Bay Area, and he expanded his résumé to include photography. From boyhood, Anton had been interested in how emotions are influenced by visual elements in art and architecture, and he'd been drawing sexy girls since he could hold a pencil. Photography was an easy way to play with angles and shadows, and document interesting architecture he came across. LaVey was already taking Weegee-like human interest shots of people at the beach and around the city. Through contacts in the burlesque theaters, he got a job taking strip photos of girls which were then bundled into small packets of six or seven pocket-sized black-and-whites and sold as stag show novelties. The photos weren't of strippers, but snaps of respectable-looking women fully clothed, in the mountains or in their apartments or at the beach, who, through the series of photos, would be shown taking off their blouses and skirts and finally posed nearly nude.

Again, the compulsion toward prurience was becoming more and more obvious to LaVey. A formula took shape in his mind which he eventually refined into the "Law of the Forbidden." When the viewer is seeing something that is absolutely not supposed to be seen, it becomes daring, nasty and therefore irresistible. The law was further reinforced when LaVey started taking photographs for the San Francisco Police Department. He was faced with the worst of human tragedy on a daily basis, racing across town to take pictures of murder scenes, suicides, auto accidents, explosions—and there were always people gathered and staring, frozen at the sight of so much blood and so shocking a scene. Forbidden, and therefore irresistible.

LaVey's chums on the force who knew of his predisposition toward the strange began assigning him to the "800" cases—complaints of ghosts, UFO sightings, unearthly moans, possession—reports no one else wanted to handle because they were weird or spooky. Anton became one of the first psychic investigators in the country and soon had an enthusiastic clientele as a ghostbuster. He became qualified as a hypnotist, counseling people who wanted to lose weight, quit smoking or vanquish some embarrassing fetish. Eventually, clients began asking Anton's advice on how to make simple charms or cast spells for love, health or vengeance. Surely someone who knew so much about the spirit world would be able to help them get their boyfriends back, or eliminate a professional rival. And so he did.

By 1956, Anton LaVey had gathered quite an eclectic social group—some of his old croonies of his circus and carnival days, some of his music and police force connections, and a growing number of his new clients and fellow occult enthusiasts. His young wife Carole and three-year-old daughter, Karla (and black leopard, Zoltan) moved into an enchanting Victorian not far from the Golden Gate Bridge that better suited LaVey's character and purpose. They began giving elaborate costume parties, attracting wealthy San Francisco eccentrics and literary iconoclasts. Though LaVey was still playing theatre organ and pipe organ at various city functions and nightclubs, more and more of his energy was going toward researching the borderland sciences and the supernatural. After a few years (and a change of mates), LaVey began giving weekly lectures on cannibalism, vampires, torture implements and methods, freaks and monsters, sex theories and aphrodisiacs, ESP, werewolves, haunted houses and homunculi. Anton also developed "Witches' Workshops," which concentrated on the skills of applied magic, enchantment, love potions, fortune telling, pulling together for the first time the laws of attraction and the power of prurience that had evolved over the course of his life. Those workshops would eventually grow into this book... and the "Magic Circle" of misanthropes who gleefully gathered in LaVey's now infamous Black House would be the same ones who stood proudly beside him evoking the Dark Gods in 1966 when he founded the Church of Satan.

Not long after establishing himself as the Black Pope and garnering worldwide publicity with a Satanic wedding, Satanic funeral and a public Satanic baptism of his three-year-old daughter, Zeena, Anton LaVey was confronted with a woman who was a living embodiment of all the Satanic witchery he'd been teaching to his students for years. Jayne Mansfield was born to the game—she knew what assets she had, both her impressive physical blessings and her mental acuity, and used everything she had to achieve her goals. She felt Satanism was the first religion to accept her exactly as she was, and the blonde bombshell was one of Anton's most enthusiastic witches right up until the day she died. LaVey delighted in Jayne's shameless displays, and learned a few more tricks to add to the compleat witch's magical repertoire.

LaVey released *The Satanic* Witch (originally published as *The Compleat Witch, or What to do When Virtue Fails* in 1970) before he wrote *The Satanic Rituals* (which came out in 1972). Though the book didn't get widely reviewed in America, LaVey and his Church continued to command worldwide attention, and the Italian translation became a bestseller. There was a short-lived paperback version published, but, in the age of feminist repression, LaVey's tips for enchantment seemed outdated and subversive to women's hard-won "freedoms." "Wicca," the newly-invented Goddess religion, tried to re-create the witch as a benevolent, white-light wise woman who would have no contact with the Devil and even less with the trappings of sexual enticement found in LaVey's naughty book. Anton LaVey's textbook for Lesser Magic soon went out of print. It turns out he was simply twenty years ahead of his time. By 1984, with the menace of our new Black Plague, AIDS, looming over the horizon, non-contact sex became the sport of choice. Role-playing games, S&M, and voyeurism became more tempting than the actual sharing of body fluids.

When Feral House approached LaVey in 1988 with the prospect of reprinting a new edition of *The Compleat Witch*, Anton knew the timing was perfect. "Women are relearning the arts of flirtation and subtle exhibitionism," LaVey said. "We must revive glamour and little-boy nastiness whether feminists yell about women exploiting their bodies or not. Women can exploit their differences to gain more power. But they must be highly evolved women. Most women will continue being sheep and buy what they're programmed, emotionally and economically. Advanced, Satanically-oriented women can choose their own lifestyle rather than have it thrust upon them. They can enthusiastically participate in all kinds of exercises, rituals if you will, to break down the brainwashing feminism has done on contemporary young women. Sadomasochistic revelries, shape-changing deviltry, discipline games—women are looking for more of that sort of thing in their private lives because it's the ideal therapy. But again they must be extremely self-aware to be willing to initiate such Satanic debaucheries. If you're just one step up from the gutter, you're too afraid of going backward to participate in vile, degrading activities. But advanced women will insist on more fantasy, formality, metaphor, imagination and magic in their relationships."

Soon after *The Satanic Witch* re-emerged, women were rediscovering the film noir and B-movie fashions of LaVey's E.C.I. period; the music, martinis and bad-girl attitude came into full swing in hip retro-bars and hot spots around the world. He also saw his influence in the Goth culture which was yet another twist on the Satanic aesthetic. Unlike many authors and cultural pioneers, Anton LaVey lived long enough to glimpse the flowering of the dark seeds he planted. He continued to release revolutionary books, grant interviews to select writers and make recordings of his evocative, haunting renditions of songs from the '30s and '40s right up to his death in October, 1997, from rheumatic heart disease. His works have influenced literally millions of people, most of whom, of course, will never know his name or the reach of his legacy.

The Satanic Witch remains an ideal introductory text, not only outlining a path to true liberation for women brave enough to risk jealous ridicule, but also highlighting LaVey's wit and general philosophy. Satanism is a system of thought based on rational self-interest, sensual indulgence, and the constructive uses of alienation—which is exactly what he advocates in this book. LaVey's Church of Satan survives as the international rallying point for new generations of iconoclasts. Some LaVey adherents use the bibliography from *The Satanic Witch* as a required reading list for advanced Satanic understanding, collecting and consuming every volume. The Synthesizer Clock has become a shorthand reference for typing people: "She's a real bottom of the clock type," or "He's a typical three o'clock." These phrases may one day enter common parlance. But for now, these truly occult ideas are reserved for the few who can tap into the power, fear and wicked fascination conjured by the Satanic witch.